Big Pictures

Problems and Solutions for Treating Outsize Paintings

EDITED BY SALLY WOODCOCK

Archetype Publications

First published 2005 by Archetype Publications Ltd. in association with the Institute of Conservation Paintings Group

Archetype Publications Ltd.
6 Fitzroy Square
London W1T 5HJ

www.archetype.co.uk

Tel: 44(207) 380 0800
Fax: 44(207) 380 0500

ISBN 1 904982 03 4

British Library Cataloguing in Publication Data
A catalogue record for this book is available from the British Library.

Typeset by Kate Williams, Swansea
Printed and bound in Italy by Printer Trento srl

Contents

Preface

This book contains papers presented at a conference held at Tate Modern in December 2000 and organised by the Paintings Section of the United Kingdom Institute of Conservation (since 2005 merged into the Institute of Conservation). The organising committee was composed of Mary Bustin, Cressida Harwood, Alexandra Walker and Sally Woodcock.

Foreword

JAMES FRANCE

An ability to envisage the bigger picture has always been regarded as a special attribute – demonstrating great insight, knowledge and experience, together with an almost sage-like breadth and depth of intuition and vision. For the artist to realise similarly grand visions on a physically commensurate scale requires additional qualities and abilities, not least exceptional stamina, perseverance and technical ingenuity. It should not surprise us to discover that those very same qualities and abilities demanded of artists in realising their large-scale creations should also be demanded of those responsible for their subsequent successful conservation.

The conservation challenges described in this publication are far from run-of-the-mill. Each describes a different set of circumstances, but all have as their central theme the challenge of dealing with exceptional scale. Everything is relative, of course, and even the treatment of large-scale miniatures, while modest in scale compared with average sized conventional paintings, can create challenges of formidable proportions.

Many conservators will, at some time in their career, face the challenge of tackling a large-scale project that tests their previous experience. While the papers contained within this publication make no attempt to prescribe a cure for all, some of the solutions have the potential for wider application, including imaginative ideas for the safe handling and transport of big pictures as well as their conservation treatment. The hard lessons and pitfalls described will almost certainly help to forewarn those preparing similar projects.

Our thanks go to the authors who have been willing to share their experiences in such an open and candid fashion. Thanks also to the team whose vision it was to organise the Big Picture Conference held at Tate Modern, following the successful restoration of Copley's gigantic depiction of *The Defeat of the Floating Batteries off Gibraltar*, which created the original context for the papers contained within this publication.

Conservation of Large Miniatures on Ivory

ALAN DERBYSHIRE

Introduction

The nineteenth century saw a change in format of the portrait miniature. The concept of the miniature as a small, usually oval, intimate portrait that could be worn as a piece of jewellery was changing. Artists felt that they had to paint on a larger scale in order to compete with exhibition watercolours and easel paintings. This necessitated an adaptation of materials and techniques, which has led to specific conservation problems.

This paper looks briefly at the historical development of the miniature in terms of materials and techniques. The particular conservation problems of large miniatures on ivory are discussed, and various approaches to their treatment considered.

History

Portrait miniatures were first painted in Europe in the 1520s. The earliest surviving miniature is one of Henry VIII, painted by Hornebolte and currently in the Fitzwilliam Museum, Cambridge. These early miniatures are painted in watercolour and bodycolour on tablets made from vellum stuck down onto pasteboard.[1] The pasteboard is often a piece of playing card. The vellum itself is extremely fine and, according to contemporary treatises[2] would have been taken from aborted calves. One of the defining techniques used in these early miniatures on vellum is the carnation. This is a smooth, opaque flesh-coloured ground layer on which the features would be painted.

There were few major changes in the materials and techniques of miniature painting until the Venetian artist, Rosalba Carriera, began painting miniatures on ivory. In 1705 she presented a portrait miniature painted in watercolour on ivory as her diploma piece for entry to the Academy of St Luke in Rome. The demand for this new and exotic material was rapid and within 20 years nearly all miniatures were being painted on ivory, as opposed to vellum. However, as a painting support, ivory is not a particularly suitable material. It is difficult to paint on as the watercolour is not adsorbed very well by the ivory surface. Also, the ivory is very hygroscopic and will warp quite readily. The only advantage for the artist is that there is no longer a need to use a carnation layer for the flesh areas. The ivory is allowed to stand, largely unpainted, for the face area.

As the eighteenth century progressed, the materials and techniques of painting on ivory were refined. The ivory became thinner, often less than 0.2mm thick, and its translucency was exploited. For example, continental miniatures in particular often have a piece of silver foil, as a reflector, placed between the ivory and the ivory's backing paper. Also, paint is often applied on the verso of the ivory. The difficulty of getting the watercolour to adhere more readily was partly overcome by adding more gum arabic to the paint mixture and also by the addition of oxgall as a surfactant. However, from a conservation point of view, this results in miniatures painted on very thin, fragile pieces of ivory.

By the end of the eighteenth century, portrait miniatures were being produced in increasing numbers and varying quality by many artists. However, there was growing criticism of the slight manner in which some of these artists, such as Richard Cosway, painted. In many ways Cosway was using a minimum amount of paint in order to exploit the translucent nature of the ivory but his style was hard to defend when he himself boasted that he could 'paint up to twelve portraits in a day'.

Larger miniatures on ivory become more common from the nineteenth century onwards. Artists such as Robertson, who was one of those who had criticised Cosway, began to paint on a larger scale and in a more painterly style. Miniatures were no longer thought of as just portable pieces of jewellery. The large rectangular-format miniatures were commonly framed in big, gilded wooden frames. They could now be hung on the wall and compete with easel paintings and watercolours.

Materials and technique of large-format miniatures

The ivory leaves for miniatures were cut from the elephant tusk by professional ivory turners. Figure 1 shows a cross-section through a tusk. The leaves are cut tangentially down through the tusk, like cutting planks from a tree. Most of the large-format miniatures would have been cut in this way. The width of the ivory leaf is therefore limited by the diameter of the tusk. Also, there is a central pulp cavity running through much of the tusk, which would preclude cutting across its exact centre. The maximum width of an elephant tusk is about 200mm. However, in practice, it would have been difficult consistently to obtain tusks of this size

Figure 1 Cross-section through tusk.

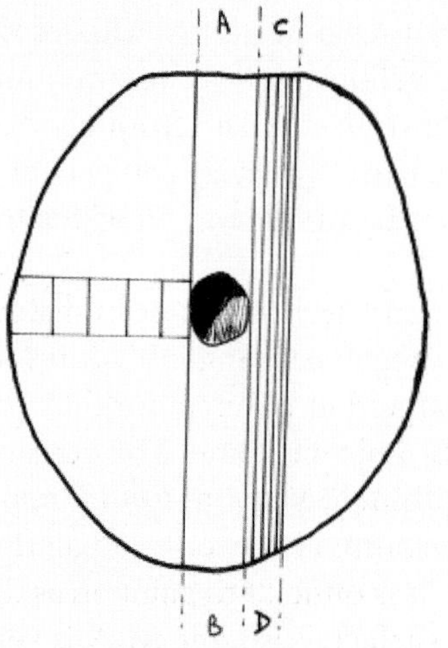

and to cut large leaves that did not contain any faults. The average size of the large nineteenth-century miniatures seems to have been about 140 × 180mm.

The parabolic grain pattern of the ivory is quite visible when a miniature is viewed in transmitted light. The density of the grain is greater at the edges of the leaf and the ivory is less flexible here. Consequently, the ivory tends to curl up slightly at the edges, which can lead to problems of cracking and warping. The ivory also tends to be relatively thick – about 1mm.

Some artists wanted to paint on a still larger scale. Sometimes they would join pieces of ivory together by sticking them down onto another support. The edges of the ivory would often be chamfered to give a good join. However, these miniatures can often become quite distorted due to the warping in different directions of the pieces of ivory.

Another technique, which was common on the continent (where ivory was more difficult to obtain than in England), was to set pieces of ivory into a support made of gesso, lined with sheets of paper. The small pieces of ivory were used for the faces and hands of the sitters, giving these areas the true translucent quality of an ivory miniature. The opaque background was painted on the gesso.

In about 1830, a Frenchman named Pappe patented a way of 'unpeeling' the ivory from the circumference of the tusk. These veneers of ivory would then be flattened using steam and stuck down to a board, ready prepared for the artist. This allowed huge pieces of ivory to be cut – as large as 700 × 3500mm. The largest veneer-cut miniature that I have seen, however, measures some 380 × 520mm. Veneer-cut miniatures tend to be in a very poor state of conservation. The ivory wants to return to its 'spiral' shape and so often a series of parallel cracks appear as the ivory pulls away from the wooden support. Occasionally, if released from the wooden support during a previous treatment, a different 'grain' pattern in the ivory compared with a traditionally cut ivory leaf can be recognised. Due to the nature of the cutting, a sine wave type pattern can be seen clearly using transmitted light.

The paint layer on large-format ivory miniatures from the nineteenth century can also differ somewhat, mainly in the method of application. When Cosway first saw one of Robertson's miniatures he could not believe it was painted in watercolour, and felt, for certain, that it must be a small oil painting. Robertson and his contemporaries wanted, indeed, to emulate oil paintings in scale and appearance. To this end they would apply layer upon layer of watercolour until they had built up a substantial and relatively thick paint layer. Only the flesh areas remained 'thinly' painted so that the quality of the ivory was retained. The artists would add quite large amounts of gum to the paint to help make it stick to the ivory and also to prevent succeeding layers from 'picking up' earlier ones.

Conservation problems and proposed treatments

Warping

One of the most common problems with nineteenth-century miniatures on ivory is warping. Miniatures on ivory nearly always warp concavely, i.e. the recto (paint surface) side of the ivory shrinks relative to the verso, which is usually covered in paper or card. The main cause of this warping appears to be the differential expansion/contraction with time of the paper backing compared to the ivory. This tendency to warp is probably 'set' when the ivory is initially laid down onto the card or paper using an aqueous glue. This would have caused expansion of the verso of the ivory relative to the recto. Nearly all miniatures would have been glued to a paper backing by the artist. This would have provided a white background for the translucent ivory and would also have reduced any initial warping during painting. Ivory miniatures from the eighteenth century also warp, of course. However, the ivory of these smaller miniatures tends to be thinner and quite even in grain density. They also tend to have only a thin paper backing. The ivory used for the larger nineteenth-century miniatures is usually thicker with a more uneven grain density at the edges. They are also, generally speaking, laid down onto thicker pieces of card. The warping of these larger miniatures tends, therefore, to be more severe.

Treatment involves removal of the backing card. This should be done dry as far as possible. Often the backing card will contain inscriptions and should be conserved and re-framed with the miniature. The warped miniature can be placed face down onto a kitchen roll covered in silicon paper during backing removal. The kitchen roll will support the curved ivory while the backing is removed using a scalpel or thin spatula. Sometimes, however, it is impossible to remove the backing card dry without slightly delaminating the side attached to the ivory. It may be necessary to sacrifice the inner layer of the card support as the rest is removed from the ivory. The final layer and any glue residue can be removed using swabs of saliva or water. Attempts to remove the whole backing card using moisture alone should be approached with caution. The ivory can curl up quite dramatically and also the slightest amount of moisture on the recto of the miniature will damage the paint layer. Often these backing papers are only attached in localised areas or at the edges. This can make their removal easier but can also cause uneven warping and hence cracking of the ivory, so this factor needs to be taken into account.

Cracking

Cracking of the ivory is usually as a direct result of extreme warping inside a tightly fitting frame. Sometimes the warping can be so great as to force the frame open. Unfortunately, the weakest component is usually the ivory, which cracks in one or several places. Normally the ivory will crack completely through the entire leaf. Occasionally, however, a crack may only be partial and a higher priority should be given to these miniatures in order to try to arrest the problem.

Treatment of warping and cracking

Often with the removal of the backing paper and glue residue, the warping of the ivory reduces to some extent. The ivory may have been warped for a long time and be set in that distorted state. It is therefore necessary to humidify the ivory in order to relax it and encourage it to remain flat. A Gore-tex system, as shown in Figure 2, can be used for this. Gore-tex is well known in the field of paper conservation and is used as a semi-permeable membrane, allowing moisture to pass through it in a slow and controlled way. Blotting paper is dampened and on top of this is placed a piece of Gore-tex, which is bigger than the blotting paper in order to avoid the risk of moisture coming into direct contact with the miniature. Silicon paper is then placed on the Gore-tex to reduce further the amount of moisture and to act as a barrier between the paint layer and the Gore-tex. Then the miniature itself is placed on the silicon paper, covered with a further piece of silicon paper and finally a piece of plastic. The miniature should be turned over every few minutes to ensure even humidification. It is also necessary to replace the silicon paper quite frequently otherwise it can become damp with a risk of offsetting of the paint layer. An alternative method is to use a humidity chamber, but this method seems less efficient. Once the ivory is flat it can be placed in a sandwich made of silicon paper and glass plates held together with bulldog clips. The miniature can be left

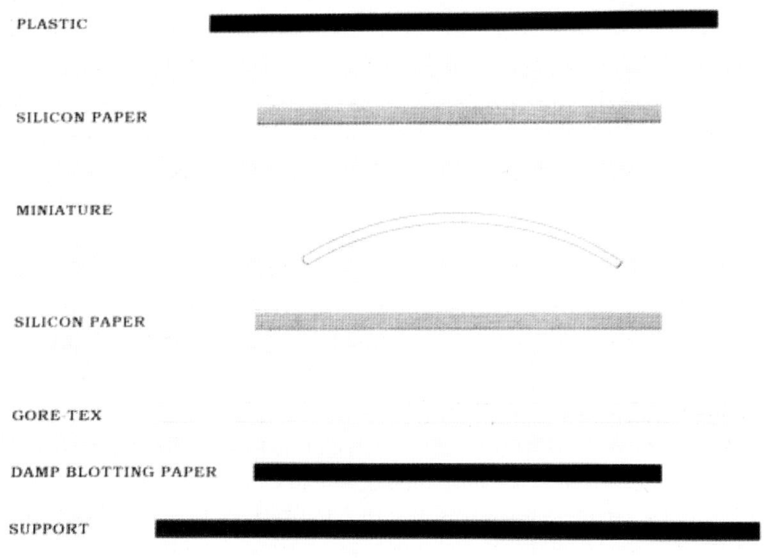

Figure 2 The use of Gore-tex in the flattening of miniatures on ivory.

in this sandwich for a few weeks, after which it should have a tendency to remain flat. This treatment is usually very successful with small miniatures. However, the larger miniatures, which are generally executed on thicker, more unevenly dense ivory, are more difficult to get to stay flat even after humidification treatment. These larger miniatures should not be forced flat and, depending on the flexibility of the ivory, it may be better not to try to keep them flat after humidification by placing between glass plates. The alternative is to allow the miniature to remain slightly warped and alter the frame to accommodate the distortion. Fortunately, this is usually possible since large miniatures tend to have been housed in wooden frames as opposed to metal lockets. To secure the miniature in the frame it can be hinged into a sink mount made from acid-free card and Plastazote. The Plastazote is flexible enough to allow the ivory to warp further if environmental conditions change. Figure 3 shows an example of such a sink mount. Cracked miniatures can be treated in a similar way. After removal of the backing card and excess glue the pieces of the cracked miniature can be relaxed using controlled humidification. The ivory pieces can then be rejoined using Japanese paper and a suitable adhesive.

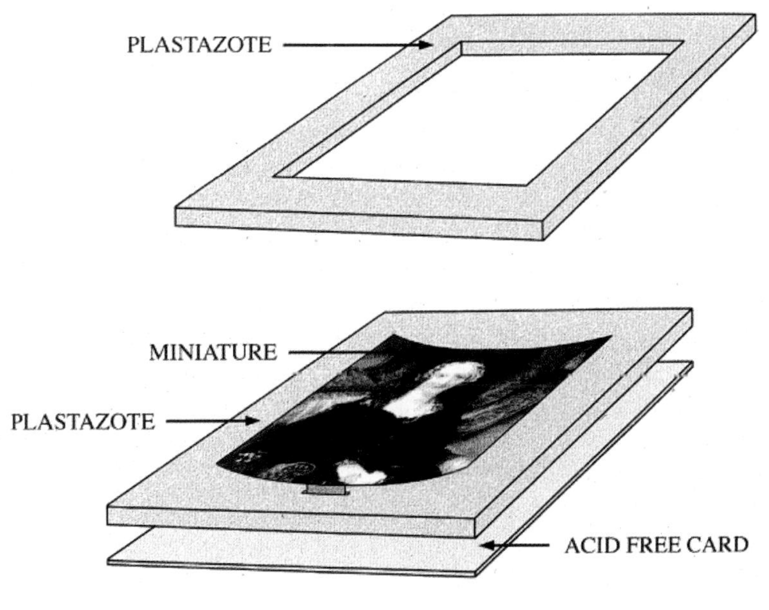

Figure 3 Sink mount for large ivory miniatures.

Mowolith DMC2 seems to have the right qualities in terms of strength, flexibility and non-yellowing ageing properties.[3] Paraloid B72 is a good non-aqueous alternative if strength of repair is not the main consideration.

It used to be common practice to lay cracked miniatures down onto a thin but strong piece of pasteboard. This undoubtedly gives a more aesthetically pleasing repair, as the two halves of the cracked miniature are held securely in plane. However, as discussed above, warping of ivory miniatures is accentuated by artists' use of paper and card backings. Therefore it seems unwise to adopt this as a method of repair. If it is decided to lay down a cracked miniature onto card it may be helpful to seal the verso of this support card with a layer of adhesive in order to help reduce its capacity to expand. Equally, an additional layer of thin card can be applied to the other side of the pasteboard to counterbalance the ivory. Having said all this, miniatures that were laid down over 30 years ago at the Victoria and Albert Museum, London, appear to have remained in good condition. This is undoubtedly due to their having been kept in reasonably stable museum conditions, but also to the methodology of the repair. Artists would not always have been as concerned in selecting the right materials or methodology. Great care needs to be taken to degrease the verso of the ivory and to make sure the adhesive is evenly applied to the support card before allowing the lined miniature to dry, between silicon paper, in a screw press.

Large veneer-cut miniatures or miniatures made up of several pieces of ivory are very difficult to conserve. It is best to do as little interventive treatment as possible and to try to rely on stabilising the environmental conditions. These conditions, relative humidity of 50% ± 5% and temperature of 19°C ± 1°C should be applied to the storage and display of all portrait miniatures.

Problems and treatment of the paint layer

Nineteenth-century miniatures were often painted more thickly and with a greater use of gum and plasticisers, such as sugar candy, than earlier miniatures. This can lead to problems of flaking and craquelure as the gum dries out and/or if insufficient plasticiser has been used. Consolidation can be achieved using methyl cellulose in a 50:50 mixture of water and ethanol, applied with a brush, using a microscope (methyl cellulose is made up to a 5% solution in water and then further diluted with ethanol). This is a standard treatment for miniatures on vellum and ivory. However, the highly gummed paint layers on some nineteenth-century miniatures can remain too water-sensitive for this treatment. The nature of the flaking often manifests itself in a particular way. These thicker, more gummy paint layers can literally peel away from the ivory. This nearly always happens in tiny horizontal strips, where the grain is running vertically, because of the inner structure of the ivory. In these cases it may be wiser to use a non-aqueous consolidant such as Paraloid B72 in acetone. The relatively thicker paint layers on nineteenth-century miniatures do not, of course, offer any substantial protection from fading, as can often be witnessed by viewing the areas protected beneath the rebate of the frame. Portrait miniatures are categorised as sensitive and limited display is recommended.[4]

Occasionally some nineteenth-century artists used solvent-based varnishes as a final layer on their miniatures. This can be difficult to detect and therefore care needs to be taken if considering solvent-based treatments.

Conclusion

Nineteenth-century miniature painters adapted the traditional materials and techniques of the eighteenth century to enable them to paint on a larger scale and with a greater depth of tone and colour. Unfortunately, this has led to a number of conservation problems, which require a different approach to that used with earlier portrait miniatures. Although this paper has outlined some of the possible interventive treatments available, there is still a need for a greater awareness of the potential for preventive action, i.e. good display and storage conditions.

Acknowledgements

I would like to thank Timea Tallian for commenting on the original draft of this paper.

Notes

1. Pasteboard is card made by sticking several sheets of paper together (alternating the grain direction) probably using flour paste and drying under pressure. This would produce a thin, yet strong, board.
2. N. Hilliard (1992) *The Arte of Limning*, edited by R.K.R. Thornton and T.G.S. Cain. Manchester: Carcanet Press.
3. J.L. Down, M.A. MacDonald, J. Tetreault and R. Scott Williams (1996) 'Adhesive testing at the Canadian Conservation Institute: an evaluation of selected poly(vinyl acetate) and acrylic adhesives', *Studies in Conservation* 41: 19–44.
4. A. Derbyshire and J. Ashley-Smith (1999) 'A proposed practical lighting policy for works of art on paper at the V&A', in *ICOM-CC 12th Triennial Meeting, Lyon Preprints*, vol. 1, pp. 38–41. London: ICOM.

The author

Alan Derbyshire is Head of Section, Paper, Books and Paintings Conservation at the Victoria and Albert Museum, London.

The Conservation of Large-Format Works of Art on Paper

A. JEAN E. BROWN

Introduction

Works of art in large format often demand a redefinition of the approach taken to the conservation of familiar problems. While the materials used and the problems presented are frequently familiar, the sheer scale of the pieces demand a reconsideration of every aspect of the work undertaken from treatment through to storage. This can be extremely challenging and exciting, as new answers are sought to old problems.

The solo-operated hoist

One of the difficulties in treating large-format works of art lies in handling the artwork during treatment. This is particularly problematic during washing, when the paper is at its most vulnerable. Clearly, there is a point at which the size of the object requires the assistance of two or more people. However, before that point has been reached, a conservator can continue to work independently providing the work is supported by the right facilities. The solo-operated hoist was developed to provide controlled aqueous treatment for large-format works of art on paper by an independent conservator. Since studio space is often restricted it was also essential that the equipment could be dismantled easily into small sections for storage.

The prototype of the solo-operated hoist

The concept for the structure was a derivation of the large papermakers' moulds used in Japan. In the Japanese model, the weight of the mould is held by a suspension system which leaves the papermaker's hands free to control sheet formation (Fig. 1).

The framework of the hoist was made up of two 'A' frames, connected by a ridge-pole, that were positioned above a washing tray (Fig. 2). A silkscreen was suspended from the pole and a pulley system developed to raise and lower it into the washing tray. At this stage, the structure was provided with rigidity by a 'bell-end' construc-

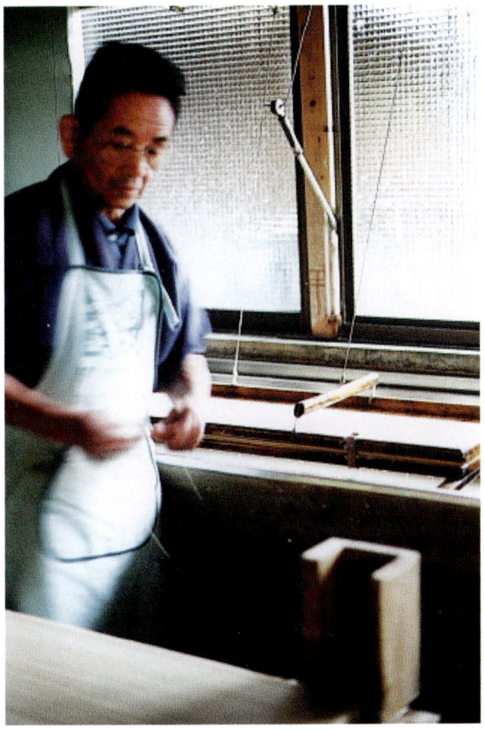

Figure 1 Japanese papermaker's mould at the mill in Yoshino, Japan.

tion and the washing tray was free-standing, rather than an integral part of the structure. The 'A' frames were made from hollow metal poles coated in white shrink-fit plastic and were secured together with wingnuts and bolts (Fig. 3) (see 'Materials and suppliers' section below for all materials and equipment used).

A fly fishing reel was used for the winding mechanism or winch. A locking system was developed for the reel to allow the silkscreen to be securely suspended at specific levels (Fig. 4). The four lines used to support the silkscreen were brought together at pulleys (A) and (B), leaving a single line to pass into the winding mechanism. This prevented the lines becoming entangled during use. However, a slight disadvantage to this part of the system was that the height to which the screen could be raised was

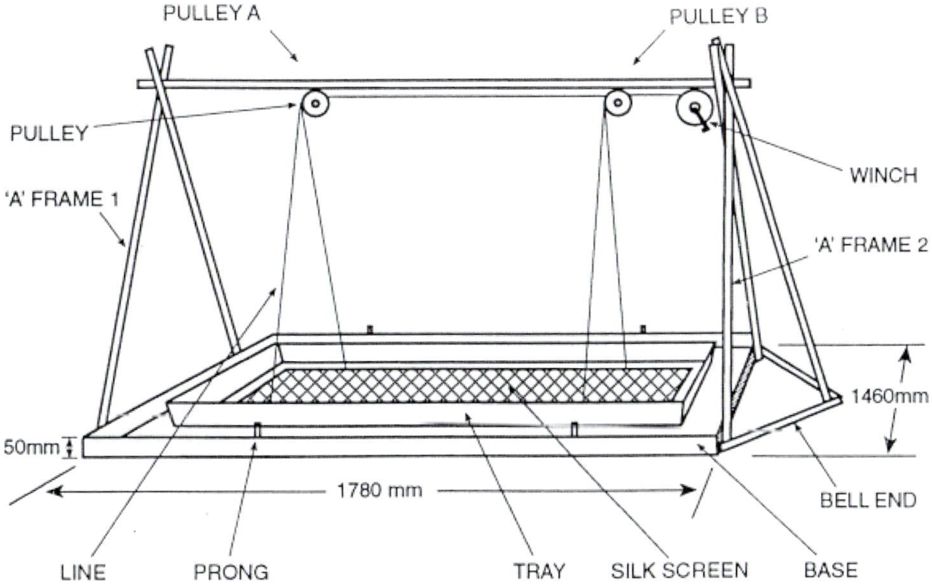

Figure 2 The prototype design for the solo-operated hoist.

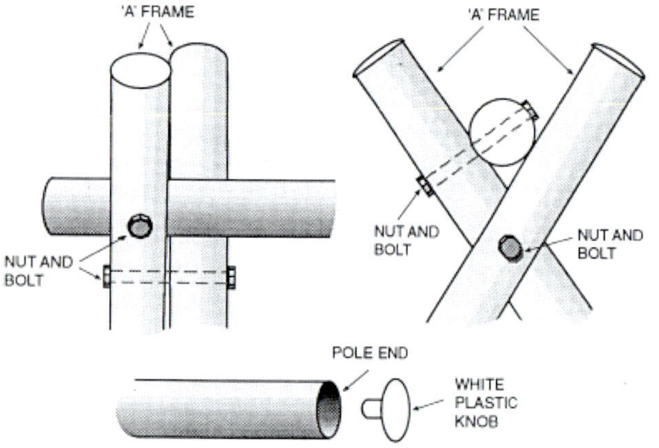

Figure 3 Detail of the wingnuts and bolts securing the poles together shown in Figure 2.

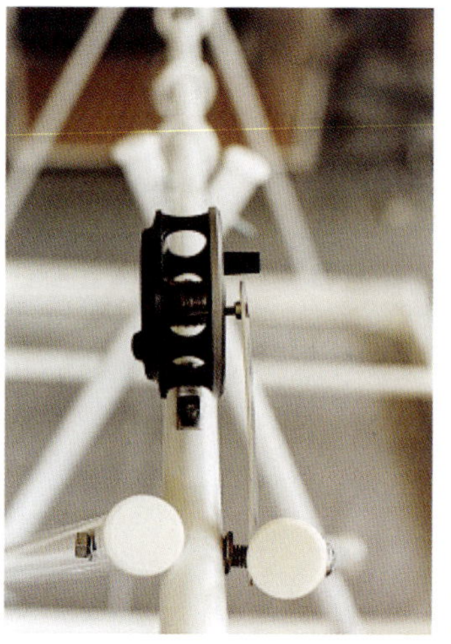

Figure 4 The winding mechanism secured in position on the right-hand side.

limited to the distance between pulley (B) and the winding mechanism. The winding mechanism was positioned at one end of the ridgepole between the two 'A' frames. Both the pulleys and the winding mechanism were initially positioned below the ridgepole (Fig. 2).

Wooden struts were placed across the washing tray in order to support the screen while placing or removing work from the screen. A hole in the end of each strut was placed over a vertical prong, positioned along the top edge of the washing tray.

The final design for the hoist

In the final design for the hoist, the 'bell end' was replaced by an extension to the ridgepole (Fig. 5). The extension was braced against the 'A' frame to form an isosceles triangle, which provided maximum stability to the structure (Fig. 6). The winding mechanism was moved along the extended ridgepole, beyond 'A' frame 1, and positioned above the pole. The increased distance between the winding mechanism and pulley (B) allowed the screen to be raised to a greater height than had been possible

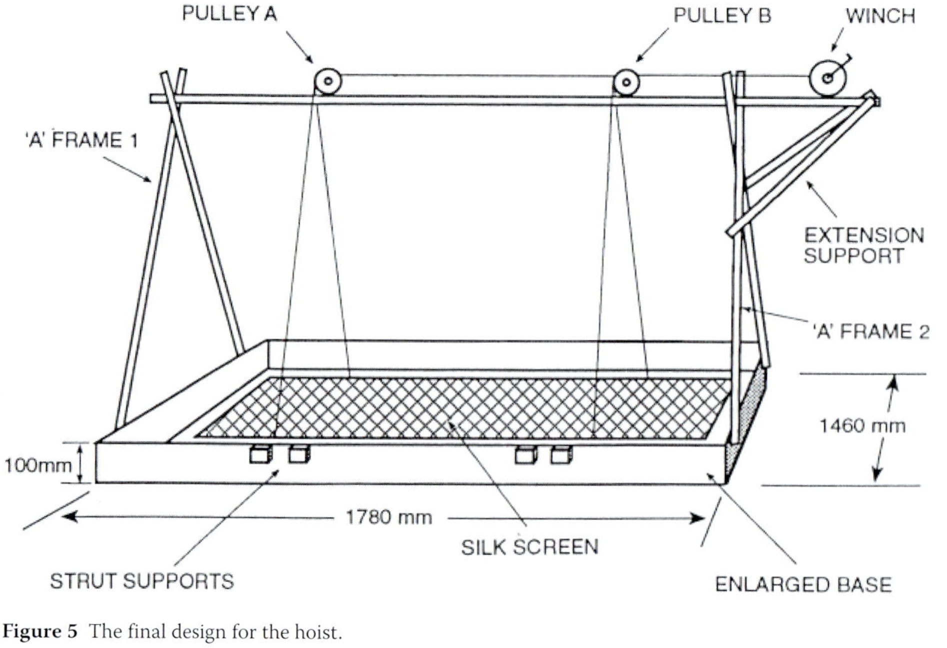

Figure 5 The final design for the hoist.

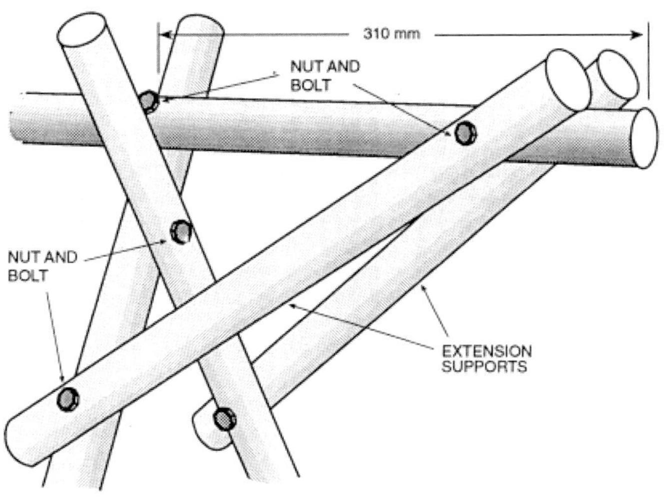

Figure 6 Detail of the extension to the ridgepole and joint at the apex of 'A' frame 2 shown in Figure 5.

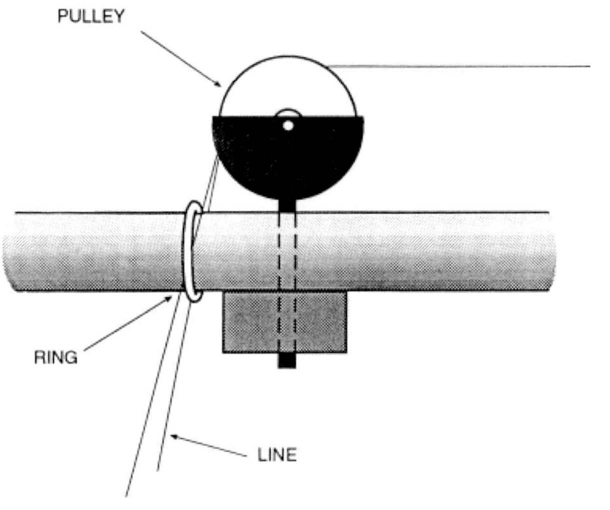

Figure 7 Detail of the pulleys repositioned above the ridgepole showing the position of the ring used to guide the suspension lines into the pulley system and prevent them wearing on the pulley casings.

with the prototype. Pulleys A and B were also repositioned on top of the pole in order to keep the support lines free from the pole structures, and a ring was introduced to guide the suspension lines into the pulley system (Fig. 7).

The washing tray

The tray was constructed from four lengths of wood, which were secured together at the corners and placed on a flat, solid surface such as the floor (Fig. 8). The structure was provided with a polythene lining which was kept in place with clips along the top edge of the tray. The wooden sides were held together with wingnuts and bolts and the rigidity was improved with corner braces. Cranked brackets were attached to the ends of the base tray to accommodate the poles from the two 'A' frames.

The vertical pegs used to secure the support struts in the prototype were replaced by a system of wooden blocks attached to either end of the struts and to the top

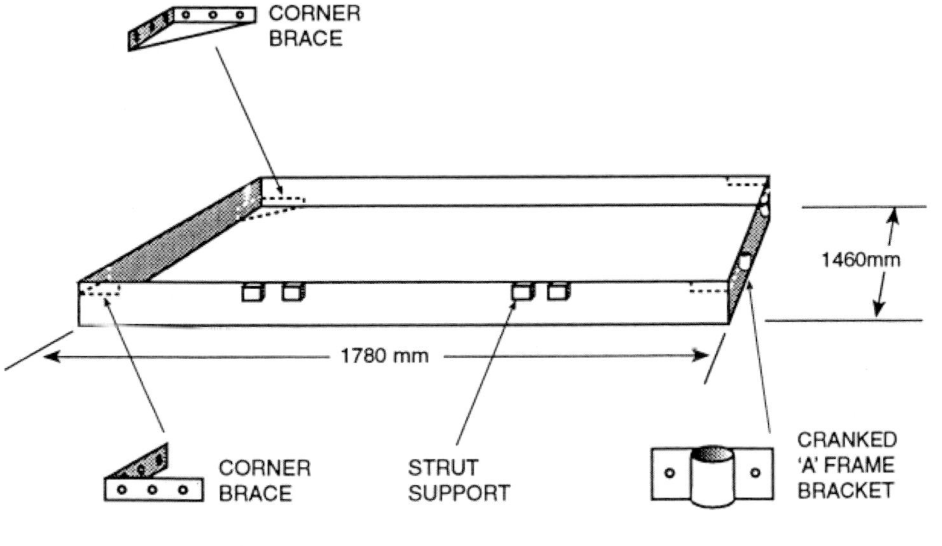

Figure 8 Detail of the washing tray shown in Figure 5 illustrating the position of the strut supports and the cranked 'A' frame bracket.

edges of the base. The advantage of this system over the earlier design was that it lay flush with the top of the washing tray, removing the risk of damage to either the object or the silkscreen during use.

The washing tray can be dismantled easily and therefore requires very little space for storage. An interim consideration for the tray design had been to make a solid structure of a material such as marine ply. However, this plan was not followed through due to the greater space that would have been required for storage.

The initial design for the silkscreen

The frame for the silkscreen was initially constructed from a single piece of angled aluminium (Fig. 9). The corners were mitred and strengthened with corner braces. The various parts were riveted and bolted together. The rivets and the nuts and bolts were prevented from rusting during use by a coat of white Hammerite paint. The screen was made of polyester net attached to the frame with an epoxy resin.

The attachment points for the support lines were provided by blind brackets, which were positioned along the top edge of the frame. A female part to these attachments was placed at the end of each of the support lines. Barrel strainers were

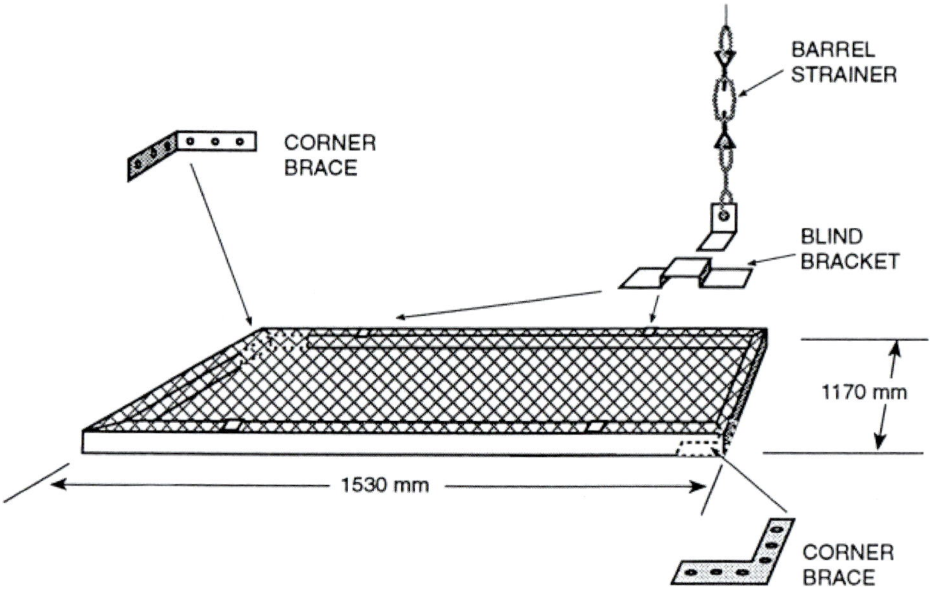

Figure 9 Detail of the initial design for the silkscreen shown in Figure 5 illustrating the location of the blind brackets along the top edge of the silkscreen and their relationship to the female part of the bracket and the barrel strainers.

Figure 10 A barrel strainer and the female part of the attachment points for the silkscreen.

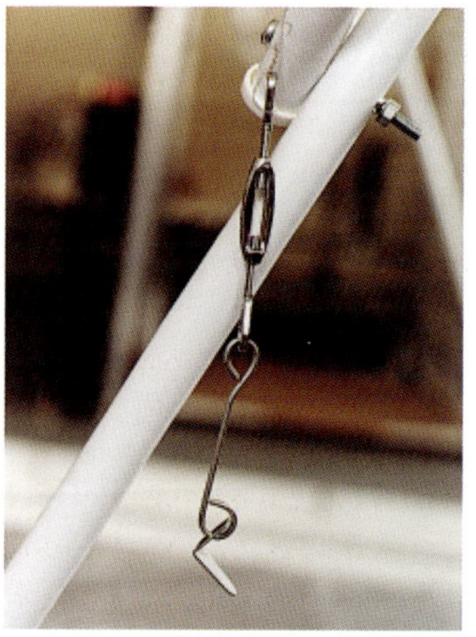

positioned above the attachment points on each of the support lines (Fig. 10). These allowed the screen to be levelled precisely on the surface of the washing solution irrespective of any irregularities in the flatness of the floor/work surface.

Modification of the silkscreen frame

The single section of angled aluminium allowed an unacceptable degree of flexing through the frame during use; therefore a method of introducing greater rigidity had to be found. Diagonal cross-bracing underneath the screen was considered but was rejected since it would prevent both sides of the screen being used. Treatment on the underside of the screen would have the advantage of requiring only a very shallow bath of solution, since the screen would be in direct contact with the bottom of the washing tray. This option could be an advantage when using expensive solutions, such as enzymes, etc. Therefore, an additional section of angled aluminium was positioned underneath the original section of frame. This provided the frame with a more rigid box-like structure when viewed in cross-section (Fig. 11).

The attachment points for the support lines were repositioned along the sides of the screen since the original location had presented a risk to the object during use. The new location also allowed the same attachment points to be used whichever side of the screen was in operation.

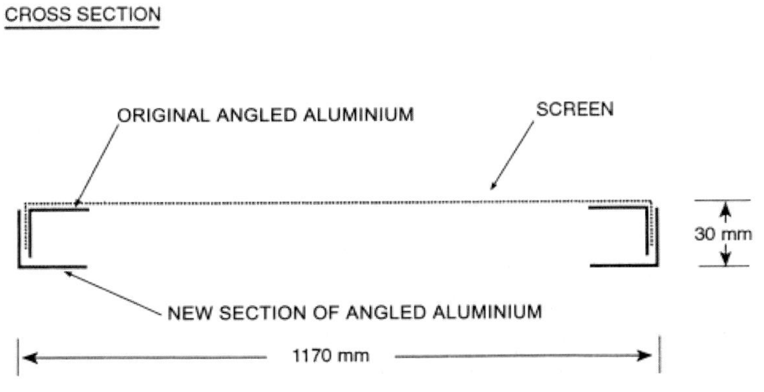

Figure 11 The modification of the silkscreen illustrating the introduction of an additional section of angled aluminium on the underside of the screen.

Operating the hoist for float washing

Prior to treatment, the correct level for the silkscreen must be established if float washing is to be carried out. In order to do this, the tray should be filled with the wash solution and the screen lowered until it rests on the surface of the water and the position marked on the winding mechanism. The level of the screen can be adjusted with the barrel strainers if it does not lie flat on the water. If the system is to be used for immersion washing, the exact level of the screen is not critical.

The object should be supported during treatment by a permeable material with good wet strength such as a non-woven polyester, i.e. Bondina or Remay. Prior to placing the object on the silkscreen, the screen must be raised and supported on the wooden struts (Fig. 12). The support lines must be detached from one side of the screen to provide clear access to the surface. Once the object has been positioned on the screen and the support lines reattached, the wooden struts can be removed and the screen lowered and locked in place at the predetermined level for float washing (Fig. 13). After washing has been completed, the screen is raised and replaced on the

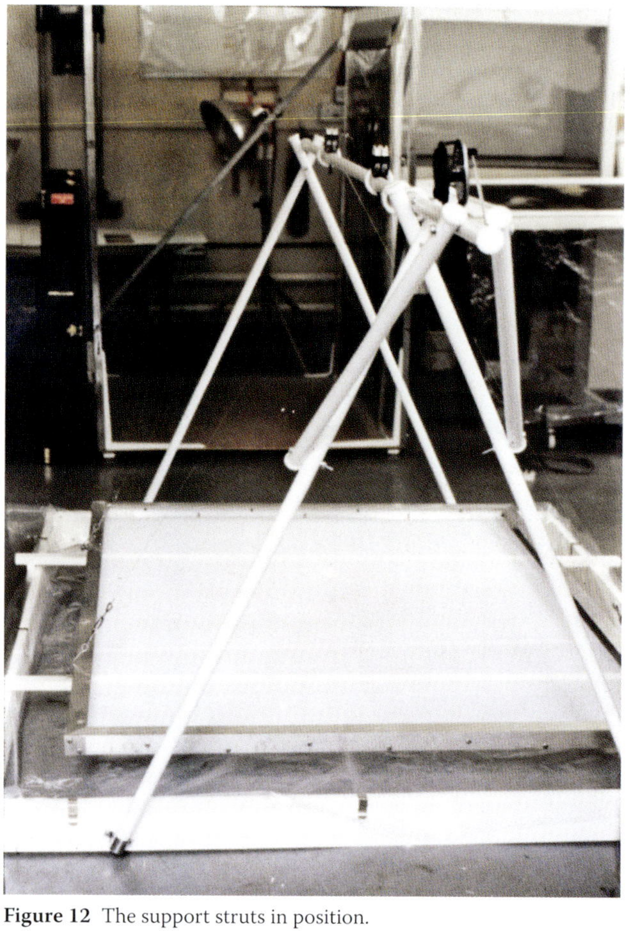

Figure 12 The support struts in position.

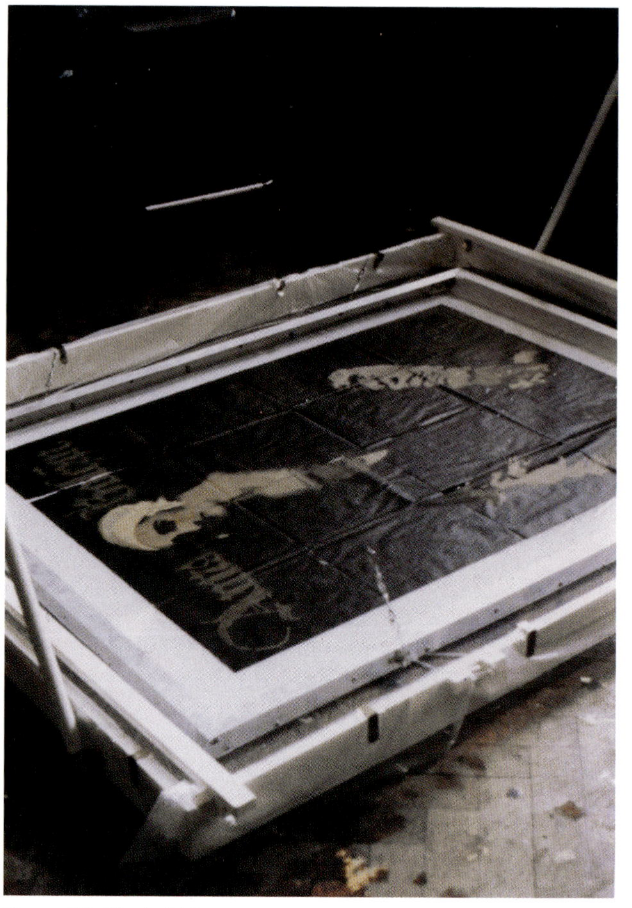

Figure 13 The hoist in use.

struts to allow the object to drain and, if appropriate, to dry. After use, the aqueous solution can be removed with a battery-operated pump (Fig. 14).

Summary

The equipment was simple and economical to construct. It could be used easily and safely by one conservator to provide effective aqueous treatments on large-format works of art on paper. The winding mechanism could be locked in place allowing the silkscreen to be suspended at any level. The equipment could be dismantled easily and required a minimum amount of space for storage. The system was particularly well suited to large, brittle objects which were unable to withstand handling and flexing.

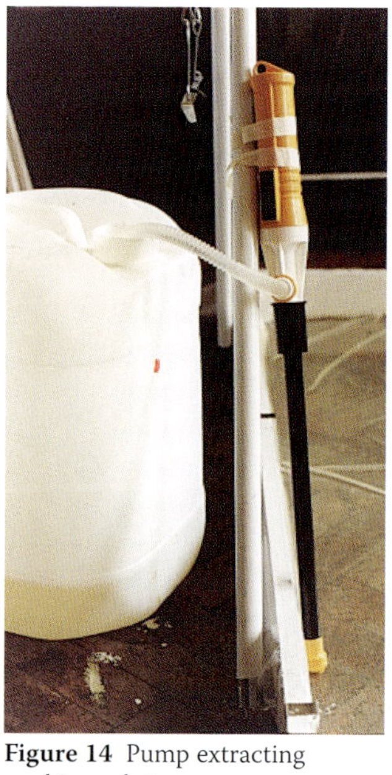

Figure 14 Pump extracting washing solution.

The hanging storage system

The equipment was developed to provide an economic storage system for a collection of large-format posters of varying sizes. Prior to conservation treatment, the posters had been folded and stored in a plan chest drawer. Refolding after conservation was not desirable; therefore an alternative storage system had to be developed. A standard plan chest was not considered viable since it would have required the posters to be stored one on top of another. This practice makes the location of individual posters difficult and can result in mechanical damage, especially where large objects are concerned. A purpose-built plan chest, with a shallow drawer for each poster, was considered, but was both too expensive and too large for the space available in the storage area. Although hanging storage systems can be purchased commercially, they are invariably more expensive than those that are built in-house.

Advantages of the hanging storage system

- It can provide safe storage for a range of different sizes of large-format objects within a limited space.
- The objects are not subjected to the stresses of folding or rolling. Objects made from lightweight materials can be provided with the rigidity required for vertical storage by attachment to a more rigid secondary support.
- Individual objects can be located easily without risk to adjacent objects.
- It can be used in conjunction with transparent polyester storage sleeves thereby providing good visual access combined with sound physical protection.
- It can be produced at a competitive price.

Design of the hanging storage unit

The dimensions of the unit were determined by the size of the collection. The unit consisted of an angled aluminium framework, with a solid roof and base, which could be moved around easily on a set of four casters. Each poster was provided with a clear, protective polyester storage envelope. The top edge of each envelope was attached to a runner, which could be slotted into a tracking system attached to the underside of the solid roof.

The prototype of the storage system

Angled aluminium sections were used to construct a framework for the storage system (Fig. 15). The angles of the joints were cut into the aluminium with a hacksaw and the structure was cross-braced on three sides to provide the structure with rigidity – the fourth side was left open to allow access to the storage facility. Initially the cross-bracing was positioned diagonally between opposite corners. The joints within each panel were riveted together with Spiralux rivets to provide maximum strength and rigidity. The remaining joints, between panels, were attached with nuts and bolts. This allowed the unit to be dismantled for transportation to the storage area; it also avoided the dimensional limitations to which a rigid unit would be subjected by the dimensions of the doors providing access to the storage area.

At this stage, the base of the unit had an open framework of angled aluminium. The roof was constructed from 12.5mm (½in) plywood, which was supported by, and bolted to, angled aluminium on all four sides (Fig. 16). The corners of the angled aluminium used in the base and roof sections were all mitred. A commercial curtain track system was attached to the underside of the board with epoxy resin and small countersunk screws (Fig. 17).

The modified design for the hanging storage system

The original design for the storage unit lacked rigidity and required a number of modifications. A board of 12.5mm (½in) plywood replaced the original open structure of the base, the ends of the cross-bracing were moved away from the

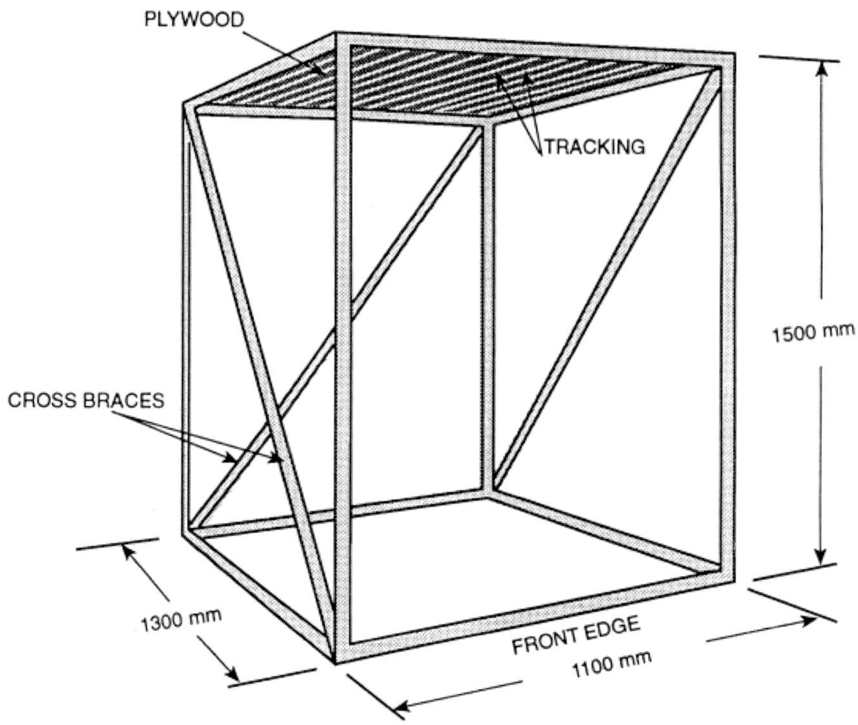

Figure 15 The prototype of the hanging storage system, showing diagonal cross-bracing and the open framework of the floor.

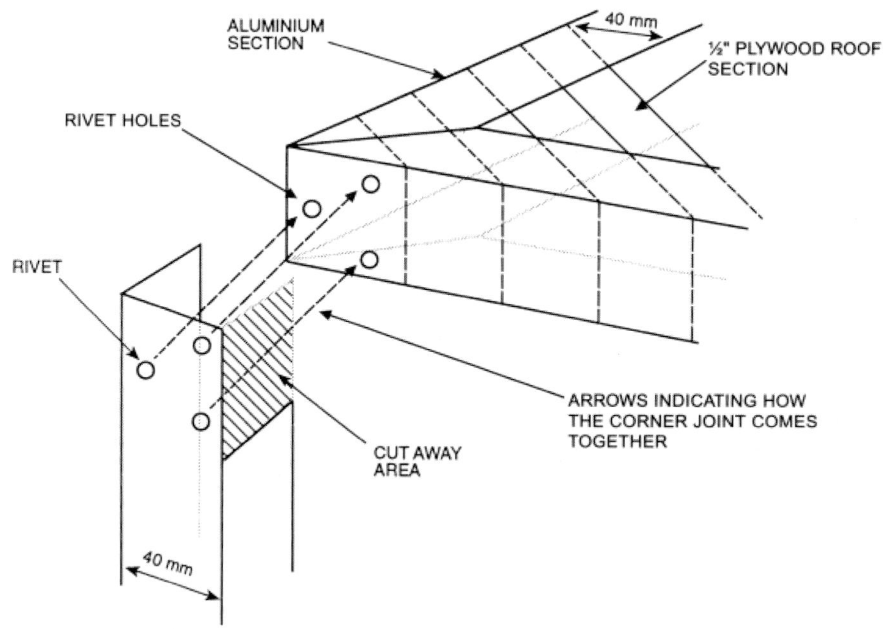

Figure 16 Detail of a corner joint used to attach the roof of the storage system to the side supports.

corner joints and corner braces were positioned at the bottom corners of the front opening (Fig. 18). The top and bottom corner joints of the unit were both cut to form a smooth, strong joint with the upper and lower framework (Fig. 19). Rivets were used to attach the various pieces together. All the cross-braces were attached in the same manner at the top and bottom of the framework. A set of four lockable casters was attached to the underside of the base to facilitate ease of movement when desired.

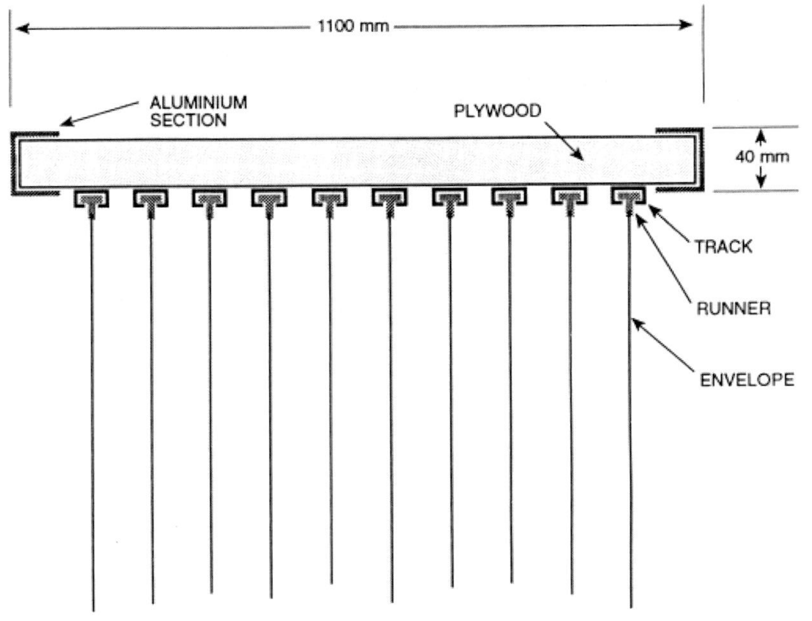

Figure 17 Cross-section of the roof board that is bolted on all sides to the angled aluminium by which it is supported. The tracking is attached to the underside of the board as illustrated in Figure 15.

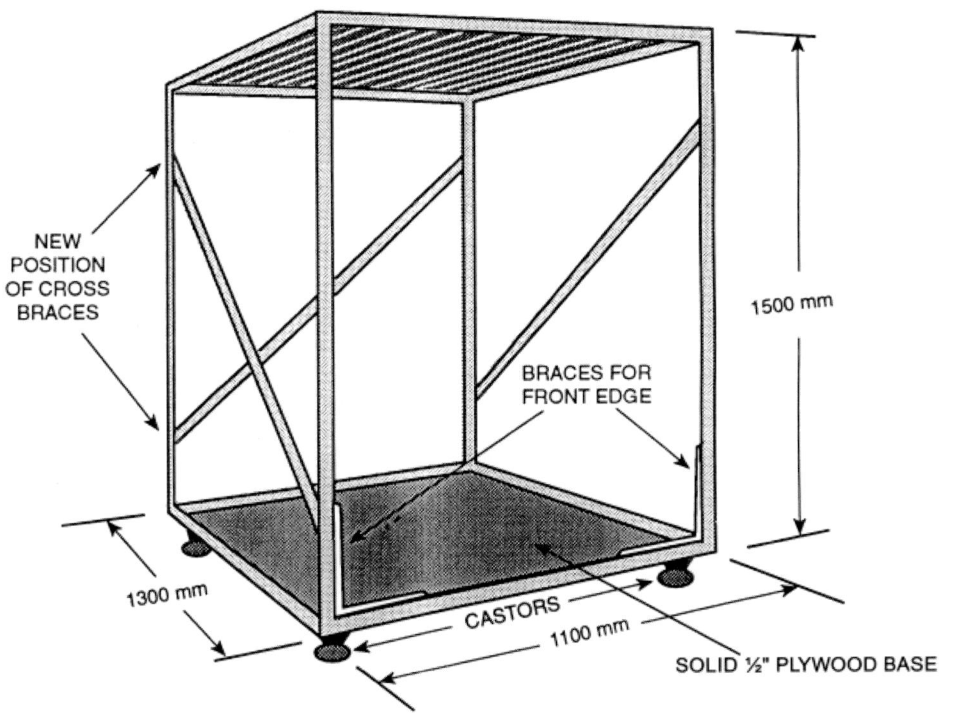

Figure 18 The modified design for the storage system.

The runners and tracking

The runners were made from strips of a rigid white polymeric material which was available in T-sections (Fig. 20). The material was originally produced to seal the gaps between workbenches. Horizontal slots were cut through the lower vertical part of the strip to facilitate the attachment of the storage envelope. The ends of each runner were provided with a loop/pulley with which to draw the storage envelope

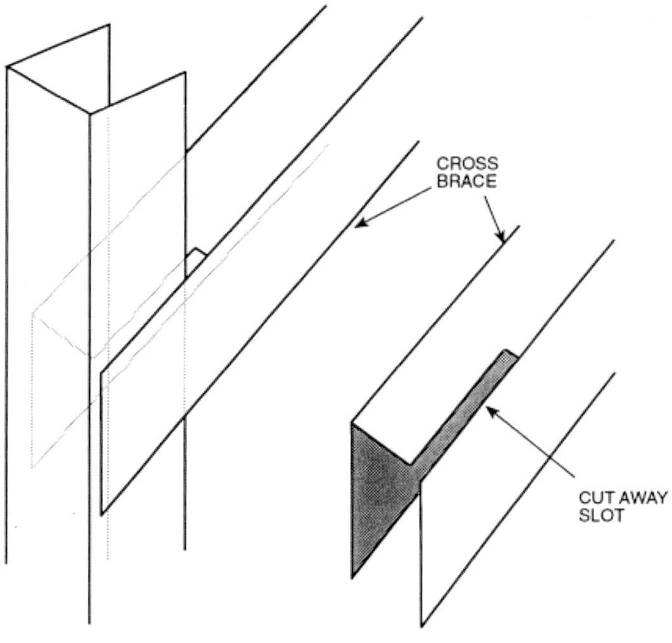

Figure 19 Detail of the attachment of the cross-braces to the uprights. All the cross-braces were attached in the same manner at the top and bottom.

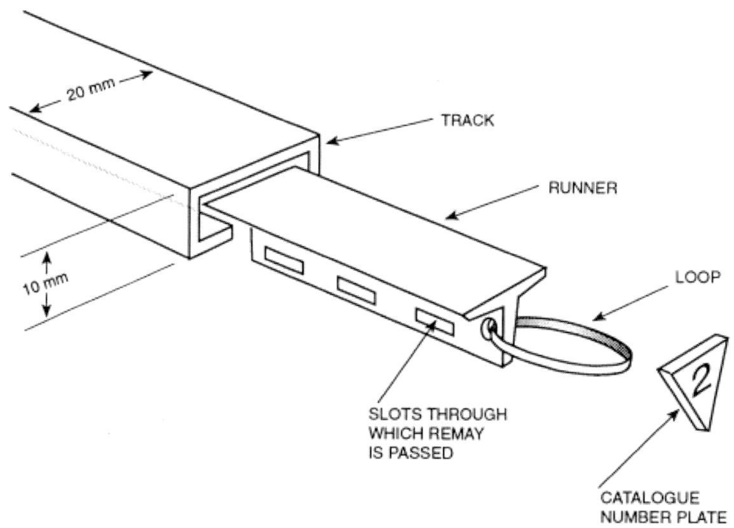

Figure 20 Detail of the runner that slots into the tracking.

along the tracking system. A plate was also provided on the end of each runner for the catalogue number of each poster.

The storage envelope

The storage envelope was made from two types of polyester which were welded together ultrasonically (Fig. 21). The recto of the envelope was made from clear polyester (polyethlene teraphthalate), which provided good visual access but had limited flexibility. The verso was made from non-woven polyester, which was opaque but provided a greater degree of flexibility. The use of clear polyester for both sides of an earlier envelope had resulted in a structure which was too rigid and introduced

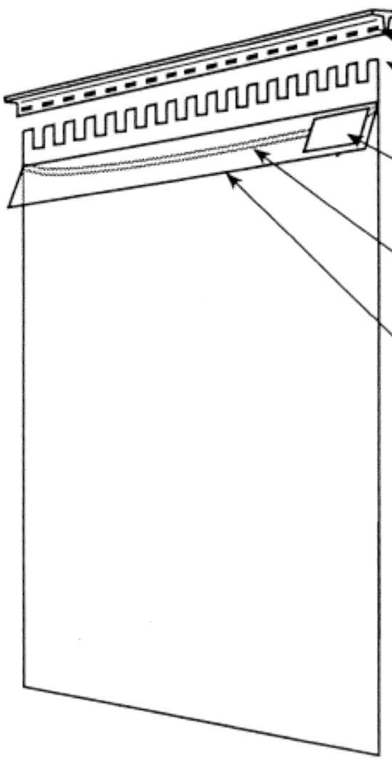

Figure 21 The design of the storage envelope with a clear polyester recto and a non-woven polyester verso.

difficulties when inserting or removing the posters. It was also found that the two types of polyester formed a stronger, more robust bond than was achieved between two pieces of clear polyester, which tended to crack when subjected to repeated flexing. The opening of the envelope was covered by a flap, which protected the contents from airborne particulate matter etc. The sharp edge of the clear polyester at the opening of the envelope was covered by a strip of the softer non-woven polyester, which was also welded into place ultrasonically. The non-woven verso extended beyond the top of the envelope and was cut into strips, which were passed through the slots in the runners and welded into position.

Summary

- The equipment was simple and economical to construct.
- It could be used easily and safely to provide storage for a range of different sizes of large-format objects within a confined space.
- The equipment could be dismantled with ease thereby avoiding the dimensional restrictions that would otherwise have been imposed by the size of the doors providing access to the storage area.
- The objects were easily attached to rigid secondary supports prior to placing in the storage envelopes thus avoiding the stresses imposed by alternative systems of folding or rolling (Fig. 22).
- Individual objects could be located without risk to adjacent objects (Fig. 23).
- The use of transparent storage sleeves provided good visual access combined with sound physical protection for the posters during storage and use as a study collection.

Conclusion

The conservation and storage of large-format paper-based objects can be challenging, but such problems are rarely insoluble. It can be exciting to discover that

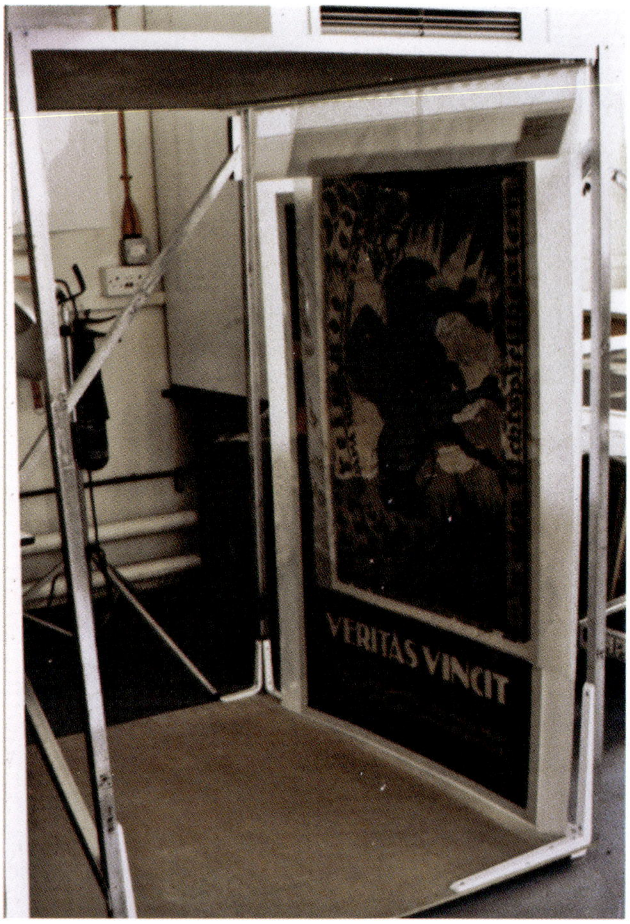

Figure 22 The storage unit in use.

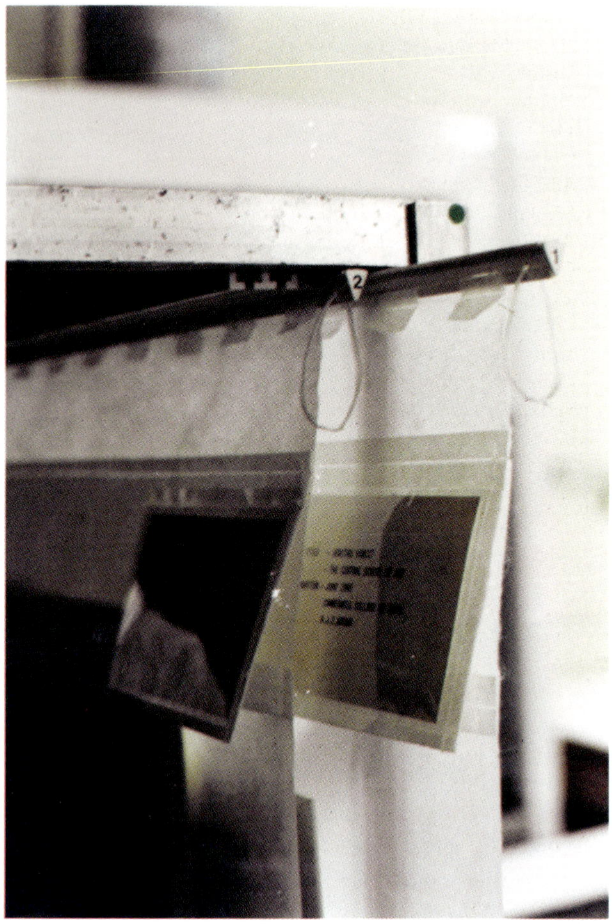

Figure 23 The storage envelope, tracking and runners.

the solutions are often well within the resources of both independent practitioners and small collections.

Acknowledgements

Many thanks to Gillian Roy and the Camberwell School of Arts where the work was carried out, and also to Sylvia Blackmeyer, Director of Learning Resources at Central Saint Martins School of Art for whom the work was carried out.

Materials and suppliers

The following materials can be obtained from most hardware or DIY stores.

- The hoist system
  White plastic-covered tubing [Coloroll]; cranked tubing brackets [Coloroll]; white style knobs [B&Q]; metal clips [Welpac]; clear polythene sheeting [Conservation by Design]; ½in thick wooden sections [B&Q]; M6 and M5 washers, screws, nuts and wingnuts [Welpac]; corner bracing [B&Q]; two pulleys [Welpac]; a fly fishing reel with an additional locking attachment; 40lb fishing line; barrel strainers [Welpac].

- Silkscreen for the hoist
  Angled aluminium sections [B&Q]; rivets [Spiralux]; M6 nuts and bolts [Welpac]; corner bracing [B&Q]; white metal paint [Hammerite]; woven polyester netting [Conservation by Design]; epoxy resin by Araldite; blind brackets [B&Q].

- Materials used in the construction of the storage unit
  2in angled aluminium sections [B&Q]; medium rivets [Spiralux]; sheets of ½in plywood [B&Q]; curtain track [Swish]; T-section strips of rigid unit sealant in a white polymeric material [B&Q]; Non-woven polyester (Remay) [Conservation by Design]; clear polyester (Melinex) [Conservation by Design].

- Addresses/websites

– B&Q plc, Portswood House, 1 Hampshire Corporate Park, Chandlers Ford, Eastleigh, Hants SO53 3YX (www.b&q.co.uk).
– Coloroll, CW Textiles Ltd., Heasandford Industrial Estate, Widow Hill Road, Burnley, Lancs BB10 2TJ (www.coloroll.co.uk).
– Conservation by Design, Timecare Works, 5 Singer Way, Woburn Road Industrial Estate, Kempston, Bedford MK42 7AW (www.conservation-by-design.co.uk).
– Hammerite: www.hammerite-trade.com.
– Spiralux: Mastercraft Tools Ltd, Gillingham, Kent.
– Swish: www.curtain-rails-direct.co.uk.
– Welpac plc, 43 Thames Road, Barking, Essex IG11 0HQ.

The author

A. Jean E. Brown is Senior Lecturer and Programme Leader of Preventive Conservation of Fine Art at Northumbria University, Newcastle upon Tyne.

The Conservation and Reinstatement of the Lonsdale Frieze, Mount Stuart

CLARE MEREDITH AND COLLEEN DONALDSON

Introduction

The Isle of Bute lies off the west coast of Scotland and the present Mount Stuart is situated on the sheltered east side of the island, within 300 acres (120 hectares) of eighteenth-century woodlands and formal gardens. The original house of 1719 was gutted by fire in 1877 and, in 1880, work on the ruined site began on 'one of the most astonishing monuments of the Victorian Age'.[1]

Mount Stuart is a spectacular Victorian Gothic house, the architectural fantasy of the 3rd Marquess of Bute (1847–1900) and the architect Robert Rowand Anderson (1834–1921). The 3rd Marquess was a scholar, archaeologist and mystic, as well as one of the wealthiest and greatest patrons of the arts of his day, and his new home reflected his artistic, astrological and religious interests. The principal rooms were fitted out for Rowand Anderson by a fellow architect, William Frame (1848–1906), who coordinated the activities of several artists and craftsmen, including the decorative painter and stained glass artist, Horatio Walter Lonsdale (1844–1919). Lonsdale had also assisted the architect William Burges at Cardiff Castle, another creation of the prodigious 3rd Marquess.

The Family Bedroom is at the centre of a private suite of rooms opening off the galleried second floor, which forms part of the cathedral-like Marble Hall at the heart of the house. Lonsdale played a central role in the decoration of these rooms, designed for the 3rd Marquess and his wife Gwendolen (1854–1932), and the principal feature of the Family Bedroom was Lonsdale's bold frieze depicting 15 scenes from the life of St Margaret. Lonsdale worked on the frieze during 1887–88 in his London studio and, in March and April 1888, the canvases and borders were fixed into place by a Mr R. Pembery, working to Frame's instructions:

> As I have before told you the borders run level all the way round, you have the sketches for each picture and for G..s sake don't make a mistake, they are all numbered and no one with any sense could do so ... what the British workman is coming to I don't know.[2]

Lonsdale designed the 15 scenes to be read in sequence, beginning at the southern end of the east wall and continuing around the room in a clockwise direction (Fig. 1). Pembery secured the frieze to the upper walls of the room beneath Frame's

Position	Lonsdale's number	Lonsdale's description	Latin text	h x w cms
East wall				
	1	Childhood of St Margaret	DEVM : COEPIT: DILIGERE	163.0 x 46.5
South wall				
	2	Landing at Wearmouth	SCOTIAM : CLITONEM : EADGARVM : CVM : SVIS : PROSPERO : VENTVS : PERVEXIT : CVRSV	162.3 x 169.5
	3	Marriage of St Margaret	SVORVM : MAGIS : VOLVNTATE : IMO : DEI : ORDINATIONE : POTENTISSIMO : REGI : SCOTORVM : MALCOLMO : REGIS : DVNECANI : FILIO : IN : CONIVGIVM : COPVLATOR	162.2 x 366.7
	4	Building of Dunfermline	NOBILEM : IBI : ECCLESIAM : IN : SANCTAE : TRINITATIS : AEDIFICAVIT : HONOREM	164.1 x 170.1
West wall				
	5	Washing the feet of the poor	PERACTO : LAVDIS : OFFICIO : SEX : PAVPERVM : PEDES : CVM : REGE : IPSO : LAVARE : SOLEBAT	166.8 x 162.1
	6	St Margaret and the merchants	FECERAT : VI : MERCATORES : RERVM : VENALIVM : SPECIES : IBIDEM : IGNOTAE : ADVEHERENT	166.9 x 163.9
	7	St Margaret holding council	CONCILIVM : STATVIT : IN : QVO : SOLA : CVM : PAVCISSIMIS : SVOREM : CONTRA : PERVERSAE : CONVETVDINIS : AFFERTORES : GLADIO : SPIRITVS : QVOD : EST : VERBVM : DEI : GRIDVO : DIMICABAT	167.4 x 333.6
	8	St Margaret and her children	FILIIS : CVRAM : IMPENDEBAT : VT : QVAM : MAXIME : HONESTIS : MORIBVS : INSTITVERENTVR	166.9 x 163.6
	9	St Margaret feeding orphans	NOVEM : INFANTVLOS : ORPHANOS : PRIMA : DIEI : HORA : A : SE : INTRODVAI : FECIT : REFICIENDOS	166.9 x 163.4
North wall				
	10	Departure of Malcolm	REGEM : QVASI : FVTVRORVM : PRAESCIA : MVLTVM : PROHIBVERAT : QVOQVAM : CVM : EXERCITV : IRE	167.0 x 169.5
	11	Death of Malcolm	EODEM : DIE : QVO : REGINA : DIXERAT : FVIT : REX : OCCISVS : EDODEM : QVIPPE : TEMPORE : CONIVGEM : AMISERAT : FILVM : PERDIDERAT : SEIPSAM : INFIRMITAS : AD : MORTEM : VSQVE : CRVCIAVERAT	162.5 x 336.5
	12	Death of St Margaret	FILIVS : EIVIS : EADGARVS : REDIENS : DE : EXERCITV : CVBICVLVM : REGINAE : INTRAVIT	167.4 x 168.4
East wall				
	13	Watching the corpse	IN : PACE : AETERNA	168.6 x 45.7
	14	Burial of St Margaret	IN : ECCLESIA : OVAM : IPSA : CONSTRVXERAT : SEPVLCA	164.4 x 101.1
	15	Translation of the relics	TRANSLATAE : RELIQVIAE : XIII : KAL : IVL : MCCL	163.2 x 101.2

Figure 1 Description, in English and Latin, with position and size of each painting.

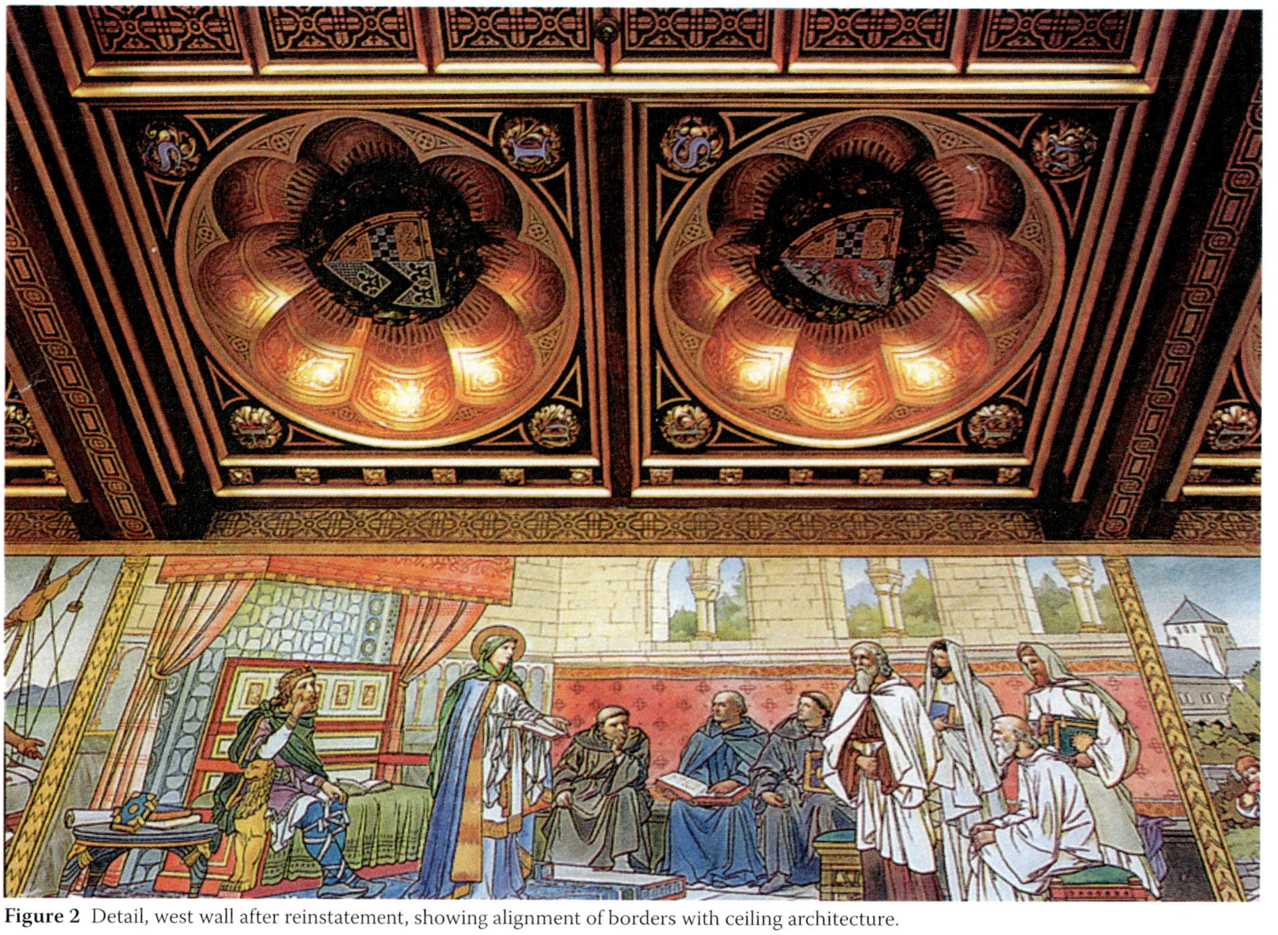

Figure 2 Detail, west wall after reinstatement, showing alignment of borders with ceiling architecture.

richly decorated ceiling; the two were tightly designed and the proportions of the frieze precisely complemented the grid-like structure of the decorative extravaganza above (Fig. 2). Gilded borders were secured to all four sides of each canvas, creating a gilt-frame effect. The section beneath each scene bore a related Latin description written in Lombardic script (Figs 1 and 3).[3] Beneath the paintings were hung 'tapestry drapery fitted to walls of room with silk embroidered flowers in colours in alternate blue and gold panels, fringe borders'.[4]

In the 1940s, the canvases and borders were removed from the walls because of water damage, and were rolled and stored in the attics at Mount Stuart. In 1992, John

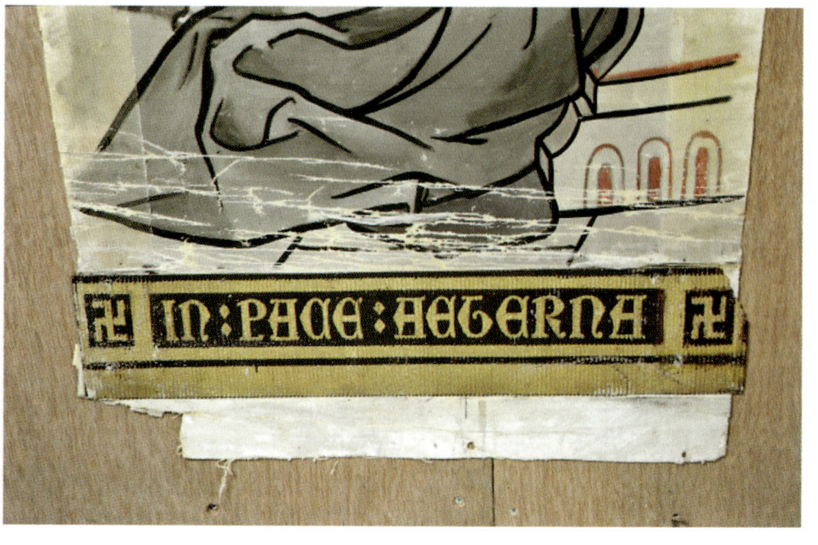

Figure 3 Detail, *Watching the Corpse*, before recent treatment, showing creases with paint loss and border with Lombardic script.

Bute, the 6th Marquess, commissioned the wall paintings conservators Donald and Rachel Smith to assess the condition of the frieze and carry out preliminary treatments. However, work was suspended upon Lord Bute's death in 1993. In 1997, the project was revived by Johnny Bute, Chairman, Mount Stuart Trust.

Identification

Since 1993, the canvases had been stored stacked one on top of the other and, although several had been faced by the Smiths to secure flaking paint, most remained in a weak structural condition. The first step was to lay out the canvases, measure them, and identify the scenes using Lonsdale's list. The borders had been stored rolled or flat in boxes, whole or in pieces, and these too were laid out to help understand what was present and what might be missing. It was deduced that:

- All the paintings were present.
- Approximately 25m of plain gilded border was present but about 30m was missing.
- 75% of the borders with Lombardic script was intact, and most of the remaining 25% was present in the form of detached fragments.

Brief reports with broad proposals were subsequently prepared. Further evidence that helped to solve this fragile jigsaw-like puzzle included:

- A single black and white photograph, *c.* 1907, taken from the south end of the room.
- Lonsdale's exquisite watercolour sketches showing, on a miniature scale, the 15 scenes in sequence.
- Archival evidence of the Latin text painted in Lombardic script beneath each scene.
- Residues of original glue, paint and plaster marks on the west wall only, the other three walls having been lined with paper.

Two years later, in November 1999, detailed reports, proposals and estimates were produced and, in December, the conservation and reinstatement of the frieze was commissioned, to be completed in time for the reopening of the house to the public for the summer 2000 season.

Condition

The paintings were unvarnished and executed in thin, flat oil paint on commercially prepared, medium weight, tabby weave canvases, with off-white priming extending to the edges of the tacking margins.

In his report of September 1992, Donald Smith noted that the canvases had been folded around paper and were 'in a particularly sad condition, the paint layer and canvas now set in a series of narrow creases. Due to pressure at these folds, flaking and crumbling of the entire paint layer is widespread.' He and Rachel Smith subsequently carried out humidification treatments to relax the canvases from this rolled, brittle state and they consolidated fragile areas of paint with wax-resin adhesive and facing tissue.

The canvases had remained flat and fairly flexible since these preliminary treatments but their condition varied: a third were in poor condition (severely creased,

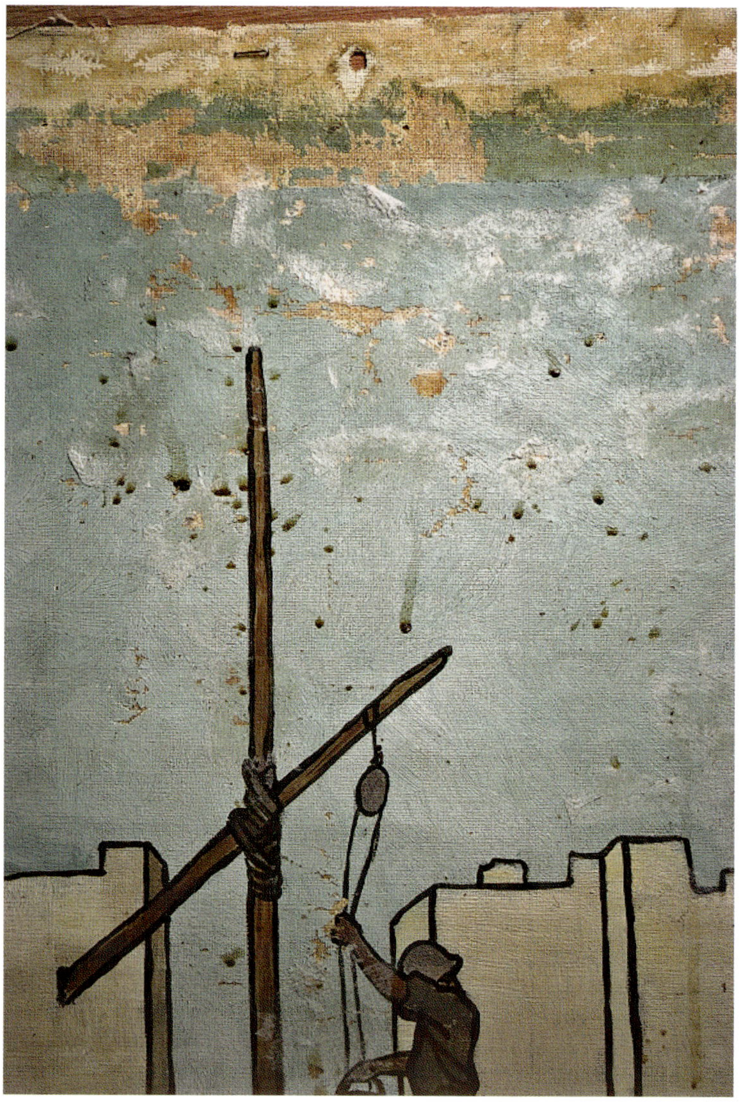

Figure 4 Detail of *Building of Dunfermline*, before recent treatment, showing faced flaking paint, paint loss and splashes of dried animal glue.

with small tears and numerous losses, with facing tissue applied to remaining fragile paint); a further third were in a fair condition (as above, but with fewer losses and less consolidation carried out) and barely a third were 'satisfactory' (with only minor creases and losses). One painting, *Landing at Wearmouth*, had been faced because of extensive delamination caused by Lonsdale's reworking of the entire composition with a lighter palette which proved to be poorly bound to the darker-toned original layer beneath. Splashes and drips of dried, discoloured animal glue were noted on the surface of some paintings, probably from glue applied by Pembery when fixing the borders in place (Fig. 4).

All the canvases had residues of household paint, plaster and animal glue on the reverse. Surface soiling on the paint surface was surprisingly light. Pollution at Mount Stuart is minimal and the paintings had been stored for some 50 years; all that was present was a fine layer of soft, grey dust.

The borders were made of a linoleum-like composite (animal glue, linseed oil and fibres) and were originally secured to the canvases with animal glue. The width of the top and side borders was 125mm; the bottom borders, with the Lombardic script, were wider at 175mm; all were 3mm thick, with a ribbed texture and a gauge of 8 ribs per 50mm. The surface finish consisted of a layer of brown oil paint followed by an oil size and gilding. They were, when first examined in 1997, in a generally fragile state. Over 75% of the bottom borders with Lombardic script was intact and remained adhered to the canvas, but was brittle and easily fractured

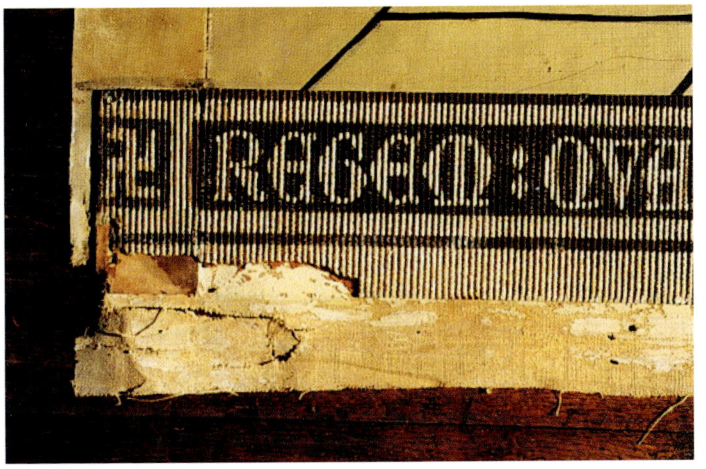

Figure 5 Detail, *Departure of Malcolm*, before recent treatment, showing damaged border and canvas.

when handled (Fig. 5); most of the remaining 25% was in small sections or fragments with friable edges. Only 25m of the plain gilded borders remained from an original quantity of approximately 55m. These lengths were generally in a good condition but, overall, they were distorted and could not be laid completely flat as cracking had occurred through the material in many places.

Treatment: constraints

Five key factors determined the final choice of materials and treatments:

1. The canvases and borders were originally secured directly to the plastered walls with animal glue; repetition of this method was not considered, as reversibility would be compromised and a lining-based system was needed for the weak canvases.
2. Access to the Bedroom was awkward, through two doors creating a tight right-angle; unless all structural treatments were to be carried out within the Bedroom itself, marouflaging the canvases onto rigid supports would not be possible.
3. The precision of the underlying structure of Lonsdale's grid-like design for the decorative scheme of the room imposed restrictions. No bulk or increased depth could be added, such as stretchers or strainers behind lined canvases, as this would interfere with the final alignment of canvases and borders.
4. The slight, but detectable, undulation across the surface of the plastered walls would make the securing of battens, or similar secondary supports, problematic should a system of stretched or marouflaged canvases be chosen.
5. The plastered walls were not sound throughout and it was not a safe option to secure over 45m^2 of marouflaged canvas on rigid supports to them.

Treatment: choice of materials

All 15 canvases were to be lined, to ensure the consolidation of unstable paint, as well as the repair and reinforcement of damaged and weak canvases. The paint layer was tested for heat sensitivity and BEVA 371 was selected as the lining adhesive. Refixing lined canvases directly onto the walls was, from the outset, the preferred option, but the difficulty lay in finding an appropriate material to perform as a suitable secondary lining support. Polyester sailcloth[5] would act as a satisfactory interleaf enabling future reversibility but additional material, both strong and flexible enough to conform to the surface of the uneven walls, was required. The preferred material was polyester film, 200–500μm thick and wide enough to accommodate the 1700mm depth of the frieze without joins. In the UK the maximum width stock size of Melinex or Mylar is 1500mm; however, one supplier was found who had in stock the remains of a special order of 250μm thickness Mylar 'A', 1850mm wide.[6]

A water-based contact adhesive was required to adhere the double-lined canvases to the prepared walls that would:

- Bond polyester film to a porous paper-covered plaster substrate.
- Achieve a good, early bond of heavy, slippery material to a vertical surface.
- Allow some repositioning.
- Develop a long-bonding range.

Reversibility was not an issue because BEVA 371 adhesive was used between the reverse of the paintings and the polyester sailcloth interleaf, as well as the sailcloth and Mylar. 3M's Fastbond 40[7] met the criteria for the contact adhesive and was tested on a small scale. The reality was, on a project of this scale and in the time available, that no realistic tests could be carried out to replicate the porous substrate and the weight of unwieldy, heavy double-lined canvases.

Thirty metres of the original plain ribbed gilded border was missing and it was decided to use acid-free corrugated[8] paper as a substitute because it was stable, light and easy to handle. A supply was found which closely matched the 3mm thickness of the original linoleum-like material and the gauge of the rib.

Treatment: offsite

From an early stage in the planning it was decided that all conservation and restoration treatments would be carried out offsite because:

- Pre-existing commitments could be met by work continuing in the Thistle Street workshop (Donaldson) and Hopetoun studio (Meredith).
- Conservators could work flexibly from an Edinburgh base.
- Studio equipment and materials would be to hand.

A temporary workshop was rented in Edinburgh, 10 miles from the Hopetoun studio. This decision was taken because (1) the Hopetoun studio was not big enough to accommodate so many large canvases that needed to be treated flat as well as upright and (2) the borders and canvases could be treated together.

At Mount Stuart, the borders were wrapped in acid-free tissue and packed in a purpose-built box; a suitable crate was also made for the canvases, which were packed laid on top of each other, interleaved with acid-free tissue and with extra tissue around the fragile borders which remained attached along the bottom of many canvases. An inner lid was fitted within the crate to ensure that the canvases could not move around inside the crate itself. The crate was transported flat, by lorry, and delivered on 13 January 2000 to the temporary studio.

The lining of 12 canvases was subcontracted to conservators with access to a vacuum table of suitable size; the three biggest canvases, however, were hand-lined in the temporary studio. The system for both hand and vacuum linings was as follows: paint and glue residues were removed mechanically from the reverse of the canvases (eye protection and masks were worn during this process as the residues included lead-based paint); tears and holes were aligned and repaired with polyamide welding powder; BEVA 371 adhesive film[9] was tacked into place between the reverse of the canvas and the polyester sailcloth interleaf, and also between the interleaf and sheet of Mylar 'A'. Hand lining was carried out with polyester sailcloth stretched across a loom; the canvas was positioned face down beneath the sailcloth and the Mylar was positioned within the loom above. The structure of the sandwich was reversed for vacuum lining, with the Mylar at the bottom.

Cleaning the paintings was straightforward because the thin, flat oil paint layer was unvarnished and there had never been any previous restoration. Surface dirt was removed using a 2.5% solution of tri-ammonium citrate in deionised water and cleared with deionised water; splashes of dried glue and other accretions were removed mechanically. Acrylic paints were used for retouching repairs to tears as well as losses from previously unstable areas of paint; all the canvases had incurred extensive paint loss from creasing through handling over the years. The paintings were left unvarnished.

The linoleum-like material of the gilded borders was fragile and the reverse was dry-scraped to remove residues of animal glue. The front, gilded surface was first cleaned with a soft brush, followed by swabbing with warmed deionised water; stubborn dirt residues were removed with a 50:50 solution of water and IMS. Friable areas were consolidated using PVA adhesive (neutral pH) in conjunction with a heated spatula; the brittle material, once softened and relaxed by the moisture of the water-based adhesive and the warmth of the spatula, was weighted overnight. Intact but distorted lengths of original border were laid on boards and weighted for several days until flattened.

New sections of corrugated paper were toned with watercolour to match the original brown oil paint layer and 23¾ carat Italian gold leaf was applied on top of this watercolour wash. The newly gilded surface was brushed with rottenstone to distress and dull the gold so that it matched the original finish. This replacement gilded material was trimmed to fit the missing sections of the border and acid-free tissue was adhered to the reverse of the replacement sections before attaching them to the canvases with PVA. Reconstruction of missing fragments of Lombardic script was carried out on top of the gold leaf using pigments bound in thin shellac (a mixture of 75% IMS and 25% pale lemon superior shellac flakes).

Treatment: reinstatement

On 3 April 1888, Frame again admonished Pembery: 'take note, if there is one single picture wrongly fixed, you will have to take it down and refix at your own personal expense, so take care'.[10] Frame's words loomed large when, on 21 March 2000, the crate was unpacked in the Marble Hall. The paintings were laid out and their sequence double-checked against Lonsdale's sketches as well as archival evidence. To ensure that the canvases were no bigger than when Pembery first fixed them in place, any projecting sailcloth and Mylar laminate was trimmed with scissors from the top, left and right edges. The canvases were then stapled to wooden battens through the laminate, which still extended beyond the bottom edges, for safe handling up the stairs.

One floor up, the weak and damaged plaster of the walls of the Family Bedroom had been made good and lined throughout with two layers of heavy grade lining wallpaper. Close-boarded scaffolding had been erected across the room at a suitable working height, with a hatch large enough to take the longest canvas.

Having carried each canvas up the stairs to the landing outside the Bedroom, the batten and staples were removed and the canvas eased through the doors

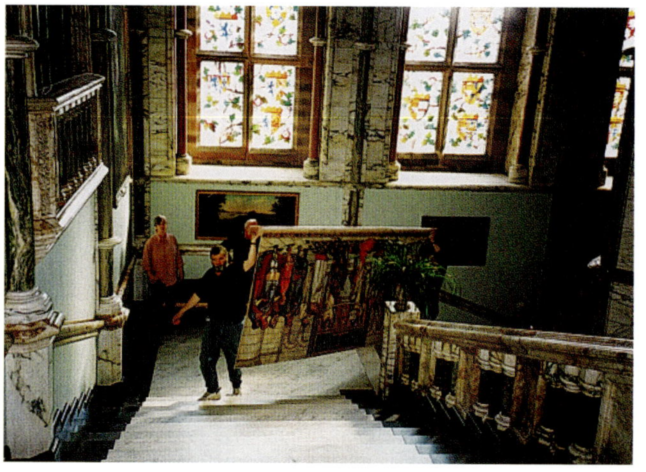

Figure 6 Carrying *Marriage of St Margaret* upstairs to the Family Bedroom.

and then lifted up and onto the scaffold floor (Figs 6 and 7). It was important to maintain tension along the length of the consolidated borders, and manoeuvring the largest canvases required five or six people on and below the scaffold.

Reinstatement of the canvases took three days. Lonsdale had originally cut the canvases to fit precisely the length of each wall and, when again positioned edge-to-edge, the result was a snug fit (Fig. 8). Accurate horizontal alignment of the complex design was another matter but, by judging the positions of the bottom borders with their Latin texts by eye, a straight horizontal border around the room was achieved.

The canvases were temporarily stapled along their top, unpainted edges and their positions on the walls marked with pencilled lines. Starting with the smallest canvases from the east wall, a thick coat of adhesive was brushed onto the wall and the canvas was then immediately positioned. Repositioning was possible but only during a bare 10-minute period rather than the 30 minutes suggested by the manufacturer. This acceleration of the bonding time, due to the porosity of the

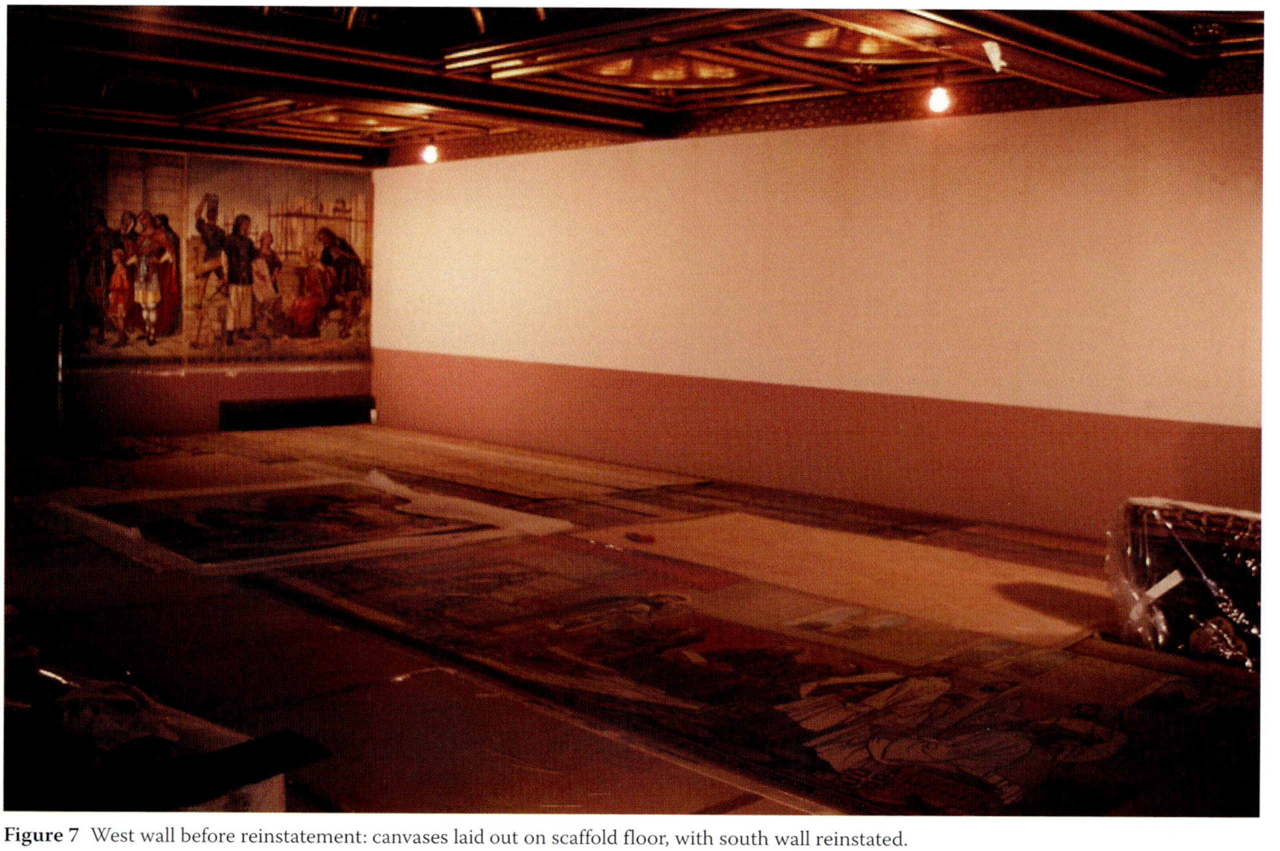

Figure 7 West wall before reinstatement: canvases laid out on scaffold floor, with south wall reinstated.

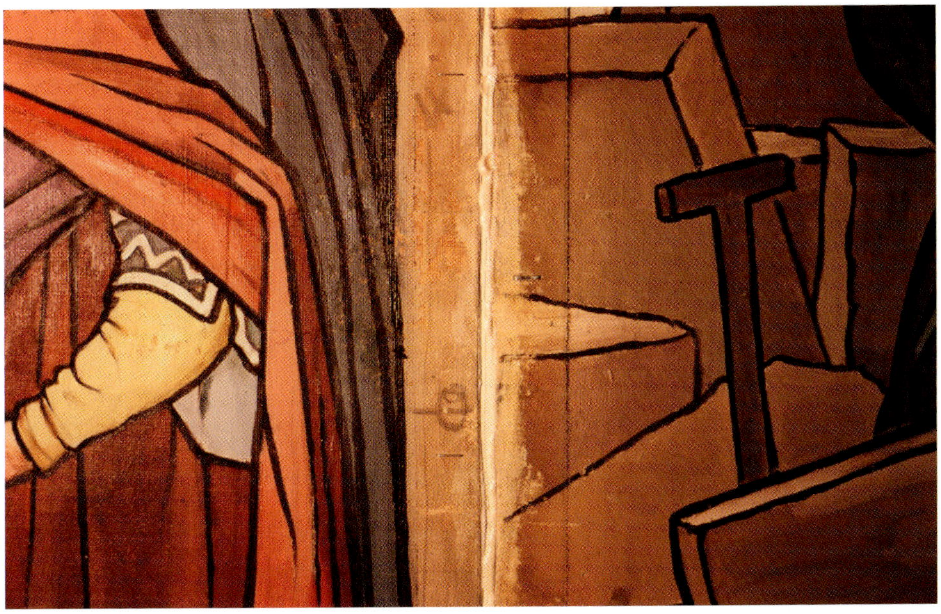

Figure 8 Detail of *Marriage of St Margaret* and *Building of Dunfermline*: excess adhesive showing at join to be covered by new border.

paper and plaster, was a problem with the three largest paintings. Here, a few air pockets remained despite the application of thick coats of adhesive by brush or roller to both the Mylar and the wall to achieve maximum repositioning time with a wet bond. In each case, small air pockets occurred in the lower central left area, reflecting our working pattern across the 1.7 × 3.7m surfaces. An excellent bond was otherwise achieved by quickly smoothing the surface with hands and small rollers (an exercise that would have been complicated by impasto or a varnish layer). The canvases were further secured to the walls by 14mm staples through all four unpainted edges around each painting.

Once the canvases, complete with their bottom borders, were in place, the borders for the remaining three sides of each canvas could be attached. By precisely correlating tack holes through both the canvas edges and gilded borders, it was confirmed that the entire top border for the west wall was present. Similarly, matching original markings and measurements dictated the positions of the five original west wall decorative uprights. However, five further original plain upright sections remained and, without evidence to identify their original location, the decision was taken to keep original material together as much as possible; four were, therefore, secured as uprights on the south wall and the fifth in the north-west corner. All remaining top and vertical sections were of new material.

The borders were lifted onto the scaffold wrapped in acid-free tissue and taped to a wooden batten. Both the original and the reconstructed borders were attached to the unpainted butt-joined canvas edges using PVA (neutral pH) and, when aligned in position, brass pins were tacked into the wall through border and canvas using original tack holes. The pins secured the borders while the adhesive dried and ensured uniform anchorage.

Final repairs to areas of loss on the edges of Lombardic script between two canvases could only be accurately carried out once the canvases were in position. It was also critical that new swastikas, found at the bottom of each upright, were accurately positioned. PVA was used to secure the inserts and repairs; new swastikas were painted with pigments bound in shellac, which was also used for the final toning to integrate new with original material. In-painting and in-gilding was also carried out on new material to complete the intended effect of parallel lines around each painting.

'All your pictures are now fixed'[11] Frame told Lonsdale on 4 April 1888; 102 years later, almost to the day, the Chairman, Mount Stuart Trust, was given the same news.

Acknowledgements

Henry Matthews and Clare Herbert hand-lined the three larger canvases; Sally Cheyne and Owen Davison vacuum-lined the remaining 12. Henry, Clare and Sally, together with Ines Santy, cleaned and retouched the 15 canvases. Lynda Robertson assisted with the conservation and reinstatement of the borders, as well as with the reinstatement of the canvases. Suggestions from Liz Rose improved the outcome of the project as well as the final appearance of this paper. Everyone at Mount Stuart Trust was extremely helpful, but particular thanks are due to Andrew McLean, the Trust's archivist.

Notes

1. G. Stamp, *The New Mount Stuart*, Mount Stuart guide book, edited by A. McLean, 2nd edn (1999), pp. 7–11.
2. Letter from Frame to Pembery, 31 March 1888, William Frame's letter book, p. 511, Mount Stuart archive.
3. The source of 13 Latin texts is St Margaret's biography, written by her confessor Turgot shortly after her death in 1092.
4. Mount Stuart inventory, 1910; also identified in the only known photograph of the Bedroom with its original furnishings, *c.* 1907.
5. Polyester sailcloth supplied by John Heathcoat & Co Ltd, Westexe, Tiverton, Devon EX16 5LL.
6. Mylar 'A' 250 micron ML250/1850kg supplied by Kensulat plc, Lower Hollin Bank Street, Blackburn, Lancs BB2 4UB.
7. 3M Fastbond 40 supplied by NBT Inveresk Ltd, 1 Rutherford Square, Brucefield Industry Park, Livingston, West Lothian EH54 9BU.
8. Corrugated paper supplied by Calligrane, Papier Fibres, 6, rue du Pont Louis Philippe, 75004 Paris.
9. BEVA 371 film supplied by Preservation Equipment Ltd, Vinces Road, Diss, Norfolk IP22 4HQ.
10. Letter from Frame to Pembery, 3 April 1888, William Frame's letter book, p. 513, Mount Stuart archive.
11. Letter from Frame to Lonsdale, 4 April 1888, William Frame's letter book, p. 514, Mount Stuart archive.

The authors

Clare Meredith was an independent paintings conservator, but is currently Acting Head Conservator at the National Trust for Scotland. Colleen Donaldson is an independent gilding conservator based in Edinburgh.

Installation of *L'Escargot*, by Henri Matisse

CALVIN WINNER

Introduction

L'Escargot, the large collage by Henri Matisse (1869–1954) (Fig. 1), was moved from Tate Britain to Tate Modern, London, on 8 March 2000. The work is not especially fragile but is surprisingly heavy, fitted with plate glass in the late 1960s, and an astonishing 7mm thick. *The Snail*, as it is popularly known, had arrived at the Tate unframed but, after some years a frame was fitted. A little later glazing was added and subsequently, because of its increase in weight, it was not moved more than a very short distance in 30 years. For the move across the River Thames, a carrying cradle was made to hold the work during transit, literally from when it left the wall at Milbank until it reached its final destination at Tate Modern. The move was carefully considered but it is never guaranteed that every eventuality has been covered. The door spaces were measured, but would the work squeeze through? There were also concerns about the frame, which was not designed to hold such weight.

Making the collage

After 1948 Matisse was prevented from painting by ill health but, although confined to bed, he produced a number of works known as *gouaches découpées*. *The Snail*, completed in 1952, is one of the larger examples at almost 3m square. It is made up of 22 hand-coloured paper sections attached to a thick paper support, itself in two parts overlapping down the centre. His assistants would paint out sheets of Canson paper with gouache paints from Linel of Paris '*extra fines*'. These pre-painted sheets would form a stockpile in the artist's studio. Matisse had begun to use Linel gouaches in the mid-1940s, when his paper cutouts, such as *Jazz*, were destined for publication. He considered these gouaches a very close match to printers ink colours and therefore guaranteed exact reproduction. Matisse would begin cutting with scissors or tearing coloured shapes from this prepared paper, producing the shapes and sizes he desired. He compared this work to carving and once he had his shapes he could arrange them at leisure by pinning them to the wall of his studio. This work would take some time and the collage segments

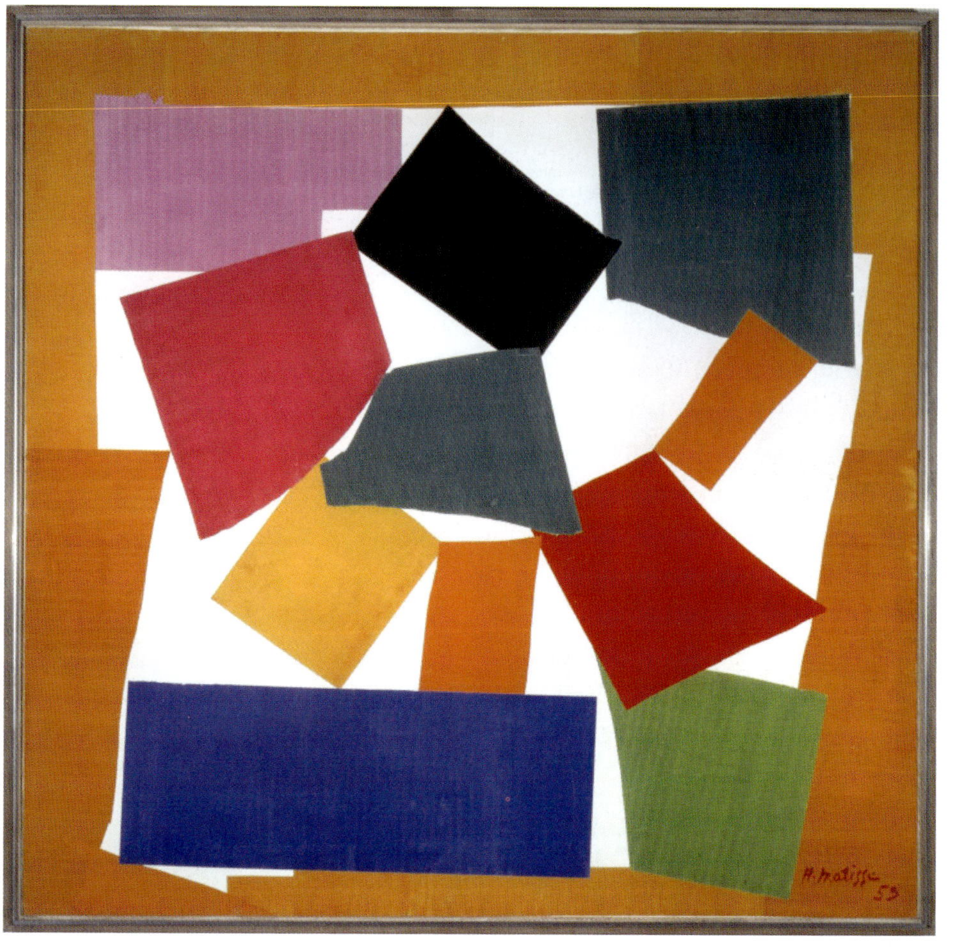

Figure 1 *L'Escargot*, by Henri Matisse.

Figure 2 Collage element illustrating damage such as scuffs and smudges caused during the making of the work.

exhibit numerous pinholes, scuffs, creases and tears as evidence of this working process (Fig. 2). One anecdote recalls summer days when the studio windows were open, with collage segments gently flapping in the wind and occasionally pieces blowing gently across the room.[1] Not until he was certain of his arrangement and all the pieces had been secured would he then authorise his assistants to go to work and fix them down to an overall paper support.

His secretary, Mme Lydia Delectorskaya, described the making of *The Snail* in a letter to the Tate Gallery (30 March 1976):

> The Snail was made in the Hotel Regina at Nice. H. Matisse had at his disposal sheets of paper painted in gouache by assistants, in all the colours he used for the 'papiers découpées'. A background of white paper – of the dimensions indicated by H.M. – was put on the wall and the assistant pinned onto it the pieces of gouached paper which H.M. passed to him indicating exactly where they should be placed. When H.M. decided that his composition was finished, it was lightly stuck to the background. The panel was taken down when H.M. needed the wall for a further work. When later on it was sent to Lefebvre-Foinet [in Paris] to be pasted down, before anything was moved, an extremely precise tracing was made to ensure that no changes were made in the composition, not even by so much as a millimetre.[2]

Maurice Lefebvre-Foinet added in a letter of 19 February 1976:

> Entrusted personally with the completion of the collages by M. Henri Matisse, we had the work pinned onto paper – two very exact tracings were made.

The supporting paper in two separate parts mentioned previously was arranged by Mr Lefebvre-Foinet and was prepared by giving an overall coating of white paint before the collage elements were pasted down onto canvas.

> We used raw canvas which had been sponged over twice and attached to a temporary stretcher. Thin paper was pasted onto this canvas to serve as a support and a means of attachment. Next the paper of the background was pasted down, then the work itself was fixed. This work was done by me with the help of M. Matisse's secretary, and completed and approved by the artist and Madame Duthuit.

The collage arrives at the Tate Gallery

On acquisition in 1962, *The Snail* arrived at the Gallery rolled face out on a large wooden roller. It was noticed that the edges of the canvas had multiple tacking holes, suggesting numerous past removals from the stretcher (Fig. 3). It appears that every time the collage had been moved it was simply taken off its stretcher and placed on a roller. A stretcher made of pine in 12 sections was assembled and the canvas re-stretched with some difficulty. In fact the edges had been reinforced in several places. It was attached to the stretcher with copper alloy tacks and then keyed out. Shortly after acquisition a simple L-section hardwood frame was made, but the work remained unglazed.

With the build-up of damage along the tacking margins, there was an obvious reluctance to maintain the practice of removing the collage from its stretcher if required to travel. By the end of the 1960s, loan requests were indeed tabled and subsequently declined.[3] This became more of an issue by the late 1960s, when a decision was taken to glaze the collage. Up until this time it had been reasonably mobile: large, yes, but not particularly heavy. If taken off its stretcher it was arguably even more manageable. However, with the above concerns about the tacking margins heeded, there was now a desire to offer further protection by glazing as a result of alarm concerning the accumulation of surface dirt and fingerprints. The delicate-coloured surface will tolerate very little surface cleaning; therefore the obvious solution was to glaze.

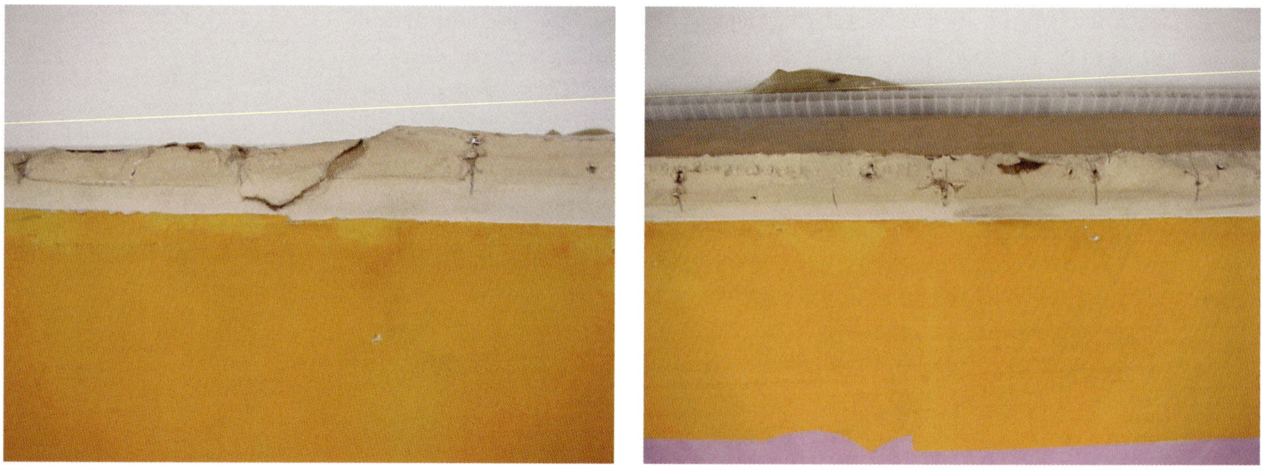

Figure 3 Two illustrations showing the extent of the damage to the tacking margins as a result of numerous re-stretchings.

Glazing the collage

In terms of protecting artworks from an accumulation of surface dirt, glazing is probably the most effective method. Unvarnished pictures or artworks that are known to present difficulties in surface cleaning therefore tend to be glazed. Exceptions exist, however, and it is common to encounter vulnerable large works where glazing was either impossible historically, because of the lack of availability of glass in large enough sheets, or impractical because of the increase in weight or unacceptable change to the artist's presentation of an artwork. The aesthetics of whether to glaze cannot be discussed fully here, but in the case of *The Snail*, its vulnerability undoubtedly tipped the balance in favour of glazing.

In order to accommodate glazing, the frame was reinforced by fitting alloy strips to the rebate. The chosen glass was 6.25mm crystal clear plate glass especially imported from Belgium (presumably because of lack of availability in the UK). At the time of glazing there is no recorded debate concerning what type of glazing would be preferable, but it is known that Perspex was not an option due to the size of the work. This is confirmed by a loan request in 1970 when there was discussion on whether to replace the glass with Perspex. ICI, the manufacturer of Perspex, informed the Tate that it was not available in large enough sheets, nor could it be made to order. The loan request was subsequently declined.[4]

The decision to glaze would prove very fortunate in later years. First, in 1988, the Gallery roof leaked, sending water pouring over the surface of the work. Although some water did penetrate the frame, most ran straight off and the work was moved to safety, unfitted, examined and air-dried with minimal damage. A year later the episode was repeated but the frame seal had been improved in the interim, so no water penetrated the frame and the running water could simply be dried off.[5] The decision to glaze was obviously the right one, but the collage had now become a very difficult work to handle and all future loan requests were declined. So, what had begun its life as 22 coloured pieces of paper was now so heavy it was considered dangerous for the artwork and handlers if moved.

Breaking the glass during handling has always been a terrifying prospect but, because the glass is so thick, laminated glass has never been contemplated. Perhaps one day a bespoke piece of low reflective and laminated glass may be considered but, inevitably, this may well increase the weight yet further. It is not unusual even today to debate whether to glaze large pictures with vulnerable surfaces. At Tate Modern, three oil stick drawings by Bill Woodrow (*95/04 Untitled*, *92/03 Untitled* and *94/03 Wilson's Phalorope*) are extremely sensitive to the touch and almost impossible to surface clean. In order to glaze these works, the artist's frames would need replacement and this is currently considered a step too far in compromising the artist's chosen presentation. Anselm Kiefer's *Ways of Worldly Wisdom*, currently on loan to the Tate Collection, is a composite work consisting of a series of printed woodcuts on paper, stuck to stretched canvas and overpainted with oil paint and shellac. At 3.6 × 3.4m the work is unframed and not glazed. Interestingly, it is not simply rectangular as there is an attached section along the right-hand side. This complicates glazing and framing, although probably does not rule it out completely. As with *The Snail*, the work is very difficult to surface clean and the accumulation of surface dirt is currently being monitored.

The move to Tate Modern

The Art Handling Department at Tate headed by Jim Grundy designed the transit cradle after much discussion on the best way to hold the work while leaving the Gallery and during transportation. Constructed of box-section steel to an A-frame design, it was fabricated in two sections to allow for its use in future art-handling work. Angled at 45 degrees on small wheels, this would allow the collage to go through doors at Tate Modern that had been set at just under 3m in height by the architects. The cradle was intentionally over-engineered for future flexibility and each part will support one ton dead weight. There was much debate on how much the work actually weighed. The art-handling team organised a sweepstake with weights ranging from 330kg to 510kg but, in fact, the work weighed in at a healthy 285kg. Compared to many stone or steel sculptures this is reasonably light, but hanging the work would inevitably call for a certain amount of manoeuvring. Thankfully, the work is relatively robust, with all the collage elements securely adhered to the surface. However, the weight was a concern as the frame was not originally intended to support heavy glass and, although strengthened, it had never been tested to such a degree.

The collage was taken from the wall at Tate Britain using 'stackers' (small wheeled units) before being lowered into the bottom wooden shutter. It was wrapped in polythene before being lifted by hand onto the A-frame and the top shutter positioned, adding another 31.5kg to the weight. The shutters were

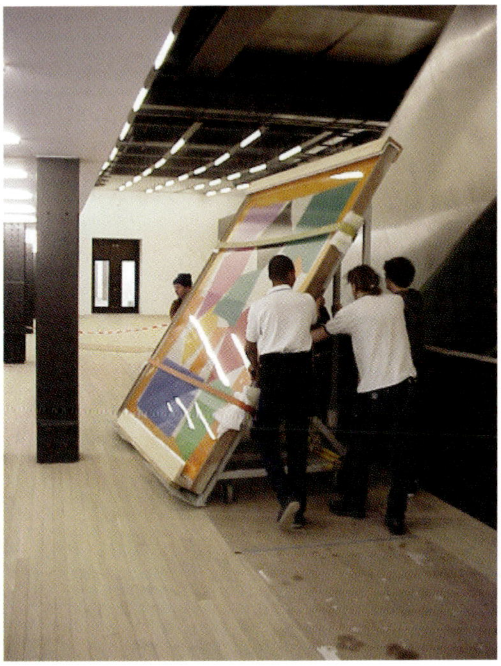

Figure 4 *The Snail* makes it way through Tate Modern on the A-frame.

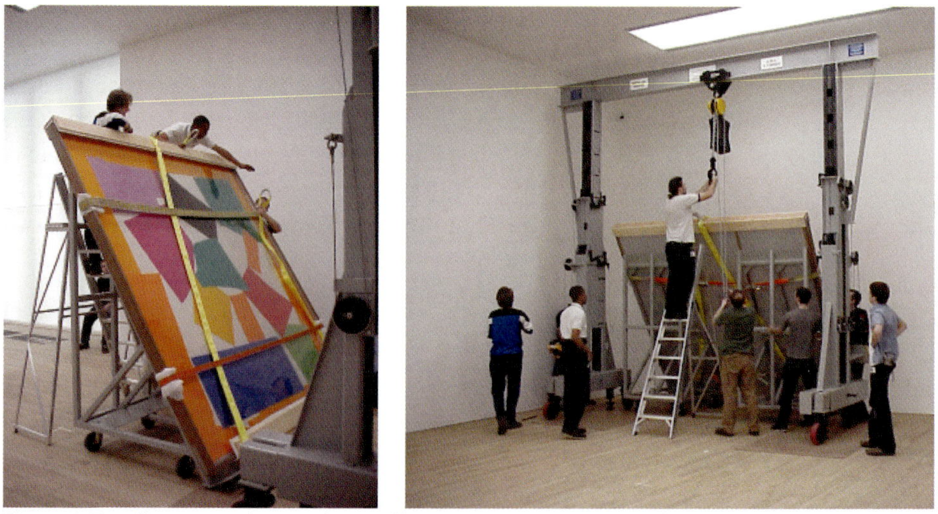

Figure 5 Two illustrations showing the installation process. First, on the left the sling is attached, ready for connection to the hoist. The strain directed at the frame is taken up by the wooden shutters at both the top and bottom and is visible here at the top of the frame. On the right the hoist is connected to the sling ready to start lifting. Once attached the collage can be moved with relative ease allowing for fine adjustments in positioning it on the gallery wall. It also allowed the conservation team to turn the work around and remove it from its frame.

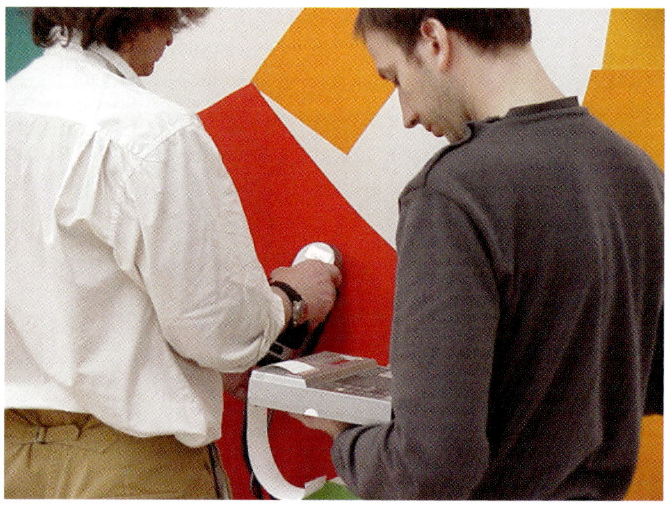

Figure 6 The move provided a rare opportunity to remove the collage from its frame. This allowed a full condition check to take place but in addition to take colour measurements of the coloured sections. This will form the first part of an ongoing programme of monitoring possible colour change within the collage.

designed to protect the frame against lifting belts to be used during the hanging procedure. Now in position, the collage could be wheeled to the waiting lorry and firmly secured to the inside. On arrival at Tate Modern the work slowly made its way to the third floor (Fig. 4), snugly fitting through the series of gallery doors. A large lifting winch had been positioned to support the weight of the collage during hanging. In theory the work could be supported while final decisions were taken on positioning. Inevitably, the final manoeuvring was by hand. It is held against the wall by metal plates and supported by steel brackets. The collage is likely to be on permanent display at Tate Modern although further moves cannot be ruled out, at least around the building.

Conclusion

The glazing of works for protection is certainly not a new idea – the glazing of drawings and prints is long established. Watercolours, prints and pastels have been glazed at least since the eighteenth century, when it became fashionable to remove them from albums for display. In 1850 a report led by Sir Charles Eastlake recommended glazing the paintings at the National Gallery in London to protect varnished oil and tempera from the polluted air of the city and from visitors to the gallery. This led to many pictures being glazed at the National and the Tate galleries (then part of the National Gallery). In modern times the rise of the conservation profession has highlighted the desire to protect paintings by glazing. Historically, the size of a picture dictated whether glazing was possible. During the nineteenth century, increasingly larger sheets of plate glass became available and later float glass made very large sheets possible, but there are still limitations to its use.

During the twentieth century, with changes in artistic practice, unvarnished works or paintings with areas of bare canvas increasingly meant that glazing became more acceptable for easel paintings. It is interesting that, because of *The Snail*'s delicate condition, it was glazed within five years of acquisition. Fortunately glass of a suitable size was available but, had it not been, *The Snail* would probably look very different today. Obviously this was a radical change to how the work had previously been seen, but the change was not questioned seriously at the time. The collage clearly needed protection and this outweighed the debate on the aesthetics of viewing the work without glazing. However, the decision to glaze had further repercussions, for example, due to its weight and the difficulty of handling, the Gallery became reluctant to lend the work. All these factors require careful consideration when dealing with large pictures and often we solve one problem only to find in doing so we create many more. The deciding factors making this particular move possible were simply that it did not involve casing the picture or complicated changes of transportation. Had these been necessary, it is likely that, as in the past, the move would not have been made.

Acknowledgements

Senior art handler Mike Hall and his team. Jim Grundy, Head of Art Handling at Tate for the design of the transit A-frame.

Notes

1. Elderfield, J. 1978. *The Cut-outs of Henri Matisse*. New York: George Braziller.
2. Entry on Internet: Description of Matisse's working practice taken from 'short text' entry written by Terry Riggs, February 1998, as part of the Tate catalogue entry. The full catalogue entry is available on the Tate Internet site: www.tate.org.uk.
3. Unpublished archival document, Tate Conservation records.
4. Unpublished archival document, Tate Conservation records
5. Unpublished archival document, Tate Conservation records.

The author

Calvin Winner was Senior Conservator for graphic art and photography at Tate Modern, London, between 1995 and 2005. He has recently taken charge of conservation at the Sainsbury Centre for Visual Arts at the University of East Anglia, Norwich.

Cy Twombly: Big Pictures in a Travelling Retrospective

MICHAEL DUFFY

Introduction

> I paint very large pictures. I realize that historically the function of painting large pictures is painting something very grandiose and pompous. The reason I paint them however, is precisely because I want to be very intimate and human. To paint a small picture is to place yourself outside your experience, to look upon an experience with a reducing glass. However you paint the larger pictures, you are in it, it isn't something you command.[1]

In 1994, Cy Twombly[2] was the subject of a retrospective organised by the Museum of Modern Art in New York. This exhibition, curated by Kirk Varnedoe, included approximately 100 works of painting, drawing and sculpture. Many works also travelled to Houston, Los Angeles and Berlin during the tour of the retrospective. In the course of the retrospective, MoMA was able to acquire three works from the artist's own collection: *Leda and the Swan*, 1962, *Untitled*, 1970, and *The Four Seasons (Quattro Stagioni)*, 1994. During the retrospective several issues had to be addressed concerning the transport and display of these oversize works, particularly *Untitled*, which at 3.9 × 6.3m (13 × 21ft) was the largest canvas in the exhibition. Handling of the huge *Untitled* canvas was complicated by its delicate surface and flimsy support. *Untitled* was on long-term loan to Bonn, prior to being transported to New York. Some of the issues concerning travelling such a huge canvas were addressed by consulting with the conservators and shippers in Bonn for the design of the crate. A MoMA conservator also went to Bonn to participate in the dismantling of the work in order to be familiar with its travel requirements and address any conservation concerns (during routine condition reporting some minor areas of flaking were discovered which required consolidation prior to moving the work). Also early in 1994, the paintings known together as *The Four Seasons* arrived from Twombly's studio in Italy a few months before the exhibition was to open. In the intervening weeks before the opening of the exhibition, decisions had to be made concerning the proper display of *The Four Seasons*, including their final format and framing. These issues were resolved in consultation with the curator of the exhibition and Twombly himself. The four canvases were intended to hang together and thus their impact is equivalent to some larger single works in terms of handling and display.

The Four Seasons

Twombly has worked mainly in Italy since 1959. One of his studios is in Gaeta, 96km north of Naples. It is here that he completed the first cycle of *The Four Seasons*, which he began in Bassano in Teverina in 1991.[3] This version of *The Four Seasons* came to MoMA to be included in the travelling exhibition and was shortly thereafter acquired by the Museum as a generous gift from the artist.

Twombly executed these large works on pre-primed canvases nailed directly to his studio walls. This enabled him to work against a solid support for these large-scale canvases for which he used pencil and oil crayon in addition to oil and acrylic paint. Twombly often refers to classical antiquity in his work, and in *The Four Seasons* floating barges recall the underworld vessels of Egyptian mythology.[4] Twombly's signature style includes melding layers of yellow and white paint to create landscapes with an atmosphere reminiscent of Turner's late landscapes. Tangles of impastoed paint contrast with washes of acrylic and large expanses of pristine white ground. Inscriptions float on the ground or emerge from under veils of thinly applied acrylic paint.[5] In addition to the pencil and wax crayon inscriptions, Twombly used oil and acrylic paint applied with a brush or his fingers. The result is a very rich, painterly surface throughout *The Four Seasons*.

The first three canvases of *The Four Seasons* were shipped freshly painted from the artist's studio and arrived at MoMA at the end of April 1994, allowing some time to devise a way to mount the works for display in September. *Summer* was the last to arrive. The paintings were transported according to the artist's instructions, rolled with tissue paper tightly face-in around tubes packed into a crate. As soon as the canvases were unpacked it became apparent that there were conservation issues that had to be addressed immediately. The works were slowly unrolled and allowed to relax. Weighting the edges with blotting paper and acrylic sheeting (Plexiglas/Perspex) strips helped to return the canvases into plane in preparation for mounting them onto permanent supports. To facilitate handling, individual platforms were constructed of Homosote board and 50 × 100mm (2 × 4in) lumber to provide a support for treatment and handling of the unstretched works.

Problems resulting from shipping the still-wet canvases could now be addressed. There was also evidence of transfer of paint to adjacent areas in the composition. Also, sometime before transit from Italy, paper towels had been applied to blot oil from the fresh alizarin paint. The paper towel became embedded in the soft paint and the tissue paper interleaf also adhered to the front of the works in several areas of impasto. To remedy this situation, the paper towelling and tissue paper were cut away and cotton swabs moistened with water were used to remove most of the paper embedded in the paint. Paper fibre residues were removed mechanically with tweezers, under magnification.

As a result of compression of the paint from rolling during transport, whole sections of impasto were locally curled up and lifting. In most cases delamination occurred between the ground and paint layers. Fortunately, the paint was still quite flexible and the impasto could be coaxed gently back into place and re-adhered with acrylic emulsion. These areas were weighted overnight. Drying cracks, resulting from thick applications of acrylic paint over oil, were also consolidated with adhesive to prevent any future delamination of paint occurring.

Once the paint layers had been secured, the structural needs of the canvases were addressed. The canvases were measured and stretchers were custom-made by a local stretcher maker to our specifications. Stretchers, made of heavyweight sugar pine,[6] were constructed to a traditional design which included an added lip and expandable joints. Deciding on the final dimensions of the works involved consultation with the curator and Twombly, who marked the dimensions in crayon directly on the canvas. Because the works were slightly off-square, Mylar (Melinex) templates indicating the exact sizes of the canvases were prepared for the stretcher maker in order to maximise the amount of original canvas that would be presented. Twombly's compositions generally extended up to the edge of the canvas (and sometimes onto the adjoining wall of his studio), therefore it was critical to have precisely made stretchers. The stretcher supports were prepared by first covering them with medium-weight polyester fabric, which is commercially available in oversize widths.[7] Strip linings of the same material were prepared with BEVA 371 adhesive. With the canvases laying face up on their platforms, the strip linings were attached with the aid of a large diameter tube that had been covered with silicon Mylar. The canvases were rolled around the tube and the strip lining attached to the verso using a hot spatula to activate the adhesive. The strip-lined canvases were then mounted on their individual stretchers and the tension adjusted with pushpins. Finally, the strip linings were attached to the verso of the stretcher with staples and the wooden keys inserted into the joints and tied. For additional protection during transportation, the versos were covered with a lightweight foam board and fitted with fabric strap loops to assist in handling.

In consultation with Twombly, the curator and conservation framer designed frames for *The Four Seasons*. Simple lacquered birchwood frames were made with an 'L' profile and a bevelled face to enable the canvases to 'float' in the frame with the entire width of the canvas showing. The nail holes and irregularities at the edges were not disguised as a testament to Twombly's working methods. Additional support of the heavier framed works was required during installation, so L-shaped brackets were mounted on the walls behind the works to distribute the weight evenly.

Untitled, 1970

In 1994, MoMA also acquired from Twombly the monumental 1970 canvas *Untitled*, which measures over 3.9m (13ft) high and 6.3m (21ft) long.[8] Prior to acquisition, the painting was on long-term loan to the Kunstmuseum in Bonn, Germany. During the Twombly retrospective *Untitled* went to Houston and Los Angeles as part of the tour, where it had to be re-stretched and unstretched at each venue.

This work is part of the so-called grey-ground series that Twombly executed on a pre-primed, medium-weight canvas, washed with thin layers of grey, oil-based commercial paint. On top of this he used white *Caran d'Ache* crayon, drawing a series of calligraphic looping scrolls. Twombly apparently worked the crayon into the still-wet paint, since, in some areas, the paint and crayon have blended into a soft inscription approximating the appearance of an erased chalkboard. Like *The Four Seasons*, this work was executed on unstretched canvas nailed directly to the artist's studio wall. Varnedoe[9] notes that Twombly made these works with the assistance of his friend Nicola del Roscio who, with the artist perched on his shoulders, shuttled Twombly back and forth in front of the 13ft-high canvas, so that he could reach the upper parts of the composition. This was quite a feat of endurance considering that the canvas originally measured over 9.6m (32ft) long.[10] Varnedoe has linked Twombly's work of this period to Jackson Pollock and the legacy of Abstract Expressionism, as well as to Leonardo da Vinci and Italian Futurist artists. In the catalogue accompanying the exhibition he writes:

> The picture brims over with a nervous, obsessed energy, yet its trance-like monotony also opens out into a sense of serene, oceanic dissolution, in a nebular cloud of great depth and infinite complexity.[11]

Untitled, 1970, was brought to New York for the retrospective after being unstretched and rolled at the Kunstmuseum in Bonn. Furthermore, as the work is too large to be stored on its stretcher it is permanently housed on a tube when not on view. The tube is suspended on a cradle to prevent crushing the rolled canvas and then slides into an outer crate for travel. Because of space constrictions in MoMA storage, the stretcher is also stored disassembled in three sections. The original support for the painting was a very lightweight stretcher measuring barely 18mm (¾in) thick. It was apparently devised to transport the painting by lorry from Rome to Berlin and then on to Bonn for exhibition. While this stretcher provided adequate support for the canvas when on view temporarily, it was clear that a new stretcher would be required for the tour's subsequent venues. For the initial exhibition in New York the stretcher still required reinforcement prior to installation, and a system of ropes and pulleys had to be devised to rig the work off the floor once it had been stretched. Even with this scheme the stretcher bowed considerably and the canvas appeared to be supporting the weight of the stretcher instead of vice versa. Once it was learned that the work would be touring to two other venues after MoMA, the decision was made to replace the stretcher when the exhibition closed in New York. The new stretcher could be disassembled into three parts since a two-part folding stretcher was deemed too difficult for transport as well as unwieldy for a canvas this large. Outer members of the stretcher were constructed of sugar pine with poplar inner cross-bars providing additional strength. The design also included aluminium brackets joining the horizontal cross-members for extra rigidity. A wooden cleat was installed on the stretcher to distribute the weight across a matching cleat on the wall and to provide some lateral movement during installation.

Stretching the canvas followed the same basic procedure for each installation of the tour. The gallery space was prepared with brown paper taped to the floor so that it would not shift. The outer wrapping was removed and the roll oriented properly. This is critical since there is little room to manoeuvre in the galleries once the canvas has been stretched – it must be hoisted directly up to the wall for installation. The canvas was unrolled face down with its protective silicon Mylar interleaf onto the brown paper. Silicon Mylar was chosen for its minimal impact on the paint and crayon surface and its archival advantage for long-term storage. Runners alongside the roll allow the canvas to be unrolled without the weight of the roll crushing the canvas. The canvas has a linen strip lining attached to the original with a thermoplastic adhesive, apparently from a previous conservation treatment. Since the original tacking margins are very narrow for a painting this size, the strip lining was added to facilitate attachment to the stretcher. After the painting was unrolled face down, the strip lining was checked for security. Some local delamination had occurred after previous unrollings, so additional applications of BEVA 371 film were necessary. Minor tears in the strip lining had also occurred as a result of previous re-stretchings and were repaired locally with polyester fabric[12] using BEVA 371 film and a hot spatula. After the stretcher was assembled it was positioned over the unrolled canvas; this required the assistance of several preparators. Re-stretching was undertaken with the canvas face down after it had been properly aligned. Staples were applied through the strip lining into the reverse of the stretcher to avoid repeated stapling through the original. Ropes fitted through metal brackets on the stretcher allow the stretched canvas to be hoisted to vertical on a scissors lift. Due to the tight fit in the gallery, light fixtures had to be removed before the work could be hoisted to a vertical position. The work was then positioned by sliding it on Ethafoam blocks, prior to lifting it onto the cleat. *Untitled* is exhibited unframed in its current installation, but it is possible that in future installations with additional wall space a frame might be added that matches frames on other works of the 1970s by Twombly.

Conclusions

With the expanded exhibition space planned for MoMA it is hoped that works of this size can remain on permanent display. In the meantime, as conservators dealing with contemporary art, we will continue to be challenged by the logistics of exhibiting oversize works in our galleries and on loan. The treatments outlined here are a result of very close collaboration with conservators and curators at MoMA. Registrars, art preparators and art transport personnel also provided their input and helped to smooth the task of bringing the works from storage to wall. With this collaboration, the works can continue to command us from their well-earned place on the wall.

Acknowledgements

During the exhibition at MoMA I worked closely with Jim Coddington and Anny Aviram, my colleagues in the Department of Conservation. Suzanne Siano and Jessica David assisted with the documentation of the works for this paper. This study would not have been possible without Kirk Varnedoe who curated the retrospective and who was responsible for the acquisition of these major works by Cy Twombly for MoMA's collection. Carol Mancusi-Ungaro at the Menil Collection generously shared her considerable knowledge of Cy Twombly's technique and working methods. In Berlin, Heiner Bastian, curator, provided further insight into the artist's oeuvre, and Hana Streicher, conservator, smoothed the installation procedure. Certainly the greatest debt of gratitude goes to Cy Twombly for creating these astonishing works in a career now spanning six decades.

Notes

1. Mark Rothko (1951) 'A symposium on how to combine architecture, painting and sculpture', *Interiors* 110(10): 104. (Excerpted in K. Stiles and P. Selz (eds) (1996) *Theories and Documents of Contemporary Art: A Sourcebook of Artists' Writings*. Berkeley, CA: University of California Press.)
2. Born Edwin Parker Twombly, Jr, 25 April 1928, Lexington, Virginia, USA.
3. H. Bastian (ed.) (1995) *Cy Twombly: Catalogue Raisonné of the Paintings, Volume IV 1972–1995*, pp. 173–7. Munich: Schirmer-Mosel.
4. A discussion of Twombly's imagery for these canvases can be found in K. Varnedoe (1994) *Cy Twombly: A Retrospective* (The Museum of Modern Art, New York), p. 50, and in Bastian 1995 (see note 3 above), pp. 34–6.
5. *The Four Seasons* contain quotations from George Seferis (1900–71), Greek poet, essayist and diplomat (K. Varnedoe, personal communication, 1995).
6. Stretchers made by Simon Liu Inc., 645 Dean Street, Brooklyn, New York, NY 11238.
7. Obtained from Art et Conservation, 33 Avenue Trudaine, 75009 Paris, France. Now available from Couleurs du Quai Voltaire – Magasin Sennelier, 3 Quai Voltaire, 75007, Paris, France.
8. See entry 111 in H. Bastian (ed.) (1994) *Cy Twombly: Catalogue Raisonné of the Paintings, Volume III 1966–1971*, pp. 231–3. Munich: Schirmer-Mosel.
9. Varnedoe 1994 (see note 4 above), p. 63.
10. After working the canvas with the white crayon, Twombly cut 3.3m (11ft) off the left side, reoriented it 90 degrees and finished the partially erased canvas with looping scrolls. This second *Untitled* canvas is now on loan to the Cy Twombly Gallery at the Menil Collection in Houston, Texas. Using scanned images and PhotoShop we were able to reconstruct the original canvas by matching up the underlying drawing in the Houston picture to correspond to the white scrolls on the left side of MoMA's painting. Carol Mancusi-Ungaro, former Chief Conservator at the Menil Collection, alerted me to the relationship between these two *Untitled* canvases.
11. Varnedoe 1994 (see note 4 above), p. 43.
12. See note 7 above.

The author

Michael Duffy is a conservator at the Museum of Modern Art, New York.

Touring Robert Rauschenberg's 32-ft-long Painting *Barge*

GILLIAN MCMILLAN

Introduction

This paper describes what we regard as a safe and convenient method of preparing, rolling and stretching the very large painting by Robert Rauschenberg entitled *Barge* (Fig. 1). The painting (oil and silkscreen on canvas) measures approximately 2030 × 9800mm (6ft 8in × 32ft 2in) and was painted in 1962–63.

This monumental work in black, white and grey incorporates many of the images Rauschenberg used time and again in his 79 silkscreen paintings. He made a substantial part of this painting for the filming in 1962 of a CBS television documentary showing him at work. However, the canvas is dated 1963 by the artist on the reverse, which indicates that he added to the painting after the filming. It has been suggested that its size and the rhythm within the composition inspired the title.

It was included in a large retrospective of his work mounted at the Guggenheim Museum in New York City in 1997 and then toured to three additional venues in Houston, Cologne and Bilbao. The painting is much too large to fit in and out of any truck or museum while stretched. Prior to this exhibition and the joint acquisition of the work by the New York and Bilbao Guggenheim museums, it had been repeatedly rolled and unrolled, stretched and stapled, every time it was moved – the tacking edges are riddled with holes from the various previous staplings.

The system described in this paper has been found to be very useful when travelling or handling big pictures. We first saw a system like this used on a very

Figure 1 *Barge*, 1962–63 by Robert Rauschenberg.

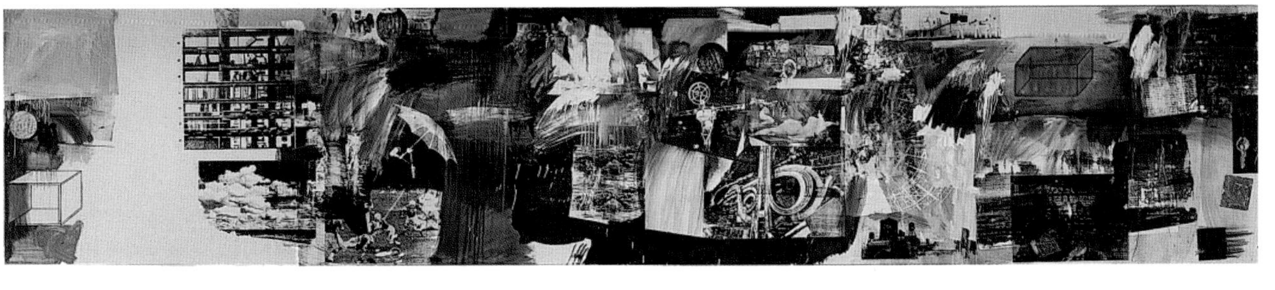

large theatre set painted by the artist Marc Chagall, which came to be exhibited at the Guggenheim in 1992–93 from the State Tretyakov Museum in Moscow.[1] We modified what we considered was an excellent idea to suit our needs. We have since used similar systems on several paintings in the Guggenheim Collection that are too large to fit into the Museum while stretched. Each one is slightly different but the principles remain the same.

First, the stretcher is designed in sections, with boards attached permanently to the front of the stretcher.[2] The boards are recessed, creating a smooth, flat surface and were attached without immobilising the stretcher's keying mechanism. The stretcher sections, when put together with metal plates, form a smooth and lightweight 'panel' support onto which the painting can be unrolled directly, face up. It can then be handled and attached to the stretcher with ease and accuracy, with none of the usual buckling of the canvas and paint layers associated with stretching a large painting on a traditionally designed stretcher face up.

Secondly, the painting is attached to the stretcher using Velcro[3] instead of staples or tacks, therefore stretching and unstretching are easy and fast and involve little or no stapling. The hook side of the Velcro is attached to the stretcher and the loop side of the Velcro is attached to the tacking edges of the painting.

Prior to coming to the Guggenheim for the Rauschenberg retrospective, the painting had been on long-term loan to the National Gallery in Washington DC. *Barge* was unstretched, rolled and packed there and was then transported to New York for treatment. We had a limited amount of time as our conservators were already committed to several other treatments for the retrospective which included approximately 400 works. We therefore commissioned a private conservator to carry out the work using our method.[4] We have treated four other large paintings at the Guggenheim using this Velcro and 'panel/stretcher' method: *Surface Veils I, II* and *III* by Robert Ryman and *Mother of Paintings* by Francesco Clemente.

The preparation of the painting

First, the old, stiff white glue and linen strip lining were removed from *Barge* and the old glue residues were removed mechanically from the tacking edges as far as was possible. Any holes or tears in the tacking edges were repaired locally. Meanwhile, the many yards of new strip-lining material were prepared. The new strip lining consists of strips of washed linen to which the loop or 'fuzzy' side of the Velcro is stitched by sewing machine. The 50mm (2in) wide Velcro strips can be pulled apart with some effort by hand in the peel direction and in the shear direction they are strong enough to secure the painting to the stretcher without any loss of tension on the canvas. The strength of the Velcro bond depends upon the width of the Velcro and how well the two components are pressed together. It can be bought in bulk on spools.

Prior to preparing the strip lining, ideally, the hook side of the Velcro is attached with an acrylic emulsion adhesive and staples to the reverse of the stretcher, a centimetre or so from the outside edge of the outer stretcher members, all around. Measurements are then taken to ascertain where on the strip lining the corresponding loop side of the Velcro needs to be stitched. This depends upon the depth and width of the stretcher bars. The placement of the Velcro is important as the two sections must match up reasonably accurately when the painting is being stretched to maximise the area of Velcro that is pressed together.

After washing and ironing the linen to be used, the strips for the strip lining are cut using pinking shears; this helps to avoid fraying of the edges and provides a desirably uneven edge to attach to the back of the painting. The strips are usually cut to approximately 150 or 200mm (6 or 8in) widths. Once the measurement from the stretcher has been taken, the loop side of the Velcro can be sewn onto the strip-lining fabric on a sewing machine. We use a straight-line stitch along the centre of the Velcro strip and zigzag stitching along both sides of the Velcro, often adding a strip of grosgrain tape[5] along the edge that will be pulled and strained the most when the Velcro is being released during unstretching. In the case of *Barge*, BEVA film was used to attach the linen strip lining. Once the strips are prepared and coated with BEVA (we usually prepare the strip linings with liquid BEVA 371 in solvent), and with the painting face down, the strip lining can be attached to the tacking edges. The side of the strip lining with the Velcro attached faces the back of the painting. Sometimes the BEVA adhesive is supplemented with hand stitching through the tacking edge of the painting and the strip lining; this takes a long time but forms the strongest bond. Finally, the corners of the strip lining are trimmed.

The roller

The roller upon which *Barge* is rolled is very wide in circumference – the tube has a 900mm (36in) diameter. A roller of 600mm (24in) diameter is usually wide enough for rolling most large paintings but *Barge* is by far the longest painting we have ever had to roll. The selection of the diameter of the tube depends on several factors such as the thickness or brittleness of the paint and ground, the type and degree of flexibility of the canvas, and the length of the painting. There is noticeable cracking from previous rollings in the ground and paint layers on *Barge*. We use a strong, hollow, cardboard tube called a Sonotube[6] which is supplied in 3.6m (12ft) lengths and various diameters (they can be joined if a longer tube is needed). Room should be allowed at either end of the tube to accommodate the tacking margins of the painting plus a little extra, just in case the painting is not rolled absolutely parallel which can easily happen. The excess is usually about 150–260mm (6–12in) beyond the size of the painting on each end.

A packing company made the roller and the packing crate for Barge.[7] Wooden spool ends with handles made to fit into the ends of the tube are glued and screwed in place. A wooden cradle was made to hold the tube off the ground and prevent it from rolling around when out of its crate. A long strip of the hook side of the Velcro fastener is attached to the length of the tube in a straight line with hot glue. The remainder of the tube is then covered with 6.25mm (¼in) thick Volara[8] over the whole surface, except for the area where the Velcro is attached. The Volara, which pads the tube, is attached with archival double-sided tape[9] and is approximately twice as thick as the Velcro. This ensures that when the painting is attached to the tube with its half of the Velcro, there is no bulge in that area when the painting is rolled over it.

Rolling the painting onto the roller

During rolling of the painting onto the roller, the turning of both ends of the tube must be synchronised to ensure the painting goes onto the tube straight. A tube as large as this can be quite heavy but it should stay parallel to the painting during rolling and tension must be kept on the other end of the painting as it is rolled. The Velcro at the shorter side of the painting is used to secure the painting to the tube first. Glassine[10] is used as an interleaf as the painting is rolled (Fig. 2); three widths of Glassine are required for *Barge*, which are overlapped generously. The Glassine is taped to the tube at the starting end. As the painting is rolled we ensure that

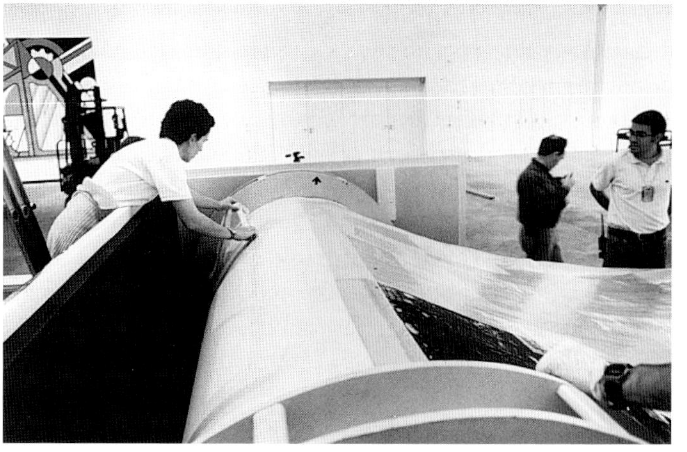

Figure 2 Attachment of the painting to the tube prior to rolling.

the Glassine stays flat. *Barge* wraps around the 900mm (36in) tube approximately three times. Two short pieces of twill tape are threaded through holes at the end of the strip lining, in the linen, and then screwed to the wooden ends of the tube. This prevents any slipping or unrolling of the painting when it is moved around. To further secure the rolled painting, long pieces of twill tape are tied around the top and bottom tacking edges after the painting is rolled, near the ends of the tube. Mylar[11] (Melinex) strips about 60mm (2ft) wide are also wrapped around the rolled painting and taped to hold the painting securely during transportation. It is then wrapped in plastic, sealed with tape and placed in its crate.

The stretcher

A new stretcher was fabricated for *Barge* as the existing stretcher was rather flimsy and inadequate. However, most stretchers could quite easily be modified by a carpenter to accommodate the panels or boards by routing out an L-shape in the front side of the outer stretcher members to accommodate the exact thickness of the boards. The centre stretcher members should be of an appropriate thickness to accommodate the boards – if they are too thick they can be planed. *Barge*'s stretcher is so large that it had to be constructed in four sections, which are packed together in a separate crate. When the painting is ready to be stretched, the sections of stretcher are screwed together with metal plates. The corner metal plates have sliding slots for the screws, which allow for expansion of the corners. More elaborate systems have been utilised for some of the other works such as the use of piano hinges and wooden pegs for the stretcher, so that it simply unfolds rather than having to be screwed together with metal plates (this is the way the Chagall Tretyakov stretcher was constructed). The essential element involved recessing a quality board material into the face of the stretcher. Although not technically an archival board, 6.25mm (¼in) Gatorfoam[12] was used for *Barge*. Gatorfoam is a lightweight board with a polystyrene core and polymeric impregnated veneer that is often used for museum mounting.

For other, more sensitive works, we have used archival corrugated board[13] covered with archival matt board to mask the slight corrugations on the side which will rest directly against the back of the painting. Whichever board is chosen, the boards are screwed into the centre stretcher members only, as this allows for corner expansion. The screws are covered with a suitable tape, as are the vertical joins between each of the four panels to create a smooth surface upon which to place the painting. Very thin and strong Tyvek[14] tape is used to tape over the joins. It can also easily be peeled away from the surface of the Gatorfoam each time the stretcher is disassembled. During disassembly, the boards do not have to be removed from the stretcher; they stay screwed in place ready for the next time it is to be used. The important point to make about this relatively minor modification to the stretcher is that when the stretcher is put together and laid flat, face up on sawhorses, the painting can be unrolled directly onto it, almost like unrolling the painting onto a flat table top. The stretcher is very stable and the canvas does not sag into the spaces between the stretcher members as it would if an unmodified stretcher were used. This is a huge advantage when stretching big pictures. Numerous conservators to whom we have spoken have experienced the awful buckling that occurs when a large painting is stretched face up on a traditional stretcher; some have often resorted to stretching large paintings face down. It can be very difficult accurately to line up the edges of the painting with the edges of the stretcher when the front edge of the painting cannot be seen. The correct alignment of the edges is particularly important when re-stretching modern paintings as they are often displayed without a frame. It is also very often inadvisable to place the vulnerable surfaces of modern paintings face down.

Unrolling and stretching *Barge*

The painting hangs from slightly angled cleats, which are screwed into the wall. The sawhorses should be set up in advance. For *Barge* we use at least 12 – if there are fewer, we make sure that they bridge the joins in the stretcher, for stability. The stretcher is removed from its crate and screwed together. This is usually done upright, leaning against a wall. The joins in the Gatorfoam are taped with the self-adhesive Tyvek tape and the stretcher is then put on top of the sawhorses with the side that rests against the painting face up.

The painting on its large roller is then lined up with the shorter side of the stretcher, making sure that the top of the painting and the top of the stretcher are properly oriented. The roller can be left in the crate and turned in place. The height of the sawhorses corresponds approximately with the height of the top of the roller, which allows for a very smooth unrolling procedure. The plastic wrapping and the wide Mylar strips are removed. The twill tapes are also removed and saved for re-packing. During this preparation and positioning for unrolling, the rolled painting should be oriented so that the exposed tacking edge is toward the bottom of the roller, allowing gravity to keep the painting from slipping on the tube while the tapes are undone.

Initially, one person is placed at each of the two free corners of the painting to maintain an even tension on the painting at all times during unrolling. It is impor-

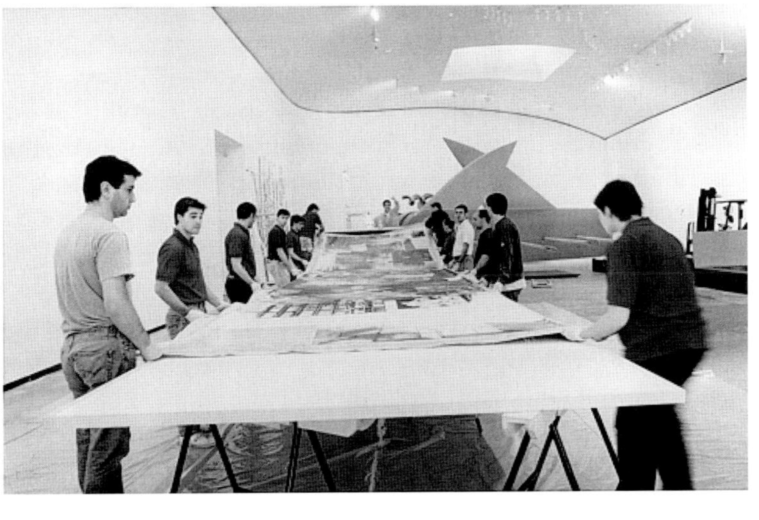

Figure 3 Unrolling the painting onto the stretcher at the Guggenheim Museum in Bilbao.

tant to keep the painting as flat as possible. Other hands come in useful along the long sides of the painting to keep it flat during unrolling and guide it safely onto the stretcher (Fig. 3). Once the painting is completely unrolled, one short end remains attached to the roller with the Velcro. The Velcro is carefully detached and finally the painting slides into place on the stretcher.

Once the painting is on the stretcher, the edges and corners are carefully lined up (this may take some time). Once well positioned several long-headed pushpins, utilising existing holes in the tacking edge, are used to attach the painting temporarily to the stretcher and keep the painting in place while being stretched.

The stretching proceeds as with any usual stretching and the pushpins are used to keep the tension on the painting. We usually only apply tension by hand: the painting is already flat on its panel/stretcher and we have found that this is all that is necessary, even for a very large painting like *Barge*. Stretcher pliers can be used, though the edges with the Velcro attached are a little more bulky and it is best to fold the linen before inserting it into the teeth of the stretcher pliers. Once we are satisfied with the positioning and tension on the painting the Velcro is pressed in place and the pushpins removed (Fig. 4). The painting can then be lifted onto the wall.

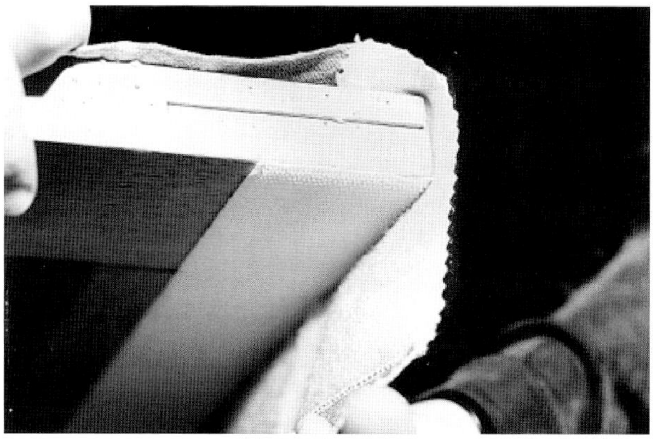

Figure 4 A mock-up of a painting showing the Velcro attachment of the painting to the stretcher.

Conclusion

In conclusion, we have found this system to be very convenient and safe for the big pictures that have to be stretched and unstretched each time they are moved. We find that it is well worth the time it takes to prepare the paintings in advance. Ultimately, it saves a lot of time during installation and de-installation, and there is much less wear and tear on the entire painting, especially the edges. This is particularly true during unstretching, when the staples usually have to be pried out of the tacking edges, which is time-consuming and sometimes even damaging. Using this system, the Velcro is simply released and the painting is ready to roll.

This system as used by the Tretyakov Museum is very beautifully and expensively crafted, with a superb stretcher and roller, and brass cogs and handles to roll the painting on and off the tube. We have made several slightly differing versions of this system and, although I have mentioned one or two, there is not space to describe all the details. However, if this system appears to suit a specific situation, modifications can be made to suit individual budgets and needs.

Acknowledgements

This was a project that required the cooperation of many people and we thank everyone involved. We especially wish to dedicate this paper to the memory of Alexi Kovalov, former Chief Conservator at the Tretyakov Museum, who first showed us this approach to touring big pictures.

Notes

1. *Marc Chagall and the Jewish Theatre*, exh. cat., Guggenheim Museum, New York (1992).
2. Stretcher made by Simon Liu Inc., 645 Dean Street, Brooklyn, New York, NY 11238, USA.
3. Manufactured by Velcro USA Inc., 406 Brown Avenue, Manchester, NH 03103, USA; supplied by Daytona Braids and Trimmings, 251 West 39th Street, New York, NY 10036, USA.
4. We thank Dana Cranmer of Cranmer Art Conservation (45 Crosby Street, New York, NY 10012, USA) for carrying out the treatment and for willingly following our design.
5. Grosgrain ribbon supplied by Daytona Braids and Trimmings (see note 3 above).
6. Sonotube manufactured by Sonoco products, 1 North Second Street, Hartsville, South Carolina 29550, USA.
7. Crate made by Artex Fine Art Services, 8712 Spectrum Drive, Landover, MD 20785, USA. Space constraints prevent inclusion of all the details of the packing crate; however, if anyone is interested in this information, please write to the author at: Conservation Department, Guggenheim Museum, 1071 Fifth Avenue, New York, NY 10028, USA.
8. Volara manufactured by Voltek, 100 Shepard Street, Lawrence, Mass 01843; supplied by Rogers Foam, 150 East Post Road, Morrisville, Pennsylvania 19067, USA.
9. Archival double-sided tape manufactured by 3M, 3M General Offices, 3M Center, Saint Paul, MN 55144-1000, USA.
10. Glassine supplied by Archivart, 7 Caesar Place, Moonachie, New Jersey 07074, USA.
11. Mylar manufactured by DuPont, DuPont Corporate Information Center, Barley Mill Plaza, P10, Wilmington, DE 19880-0010, USA.
12. Gatorfoam is manufactured by International Paper, PO Box 1839, Statesville, North Carolina 28687, USA; supplied by New York Central Art Supply, 62 Third Avenue, New York, NY 10003, USA.
13. Archival corrugated board supplied by Archivart (see note 10 above).
14. Tyvek tape manufactured by DuPont (see note 11 above) and supplied by Light Impressions, PO Box 22708, Rochester, NY 104692-2708, USA.

The author

Gillian McMillan is Senior Conservator, Collections, at the Guggenheim Museum, New York.

The Problem of the Seven Foot Door

IAN McCLURE

Introduction

Quite apart from the particular problems presented by large paintings during conservation treatment in the studio, where even moving a painting becomes a complex operation, their transport to and from the studio can prove a major factor in the whole project. While there is some literature on the transport of large paintings on canvas,[1] literature on the transport of paintings in general[2] tends to focus on small- to medium-sized paintings where complex packing systems, such as double cases, can be utilised without the constraints of extra size.

This paper describes three projects involving the movement of large paintings to and from the studio, where access to the area in which the paintings were displayed was restricted. The return to Trinity Hall College Chapel of Maso da San Friano's *Visitation* (Fitzwilliam Museum, University of Cambridge) demonstrates the problems of moving large and heavy panel paintings. The group of three paintings on canvas by Hondecoeter from the Dining Room at Belton House (National Trust) had to be removed and returned through the window that was higher than the door to the room. Finally, two paintings by Franchi had to be installed in their new home where the only access was through a series of low doors. In each situation, different solutions were employed. Unexpected factors such as the strength of the wind on the proposed day of the move had to be taken into account. In all three cases the transportation was successfully carried out, due in no small part to the large number of assistants, students, interns and staff of the Institute who could be called upon to assist, and by employing a transport firm which was very helpful and adaptable.

Maso da San Friano's *Visitation*

Maso da San Friano's *Visitation* was originally commissioned for the de' Peschi Chapel in San Pier Maggiore in Florence in 1560. The poplar panel measuring 4090 × 2480 × 40mm was estimated to weigh about 275kg. Impressions on the paint surface suggest it was transported on its side with webbing straps when the paint had not completely dried, presumably when it was installed in the chapel.

The church was demolished in 1783 and the painting was moved to Rome. There it was purchased for the Picture Gallery at Attingham House in Shropshire. In 1835 it was sold at auction at John Robbins of Regent Street, London. A label on the back of an earlier frame for the painting gives this address and adds 'per Wallis's Coach'. Sold to Henry Hope, it was lent to the Fitzwilliam Museum in 1850 and given in 1859.[3] The painting was moved to the chapel of Trinity Hall, a Cambridge college, in 1955. While the journey from Rome to England would have been by sea, it would be very interesting to learn how it was transported by land; what exactly was 'Wallis's coach'? Although the painting had structural problems requiring conservation, these were not readily attributable to transport. A series of fixed battens had induced splits and the failure of joints in the panel.[4]

The painting was removed from the chapel by erecting a platform in front of the reredos. The painting was detached from the wall behind the reredos and slid out onto the platform and manoeuvred onto its side. It was wrapped in polythene and then wheeled out of the College on a trolley to the nearest point accessible to a truck large enough to accept the painting. There was no question that the painting could travel with the grain vertical, given its height. However, as the panel was braced with three dovetailed battens and three large-section timbers screwed to the back it was judged safe to transport the painting in this orientation. Once at the Hamilton Kerr Institute, the painting was cleaned and splits and joins repaired and restored. The later, fixed battens were replaced with a steel and aluminium framework, which allowed the panel to move in response to changes in relative humidity and provided a means of fixing the panel to the wall. In transport the framework was attached rigidly to the panel.

Access to the chapel was restricted and a truck large enough to transport the painting could only get within 400m of the chapel (Fig. 1). A trolley constructed of slotted steel sections with a vertical side to support the painting was used to complete the journey to the chapel. Access to the chapel itself was restricted by the height of the door, which meant that packing of the painting was limited to bracing it to the steel and aluminium support on which it rested. Simply wrapping the painting would have made it extremely difficult to handle as it required at least six people to lift it. Packing it securely in a crate would have required lifting equipment to move it safely and the crate would have been too large to enter the chapel, necessitating its unpacking outside the building (Fig. 2). The move was carried out on a clear, bright day. The Institute could call on all its students, staff and interns to assist in the manoeuvre, with the assistance of a fine art removal firm, which meant that the handling team was experienced and could follow very precise instructions. The steps in the process of moving the panel were rehearsed

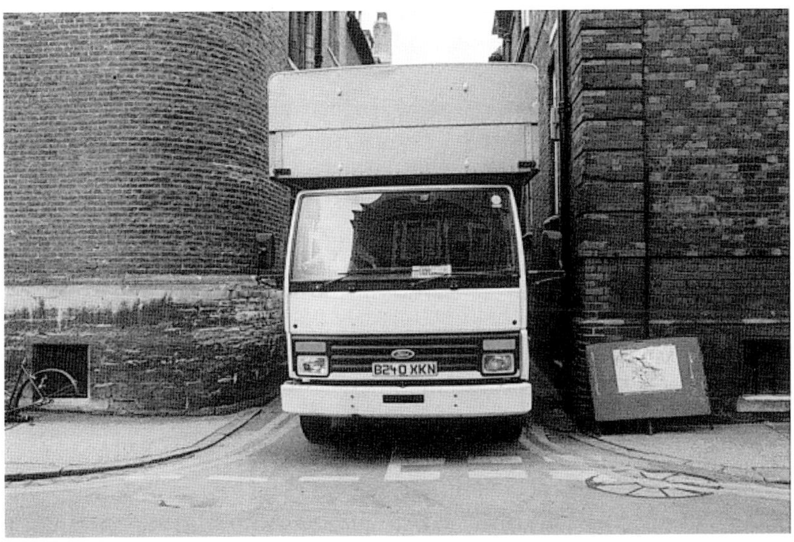

Figure 1 Limited access by road for a large painting (© Hamilton Kerr Institute, University of Cambridge).

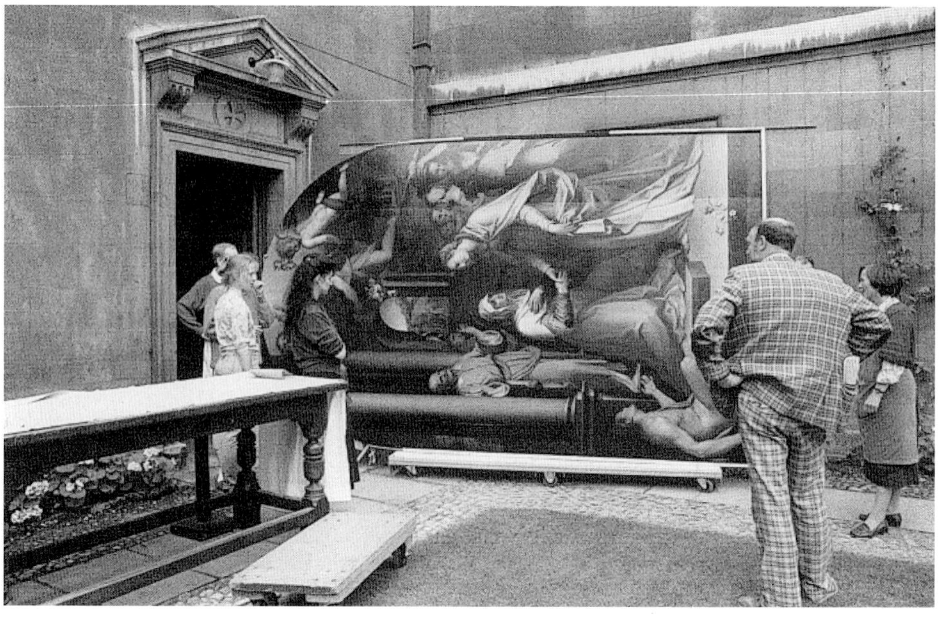

Figure 2 Maso da San Friano's *Visitation* entering the chapel at Trinity Hall, Cambridge (© Hamilton Kerr Institute, University of Cambridge).

and the panel was lifted into position by walking it up a series of stacking boxes, one side being lifted at a time.

The Belton House Hondecoeters

Canvas paintings have the advantage over panels in that the support can be curved or folded. Stretchers for large paintings on canvas seem to have incorporated folding systems from at least the early nineteenth century. *Caernarvon Castle* by De Loutherbourg (2500 × 3710mm) signed and dated 1804 (Royal Collection, Windsor Castle) is unlined and on its original stretcher. It has four corner braces and one vertical cross-member. The vertical sections of the stretcher are halved and joined with steel plates. The canvas would have been detached from the stretcher on the sides by removing the tacks, the steel plates removed and the sides of the stretcher swung out to form legs with the canvas forming a U between. Temporary cross-bracing at the end of each side would make the structure stable enough to be lifted and manoeuvred. Inevitably this system compresses the paint layer and when sufficiently aged, crack patterns would form in the bottom of the fold with tenting and flaking (Fig. 3). More sophisticated folding systems with locking devices were also developed. Again the Royal Collection has examples from the nineteenth century, often incorporating folding and locking systems.[5]

It is known that the series of three large paintings by Hondecoeter, purchased by Lord Brownlow in London for the Dining Room at Belton House, travelled from London to Grantham by train at the end of the nineteenth century. All three stretchers were designed to separate across the centre, allowing the paintings to be folded paint side in. The largest, *Landscape with Birds*, measuring 3650 × 5070mm, showed typical damage to the paint layer with losses and tenting where the fold compressed the paint.

When their removal for conservation work was considered,[6] it was clear that none would fit through the doors to the room as they were little more than 7ft (2130mm) high. The only other exits were two large sash windows approximately 4000mm above ground level, but higher and wider than the doors. All three paintings were housed in frames that were built into the wall. It was impossible

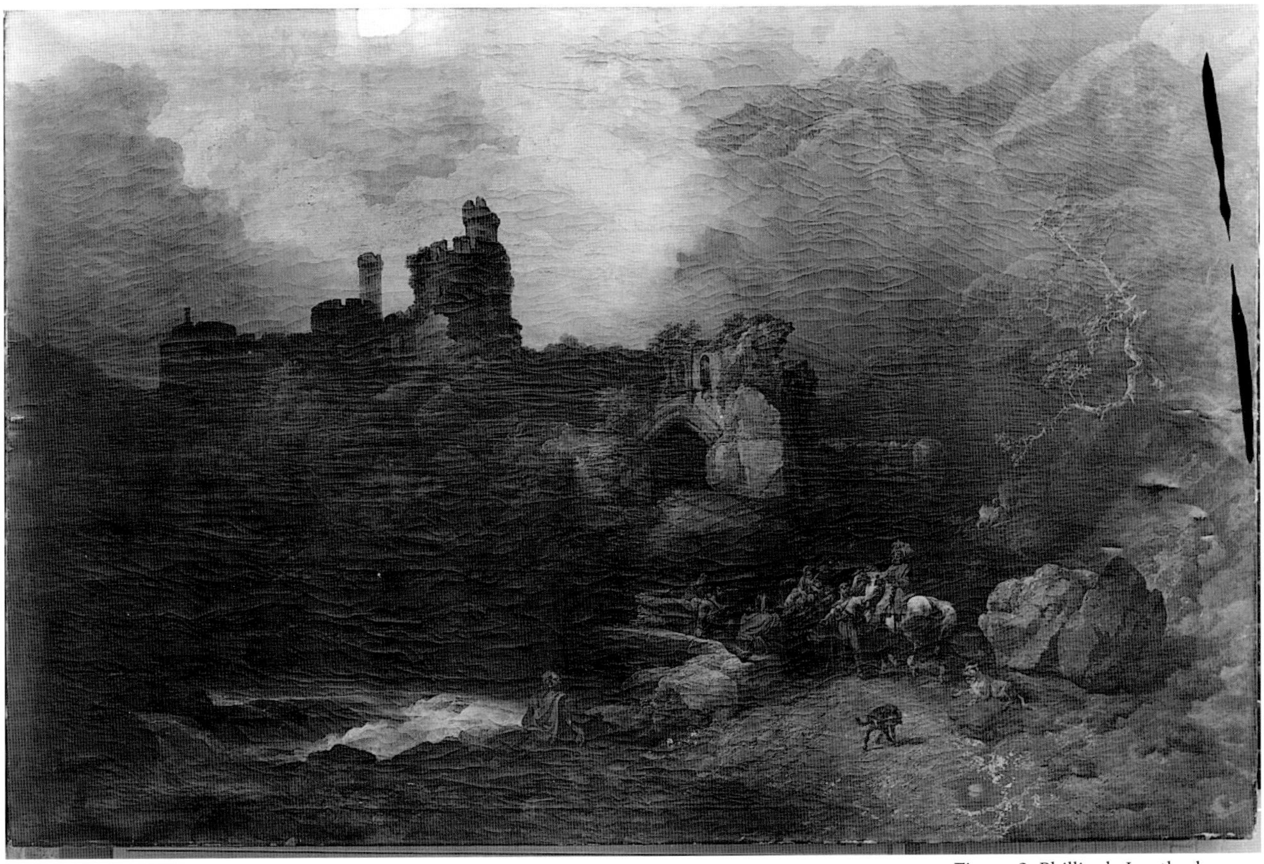

Figure 3 Phillip de Loutherbourg, *Carnaervon Castle* (Royal Collection). Photograph in raking light, showing the effects of folding (© Hamilton Kerr Institute, University of Cambridge).

therefore to obtain exact measurements and also to measure exactly the dimension of the window with the sashes removed. It was decided that the best option was to roll the largest painting along its longest dimension. To lift the painting on its stretcher through the window, should it prove possible, would require a two-tier platform so that the painting could be supported at the top when outside the window. If the painting proved too high for the window and the option of rolling the painting was taken, a different, flat platform would be required. If the painting could be transported on its stretcher, specialised transport would be required. The costs of having the transport on standby and the possibility of having to retain and alter the scaffolding platform (quite apart from the security issues) were factors in choosing the rolling option. Finally, as part of the conservation proposal, all three paintings were to be relined or strip-lined, so all three paintings would be removed from their stretchers during treatment.

A roller was constructed that was the largest diameter possible that would fit through the window, approximately 1200mm. The circumference of the roller was slightly larger than the height of the painting, so that there would be no overlap when rolled. The roller was constructed of hardboard formed round plywood disks and braced internally by wooden lathes. The roller was made in two 2700mm sections that bolted together, so that smaller and less expensive transport could be used to take the roller to Belton House. When bolted together, the roller was completely rigid and did not sag in the middle when lifted by a scaffold pole fed through the centre of the roller. If the roller had flexed there would have been a danger of creasing and paint loss to the canvas and paint layer. Triangular brackets were made to be fitted to each end once the painting had been attached to the roller to make it stable and to leave the roller clear of the ground.

The painting was laid face down on a prepared surface onto a layer of eltoline tissue over a layer of polythene. The stretcher was removed. A further layer of

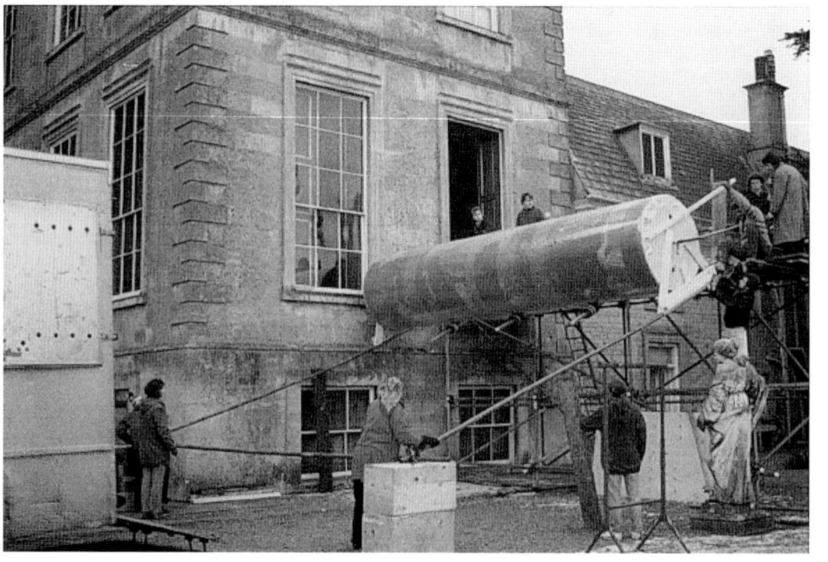

Figure 4 Removing Hondecoeter's *Landscape with Birds* from Belton House, November 1985 (© Hamilton Kerr Institute, University of Cambridge).

tissue was laid over the reverse of the canvas. The roller was placed over the painting set on 15mm lathes that ran the width of the painting to avoid pressure on the reverse of the painting. The top tacking edge of the lining canvas was stapled to the roller. The roller was moved carefully forward, picking up the painting. The lower tacking edge was secured. The brackets were attached to the painting and the roller was lifted through the window onto the platform outside.

Scaffold poles were connected to the platform to act as runners to guide and support the roller to the ground (Fig. 4). U-shaped channels were fitted to the base of the brackets at each end of the roller. Consideration was given to braking the descent of the roller but in the event the slight sagging of the poles caused the edges of the channel to grip the pole. The scaffold poles were given additional bracing and the roller drawn down. The empty stretcher was then lifted through the window with less than 20mm to spare.

On completion of the conservation treatment in 1991, all three paintings were wrapped. All were cushioned with low-density foam between the reverse of the canvas and the stretcher bars. The two smaller paintings were fitted into wooden frames to give a measure of protection. Because of space constraints the largest was simply wrapped in 12μm Melinex and polythene. Ties were attached to the top of the wrapping to act as stays when the painting was lifted and moved. A truck for theatrical removals was hired that would take the largest painting diagonally. However, the transport had to be postponed as, on the arranged day, the wind was too strong to risk taking the painting from the studio. The exit to the studio faced east and the painting would have been buffeted by wind broadside from the south-west. The transport was rearranged and an awning was built over the exit to act as a shield but on the second attempt, the weather conditions were perfect. The two smaller paintings were stowed in the front of the trailer and the larger painting was laid paint side up on a cradle built into the trailer. The painting could have been carried paint side down to reduce the risk of the canvas resting on the stretcher bars. However, without any support, the canvas would have sagged forward and the effects of movement and vibration were judged to be greater in this position. In addition, resting the paint layer on a rigid surface might have caused abrasion damage.

On arrival at Belton House the truck was driven to the rear of the house where it sank in soft ground and had to be towed by an estate tractor. The paintings were unloaded and swung up by crane onto a two-tier platform that allowed the top of the painting to be supported (Fig. 5). The crane was able to assist in lifting the painting through the window.

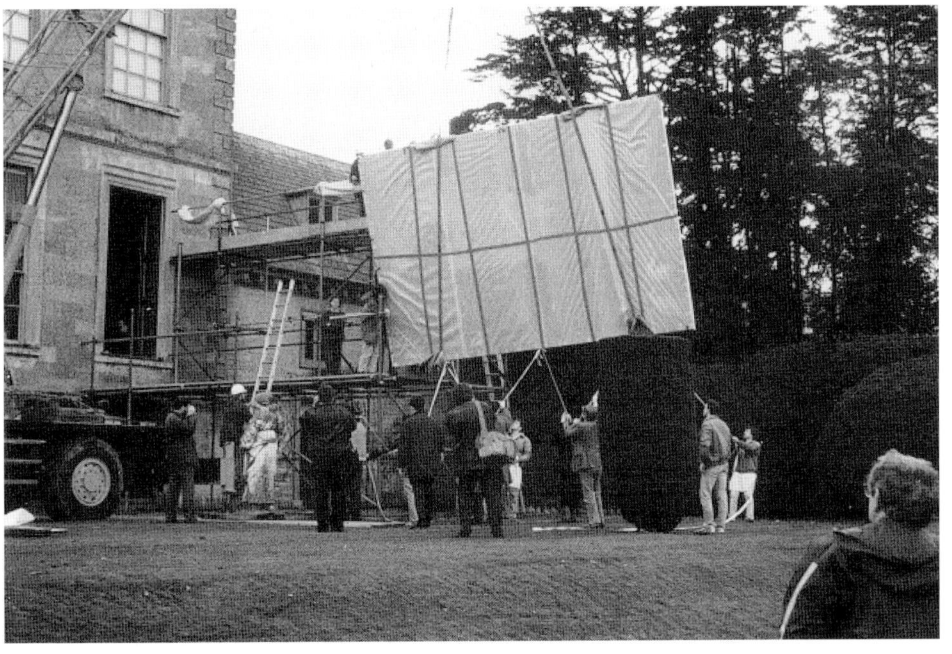

Figure 5 The return of Hondecoeter's *Landscape with Birds* to Belton House, March 1991 (© Hamilton Kerr Institute, University of Cambridge).

Franchi's *The Idolatry of Solomon* and the *Temple of Cupid*

Two paintings by Antonio Franchi measuring 2640 × 3240mm were received in 1995 for possible structural work, cleaning and restoration. Both – *The Idolatry of Solomon* and the *Temple of Cupid* – were painted for the Palazzo Rinuccini in Florence in 1670. The paintings were bought at auction in London and were intended for a private collection in Yorkshire. During conservation it was decided that the existing linings, possibly late eighteenth or early nineteenth century, were still sound and no further structural work other than consolidation of the paint layer would be required. Shortly before the completion of the project it was learnt that the only access to the room in which the paintings were to hang was through a series of doors, none of which was higher than 7ft (2130mm). In this case the windows could not be used as the mullions were of stone.

Removing the canvases from their stretchers was considered, but it was thought to be too difficult to re-stretch them to exactly the same positions after the stretchers had been dismantled and reassembled. Although the linings were in stable condition, the action of rolling might have caused local delamination that might only become apparent at a later date.

The idea of folding the paintings around a former with the removal of the central section of the stretcher was inspired in part by Ambrose Scott Moncrieff's account of folding a painting for transport.[7] A visit was made to the house to measure the doors and it was decided to build a former (Fig. 6) where the centre part of the stretcher would be cut out. One side of the stretcher would be fixed to one side of the former and the former rolled over the painting to meet the other side of the stretcher, which would then be secured. The former could then be carried by handles at each end.

The former was constructed of 12mm plywood sections and wood. Again, care was taken to make the former as rigid a possible, as any twisting or sagging would have damaged the paint layer. The curved top section was constructed of wooden lathes to which sheets of 12mm Plastazote foam (nitrogen expanded polyethylene) were adhered. The curve exactly matched the section removed from the stretcher. L-shaped steel sections were made as joining plates to reattach the central section of the stretcher. These were predrilled and fitted before the section was cut out so that the saw cuts would not reduce the length of the stretcher bars. As the

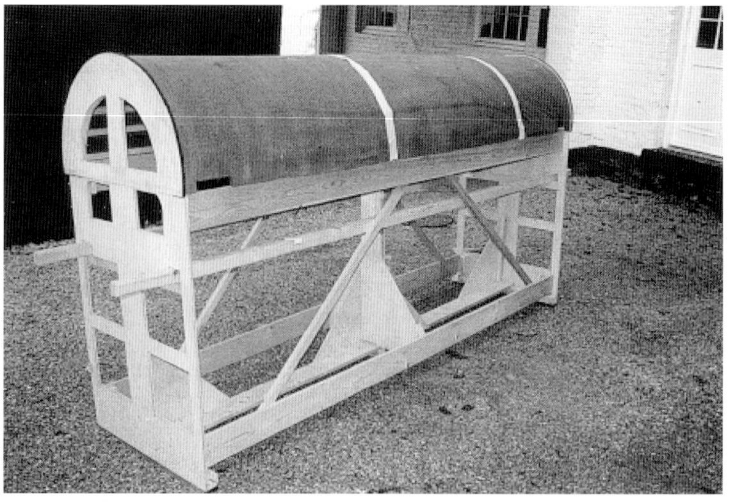

Figure 6 The former made for folding a lined seventeenth-century painting to allow access through a low door (© Hamilton Kerr Institute, University of Cambridge).

stretcher had been cut along its length, the L-sections gave greater rigidity than simple flat plates. The diameter of the semicircular top section was 770mm, again the widest possible given the width of the doors. A lip of 10mm projected above the semicircular section so that the former would not press on the painting as it collected it. Holes were cut in the flat sections of the former to reduce weight.

The painting was placed onto a prepared surface over which a layer of polythene was laid. The central section of the stretcher was removed by marking the cuts, removing the tacks, placing a protecting layer of used X-ray film under the section to be cut and using a Japanese ryobi pull saw to make the thinnest of cuts. A second layer of polythene was laid over the reverse. The sides of the former were detached and were attached to the reverse of the stretcher, rendering it dimensionally rigid. One side was screwed to the former and the former rolled over the painting (Fig. 7). The second side was then secured. The polythene was sealed to make the package as airtight as possible for the journey to preserve the moisture content during transport. The former was then loaded onto a truck and delivered to the house (Fig. 8). Unfolding the canvas and replacing the central section of the stretcher was a reversal of the packing procedure. The tacking edge of the central

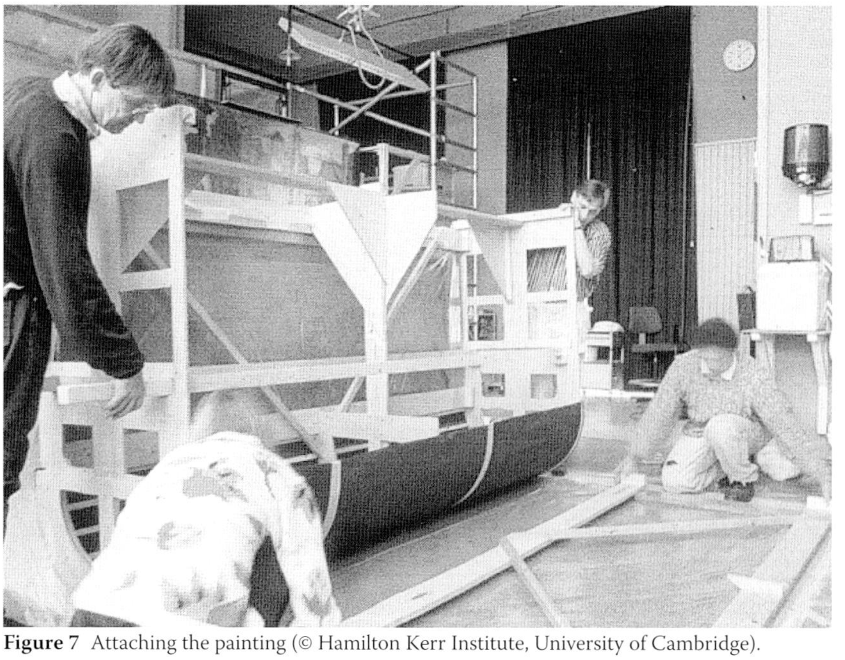

Figure 7 Attaching the painting (© Hamilton Kerr Institute, University of Cambridge).

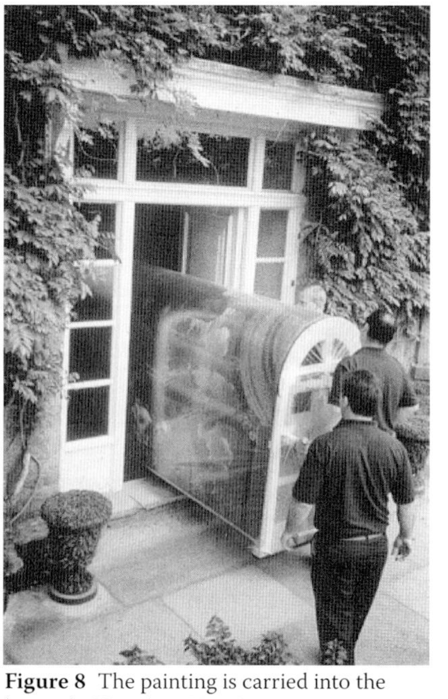

Figure 8 The painting is carried into the house (© Hamilton Kerr Institute, University of Cambridge).

section of the canvas was strip-lined with polyester sailcloth and BEVA 371 film (ethylene-vinylacetate copolymer) to assist in re-stretching.

Conclusion

In all the procedures described above, there was an element of risk which had to be balanced against other beneficial factors. For example, Figure 8 shows clearly how the intention of making the curve of the fold as large as possible increased the risk of damage to the paint surface by careless handling. The sides of the former could have hit the doorframe. However it was considered that this risk was very clear and could therefore be minimised by working slowly and using professional art handlers. Reducing the risk from handling by building greater physical protection into the packing would have caused increased physical stress to the painting by being folded around a tighter curve.[8]

Acknowledgements

I would like to thank all those students and staff, past and present, who have assisted in these projects. In particular I would like to thank Alan Doherty, who, given the instruction to 'make a completely rigid roller, four feet in diameter and eighteen feet long', went and did exactly that.

Notes

1. See N. Stolow (1987) *Conservation and Exhibitions*. London: Butterworth, especially pp. 79–87.
2. See M.F. Mecklenburg (ed.) (1991) *Art in Transit, Studies in the Transport of Paintings*. Washington, DC: National Gallery of Art.
3. Information on file at Fitzwilliam Museum, University of Cambridge. Accession no. 496.
4. For the conservation of this painting, see L. Keith (1994) 'The structural conservation of Maso da Friano's *Visitation* altarpiece', in M. Massing (ed.), *Bulletin No. 2*, pp. 78–83. Cambridge: Hamilton Kerr Institute.
5. The stretcher of *The Battle of Meanee*, 1847, by Edward Armitage (St James's Palace), measuring 4 × 6m, has a sophisticated folding and locking system. Personal communication, Dr A. Brewer. See also Chorley in this volume, pp. 119–28.
6. An account of the conservation treatments of the three paintings is filed at the Hamilton Kerr Institute.
7. A. Scott-Moncrieff (1984) 'The modification of a folding picture', *The Conservator* 8: 35–40.
8. For a stimulating discussion of risk in decisions concerning paintings, see J. Ashley-Smith (1999) *Risk Assessment for Object Conservation*. London: Butterworth-Heinemann, especially pp. 120–37.

The author

Ian McClure is Director of the Hamilton Kerr Institute, University of Cambridge.

'The Unloved Painting' by Guido Reni

CHRISTINE LEBACK SITWELL

Introduction

I have called my paper 'The Unloved Painting', not because the painting lacks artistic merit or historical interest, but because it has failed to find a permanent display location for the past 160 years. Guido Reni painted *Separation of Day and Night* on the curved ceiling of the main salon in the Palazzo Zani in Bologna, Italy, sometime between 1569 and 1604 (Fig. 1). By 1840, the painting was in poor condition as described by Giordani in his book on Guido Reni:

> ... the vault had cracked in many parts and the lime plaster was threatening to fall into pieces (although to avoid this, a type of iron wire net had been nailed to hold some of the surface together).[1]

Prince Pallavicini, the owner of the palazzo, wishing to redecorate the ceiling but realising the importance of the fresco, decided to remove it. He entrusted the work to Giovanni Rizzoli who:

> ... set out to undertake the delicate task courageously but confidently, using his own particular system ... he had to overcome technical and logistical difficulties because of the awkward position, the inclination of the curve and the large size of the painting.[2]

The description of his system involved the removal of the painted layer only as other methods that retained the thickness of the plaster were not always successful and prevented the rolling of the painting without further damage. Once removed, the painting was lined onto canvas. According to Rizzoli:

> ... the painting could now be rolled up and carried without the slightest risk of damage as though it were a real oil painting.[3]

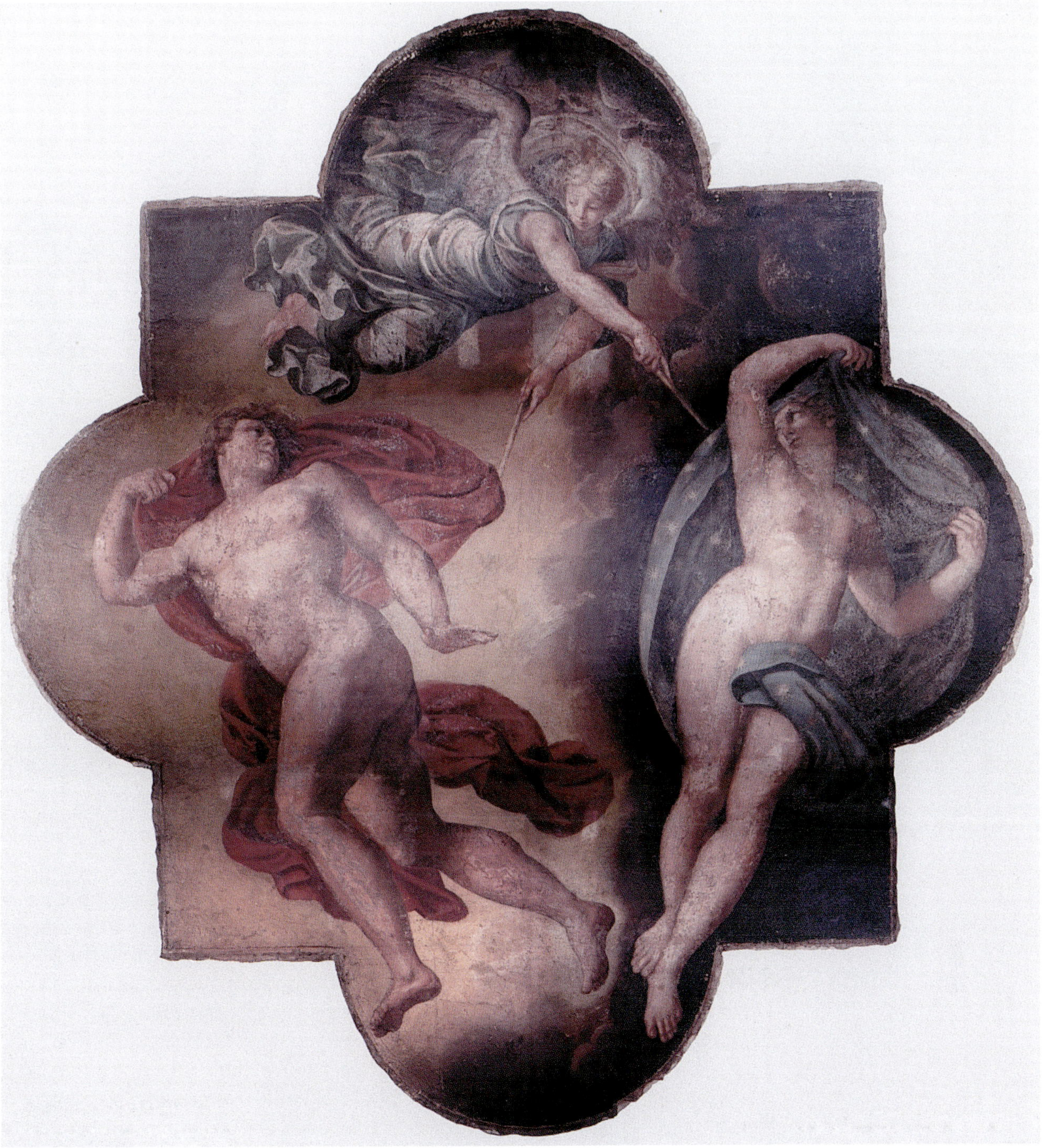

Figure 1 *The Separation of Day and Night* by Guido Reni. (Image courtesy of Angela Geary, Option 5.)

Removal to England

William John Bankes (1786–1855) purchased the painting in 1840 or 1841 for £600 and shipped it to Kingston Lacy, his home near Wimborne in Dorset. Whether or not the painting stayed at Kingston Lacy is unclear as there are conflicting references, some of which are undated and unsigned, which indicate that the painting was either at Kingston Lacy or at another Bankes property near London. There is reference to it having been seen at Kingston Lacy in 1857 but no indication is given of the location within the house. Another reference, which cannot be documented, states that in *c.* 1850 the painting was transferred to a house belonging to the Bankes family in Sheen, near London, where it hung on the ceiling of the

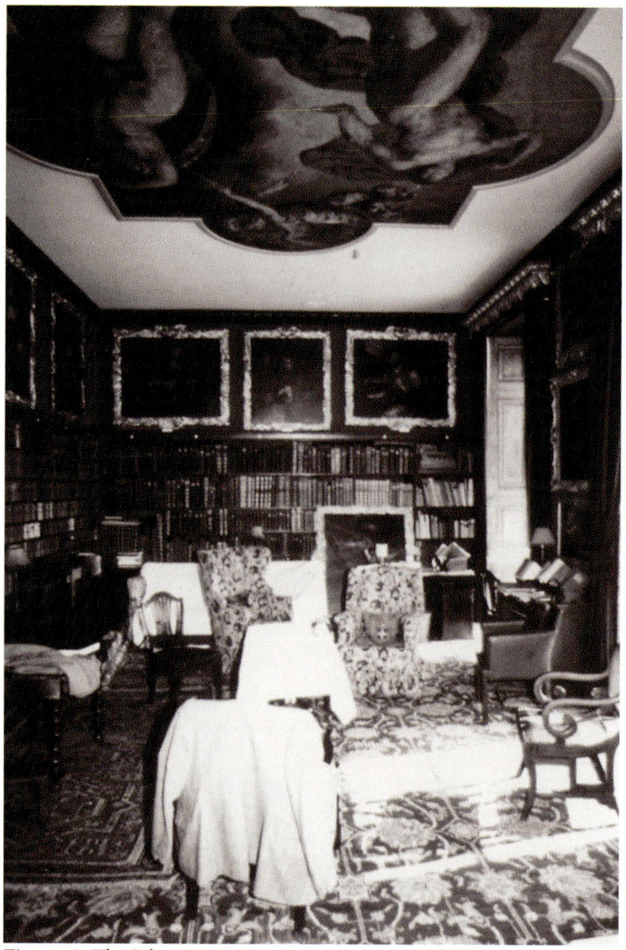

Figure 2 The Library at Kingston Lacy showing the painting *in situ*. (Reproduced by permission of the National Trust Photographic Library.)

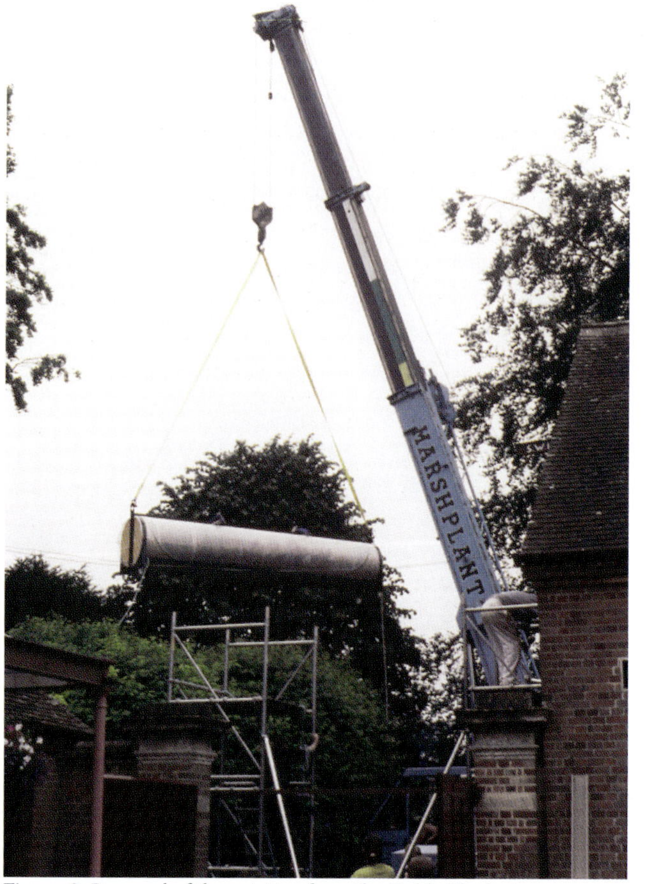

Figure 3 Removal of the painting from the Stable Block at Kingston Lacy. (Photograph: Christine Sitwell.)

Grand Staircase until 1913 when the house was demolished. However, there is a *Country Life* photograph of 1904 which clearly shows the painting on the Library ceiling at Kingston Lacy, therefore it could not possibly have been in the Sheen house at the same time. In 1981 Ralph Bankes bequeathed Kingston Lacy to the National Trust and the painting was definitely on the Library ceiling (Fig. 2).

Unfortunately, major building works at the house necessitated its removal once again. It was removed from the ceiling, faced, rolled onto a large cylinder and stored on the upper floor of the stable block. When the house was reinstated, it was decided not to return it to the Library because of its poor condition and the fact that its size and subject matter overwhelmed the relatively small interior of the Library. When William John Bankes had been making alterations to Kingston Lacy in the late nineteenth century, it appears that he had intended to raise the ceiling of the Library, but this was never undertaken. Had this happened, the painting might have been less dominating. There were also indications that it might have hung in the Dining Room, where its large size would have been visually more acceptable. However, it was destined to remain rolled up until 1999 when the Trust decided to assess its condition with a view to conservation treatment and reconsider hanging the painting in the Library, the Dining Room or possibly some other, as yet, unknown location.

Several problems became apparent immediately, the first being how to remove it from the upper floor of the stable block and where to unroll it. The painting measured approximately 4.5 × 3.92m and the roller dimensions were 4.95m in length with a diameter of 90cm. When the painting was originally placed in the stable block, it had been carried by hand, with slings, up a stepped scaffold tower through an opening on the courtyard side of the stable block. This access was no longer available and the only alternative was through a narrow doorway into an adjacent room with a door at the farthest end. The roller was suspended on wooden frames at either end and these were then replaced with a smaller, wheeled metal framework to enable the roller to pass through the narrow doors.

The area beneath the stable block opening was of insufficient size to allow a stepped scaffold tower to be used. The only feasible method for lowering the painting involved the use of a mobile crane which would manoeuvre the painting out of the building, onto two tower scaffolds, off the tower, over a row of trees while turning it 90 degrees and onto the road below (Fig. 3). As there were no buildings of sufficient size at Kingston Lacy to enable the painting to be unrolled, it was transported to Petworth (another National Trust house) where a large room in the Battery House had recently been converted to a conservation facility for large objects.

Condition assessment

The initial examination of the painting revealed that it was in relatively good condition, despite extensive areas of previous restoration, which included broad passages of overpaint. The paint layer, although friable in numerous areas, was relatively sound, and the original canvas retained a degree of flexibility. The painting appeared to have been strip-lined within the past 40 years and this contributed to the noticeable distortions at the edges. Despite having been heavily overpainted, there were passages where the original striations of plaster texture and painting technique were clearly visible. The appearance of the painting and the lack of any incised lines or boundary lines indicated that the technique probably involved the use of pigment in an aqueous medium on fresh plaster (*a secco*) rather than the true *buon fresco* method.

The National Trust had not had previous experience in the conservation of transferred fresco paintings, nor were there many conservators in this country who have had an opportunity to be involved in their treatment. Thus, it was decided to seek advice from Bolognese conservators and British colleagues regarding its condition and conservation treatment. The fact that the companion painting, *The Fall of Phaeton* by Guido Reni, remains *in situ* in Bologna, and the recognised experience of Bolognese conservators in the treatment of transferred frescoes, were important considerations in the decision to approach them. The prospect of sponsorship for the work must also be recognised as a factor.

However, the possibility of restoring the painting in Italy posed several problems which would add to the complexity of the treatment and also to the possible risk of damage to the object. The transport of the painting – its numerous removals from roller to stretcher to roller and ultimately to stretcher or solid support at its final destination – would expose the painting to possible damage from handling, vibration and shock, particularly during transit. The need for continual collaboration between the National Trust and the Bolognese conservators over the different aspects of the treatment, particularly the visual appearance, would be made more difficult due to distance and language problems.

Before any consultations could be arranged, it was necessary to commission a condition report and photographic survey.[4] There was no overall photograph of the painting and certainly no detailed images recording its condition. As the painting could not be photographed in a vertical position, it was necessary to devise a method for photographing it flat. It was decided to erect scaffold towers at either end of the painting and suspend a platform that could be moved to different heights to allow several overall as well as detailed photographs and slides. To compensate for distortions in the painting, a grid system was devised. The photographs were digitised to create a composite photograph and the slides were scanned to provide an accessible record of its condition.[5] Paint samples were also taken to provide clarification of the technique, the pigments, medium and lining adhesive.

Once the condition reports and photographs were available, the Italian conservators and curators were invited to examine the painting and discuss its condition and conservation treatment. Subsequent to this meeting, conservators from the National Gallery also viewed the painting and provided valuable advice. The conservation treatment of a large complex painting will inevitably stimulate discussion and produce differences in approach, both practical and philosophical. A fresco that has been transferred to canvas displays the characteristics of both the fresco and the canvas painting. The original appearance, altered by age, damage, structural intervention and extensive overpaint, becomes an elusive image, and the degree to which it is recaptured is influenced by factors both tangible and intangible.

Essentially, we had to establish whether or not we viewed the painting as a fresco or a fresco that displayed characteristics of an oil painting, and the level of intervention with regard to its final visual appearance. Realistically, it is not possible to specify the final appearance as this can only be assessed during the treatment, but it is essential to have a clear concept of the desired appearance.

The consultations with our Italian and British colleagues were invaluable as they discussed different approaches to the appearance and treatment of the painting. They also helped us to focus our thoughts more clearly with regard to our intentions. Suggestions regarding collaboration between painting and wall painting conservators in the conservation treatment, as well as possible assistance in scientific analysis, were offered.

Conservation options

Fundamentally, there were two conservation options. A more radical or interventive approach involved the removal of the original lining canvas and lining adhesive to regain the original texture and tonal appearance of the fresco. This recommendation was based on years of experience and the development of a methodology in the treatment of transferred frescoes. The painting would then be lined onto a series of fine canvases and attached to a solid support. The second approach retained the original canvas as it was an integral part of the plaster layer and appears to be in good condition. The painting would be lined onto a series of fine canvases or interleaving supports and then mounted onto its original stretcher or a solid support. Further clarification regarding the first approach is being sought, but our initial conclusion is that a less interventive treatment (i.e. retaining the original lining canvas) is preferable. Our acceptance of the painting in its altered state as displaying characteristics of both a fresco and a canvas painting has encouraged us to seek conservators in the UK to undertake the treatment in addition to the Italian conservators.

Relocation

In theory, the next step is the preparation of a specification to allow conservators to view the painting and provide method statements and estimates. However, we need to decide the final location of the painting before this can be implemented, as the location may have a bearing on the conservation treatment. At present, there are three possible locations: the Library or Dining Room at Kingston Lacy or a long-term loan to a museum. Ideally, the painting should remain at Kingston Lacy as it is Trust policy that contents remain at the houses, as they represent the cumulative history of collecting and display. The possibility of lending the painting to a museum is to overcome the fact that there may be no suitable place to display it at Kingston Lacy.

As mentioned previously, the painting was on the Library ceiling but its sheer size and subject matter dominated the room. There is a suggestion that the painting was intended for, or may have hung on, the ceiling of the Dining Room. The Dining Room ceiling has an elaborate carved decoration and we neither know whether it would fit within the decoration nor what it would look like. To overcome this problem, the ceiling is being measured to determine if the painting would fit. If the ceiling can accommodate the painting, the ceiling will be photographed and a digital image created. The existing digital image of the painting can then be superimposed on the digital image of the ceiling. It is hoped that photographs of the walls will also be taken so that it will be possible to view the painting from floor level.

The final location may have a bearing on the conservation treatment, as it may determine whether or not the painting is attached to a stretcher or a solid support. When the painting was removed from the Library it was placed onto the roller in the room and carried down the main staircase. We have now determined that the windows in both the Library and the Dining Room can be removed to allow access by the exterior steps at ground level. This would enable either a roller or a solid support access to the rooms. However, the weight of the solid support or the stretcher plus the painting has to be determined in advance in order to ensure that either ceiling could support them.

Conclusion

Separation of Day and Night is no longer unloved, but it is proving to be a difficult lover. Her character is complex and hidden and her final desires are demanding. However, she has made us take her seriously and seek advice from those who are familiar with her ilk. Her two suitors have offered interesting, but different, approaches that we have to evaluate carefully in light of what is best for her and fulfils our desires for her. Long-distance collaboration has its difficulties, particularly in light of our established practice of working closely with conservators. We have, however, reassured ourselves that she could be conserved in the UK despite the fact that we do not have a tradition of conserving transferred fresco paintings.

Acknowledgements

This project has been a collaborative effort and I would like to acknowledge the following: my colleagues at the National Trust, Alastair Laing, Katy Lithgow, Sarah Staniforth, James Grasby, Mary Greenacre; the staff at Kingston Lacy and Petworth; Fine Art Services; Bush and Berry Conservation Studio; Angela Geary; Peter Thuring; Ottorino Nonformale, Andrea Emiliano and David Bomford, Tony Reeve and Jill Dunkerton of the National Gallery, London.

Notes

1. G. Giordani (1840) *Cenni sopra diverse pitture staccate dal muro e trasportate su tela e specialmente di una grandiosa da Guido Reni.* Bologna, pp. 25–31.
2. *Ibid*, p. 27.
3. *Ibid*, p. 28.

4. Bush and Berry Conservation Studio was commissioned to provide a condition report and slide survey. Peter Thuring took the overall photographs for the composite image.
5. Angela Geary of Option 5 undertook the digital imaging.

The author

Christine Leback Sitwell is Painting Conservation Adviser for the National Trust.

Using Aluminium for a Stretcher: A Practical Assessment

JACQUELINE RIDGE, DAVE JONES AND JACK WARANS

Introduction

The driver for this paper was the need to make a new stretcher for *The Worship of Bacchus* by the illustrator George Cruikshank (Tate, London). Measuring 2.3 × 4m, it is one of the largest historical works in the Tate collection (Fig. 1).

The painting retained its original wood stretcher, which was designed to fold in half (Fig. 2). It was not atypical of those made for large canvas paintings but its condition and structural stability was deemed inadequate. Because of the degraded nature of this unlined canvas, a new stretcher needed to support the weight of the fabric, but was not needed to withstand active tensioning, as the fabric was too weak. Crucially, the structure required torsional rigidity to minimise skewing and possible failure of the embrittled fibres while it was being moved about. The final weight of the painting was an issue on handling and framing grounds.

In 1998 Tate borrowed *Gassed* by John Singer Sargent from the Imperial War Museum, London. Measuring 2.3 × 6.1m, its large size made it potentially weighty and difficult to handle. Stretched in the 1970s onto a hollow section aluminium stretcher with one vertical cross-member, the painting, out of its frame, proved both light and rigid. With this in mind it was decided to consider aluminium as the material for the Cruikshank stretcher.

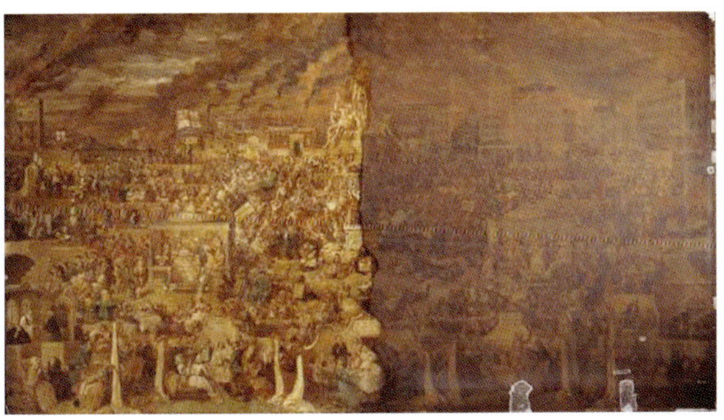

Figure 1 *The Worship of Bacchus* by George Cruikshank, during cleaning.

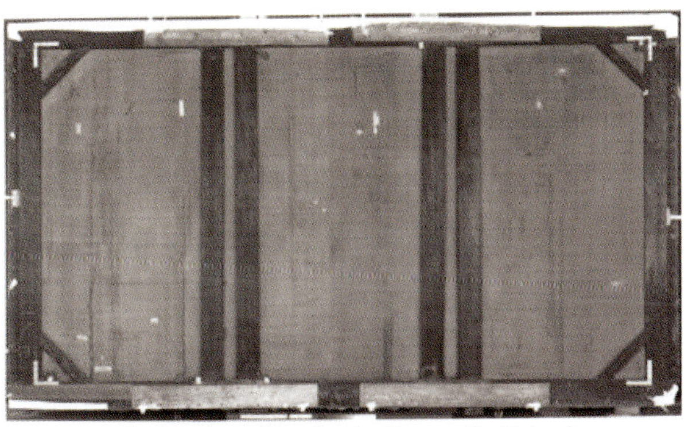

Figure 2 *The Worship of Bacchus* by George Cruikshank, reverse, showing original wood stretcher.

Wood stretcher design at Tate: factors considered

Factors felt to be particularly important when considering a stretcher for large works included:

- Weight and handling ease.
- Rigidity of structure: to support the stretched canvas with sufficient torsional rigidity.
- Rigidity of structure: to withstand stress exerted during stretching.
- Rigidity of structure: work framed or unframed.

Aspects that needed additional thought when considering the use of metal for the stretcher members:

- Tension adjustment systems.
- The number of cross-members: generally spaced about 1m apart (considered for works over 1m).
- Design of corner joints.
- How the fabric is attached.
- Aesthetic appeal.
- Attachment of hanging fitments.
- Ease of manufacture.

Other factors to be considered:

- Avoiding stretcher bar marks: chamfers, beading, canvas clearance of members.
- Profile edge required.
- Rebate of frame.

Properties of aluminium

- Rigidity: high tensile strength to weight ratio.
- Can be extruded into complex shapes (at a high cost for customised designed shapes).
- Many standard cross-sections are available off the peg.
- Cost per unit length: for box-section aluminium the cost per unit length compares favourably with timber used for large stretchers.
- Consistency of manufacture: few faults along lengths.
- Properties can be fine-tuned by selection of specific alloys.
- Aluminium can be cut without specialist equipment other than aluminium saw blades.
- The manufacturing time in-house once appropriate jigs are set up would be significantly less than for wood.
- The rapidly formed aluminium oxide skin on the metal surface provides a layer extremely resistant to corrosion and certainly to an environment likely to be experienced in the museum.
- High thermal expansion value: equivalent to about 1.8mm across a 4m length over 20°C change, therefore not felt to be critical.
- Chilling effect on canvas and paint if in close contact with aluminium might be an issue during transit situations.
- Metal/metal reactions: choice of metal for screws, hanging and framing fitments needs to be considered.
- 95% of aluminium is recycled!

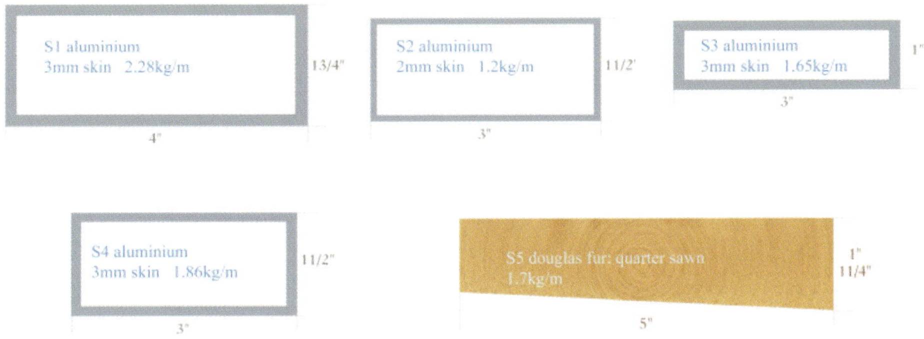

Figure 3 Samples S1–S5. Alloy type S1–3: BS 6063; S4: BS 6082.

What form of aluminium and how stiff?

For our initial prototype we considered simple box-section aluminium. It is readily available in a range of dimensions, thickness and alloy composition (Fig. 3). In order to get a feel for comparative stiffness, two simple loading experiments using a cantilever set-up were carried out. The flex achieved for 2m lengths of the samples was compared with that for a wood length of section used for our traditional large stretchers (Fig. 4).

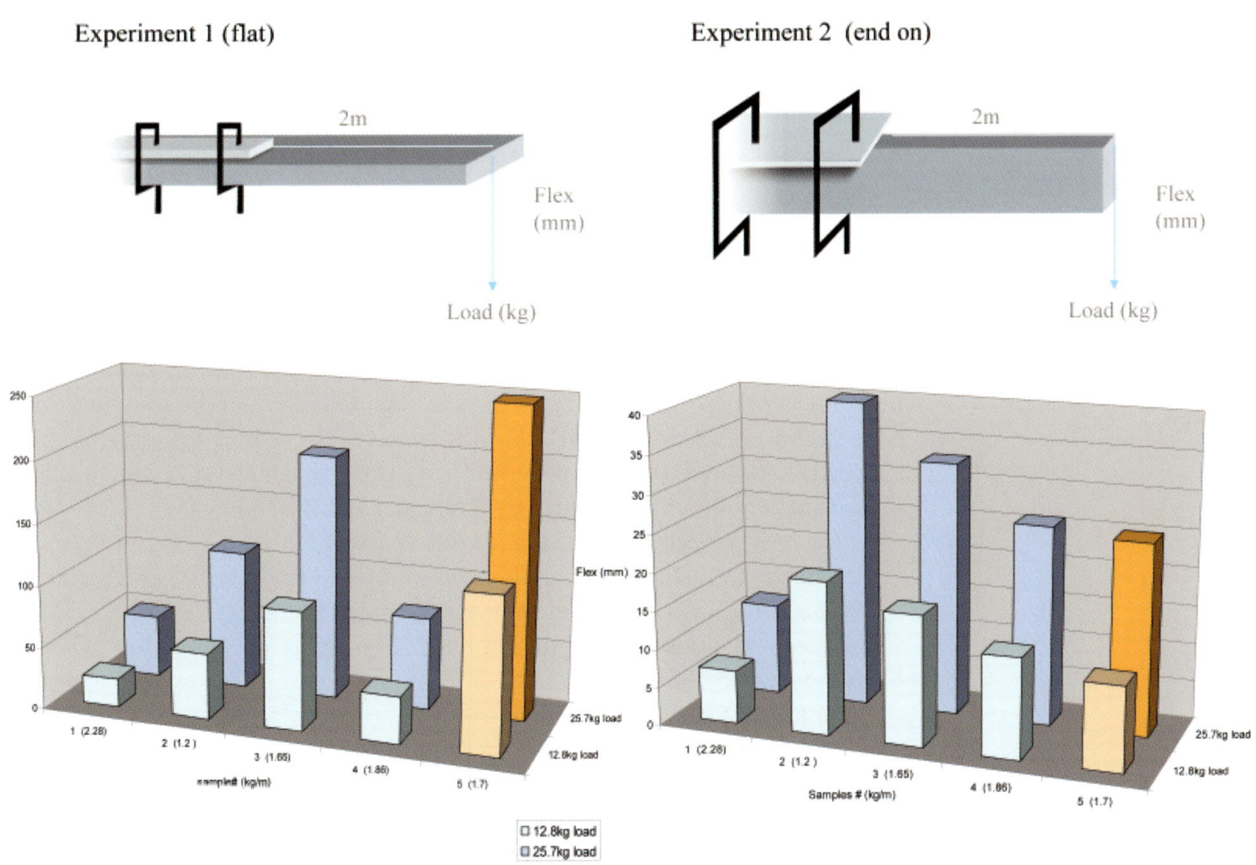

Figure 4 The two experiments with the graphical results. Experiment 1 shows that all the aluminium sections were stiffer (less flex) than the wood when loaded across their flat width. Experiment 2 shows wood to be stiffer (less flex) than S2, 3, and 4 when loaded end on. *Notes*: Theoretical calculation to determine the expected 'flex' for these samples confirms these results. In experiment 2, the flex for S2 should have been about 30mm, therefore nearer to that for the wood sample. The loadings were of a comparable order to that found to be exerted by canvas on a stretcher bar.

What does this tell us?

If we assume that for any stretcher format the stiffness of an individual stretcher member is *one* of the significant determining factors for the overall rigidity of the structure and that the standard Tate wood stretcher format provides adequate rigidity, then:

- the same format made from S1 or S4 would provide a structure of rigidity over and above that required;
- the same format made from S2 or S3 would provide a structure of lower weight but possibly of insufficient rigidity.

The relationship between sample stiffness and the overall torsional rigidity of a stretcher structure is complex. However, a structure in aluminium with less cross-members, therefore less weight, but still of adequate torsional rigidity might be achieved from S4. The impact of the decreased rigidity (S2, experiment 2 versus wood) as a function of the rigidity of the overall stretcher is difficult to assess. But this sample with appropriate numbers of cross-members may also be possible.

Weight gains

45.6kg	Weight of original Cruikshank stretcher
40.0kg	Estimated weight of typical new wood stretcher (3 vertical, 1 split horizontal members)
37.0kg	Estimated weight of aluminium stretcher (2 vertical cross-members S4)
24.9kg	Estimated weight of aluminium stretcher (2 vertical cross-members S2)
28.1kg	Estimated weight of aluminium stretcher (no cross-members S4)
32.2kg	Estimated weight of aluminium stretcher (no cross-member S1)

Other aspects

- The depth of the final structure and the corresponding rebate on the frame. We did not want to create a structure so deep that a weighty build-up would be needed on the frame. S2 and S4, although thicker than the standard wood section were felt to be acceptable.
- The hollow box-section lends itself to a simple wood insert to create a mortise and tenon joint. The extra thickness of S2 and S4 allow for a thicker joint but clearly of less area overlap. In the prototype, the joint was cut from a tri-laminate block of ash, and the aluminium sleeve routed to accommodate its shape and keys. The joint sections fit snugly in the sleeve and are further secured with steel self-tapping screws.
- Some form of beading to provide clearance for the canvas at the picture plane needed to be provided, as did a surface to which the canvas could be attached. This was achieved by adding wood strips to the side and front. These were glued (PVA emulsion) and screwed in place.

Conclusions

From this initial work it did seem possible to construct an aluminium stretcher of less weight but adequate rigidity for the Cruikshank. Simple loading experiments provided a 'feel' for the materials and gave a practical understanding of the technical data. The flex experiments carried out compared flex in a 'cantilever' set-up. A supported beam arrangement would have corresponded more closely to a stretcher, but the measurements would have been smaller and more difficult to obtain. In practice, the differences of flex in experiment 2 may not be that significant and more than compensated for by other aspects of the stretcher design. It would be of interest to assess a section with S1 dimensions but a 2mm skin.

Existing designs chosen by conservators and artists

Dante and Beatrice *by Henry Holiday (1883) (Fig. 5)*

National Museums and Galleries on Merseyside. 1422 × 2032mm, seven-member steel stretcher, not original (1960s). Steel stretcher with wood veneer, screwed spring system to tensions, canvas attached by stretching over teeth of 'carpet gripper'. Stretched over polythene sheet as moisture barrier. The stretcher is extremely heavy and very rigid.

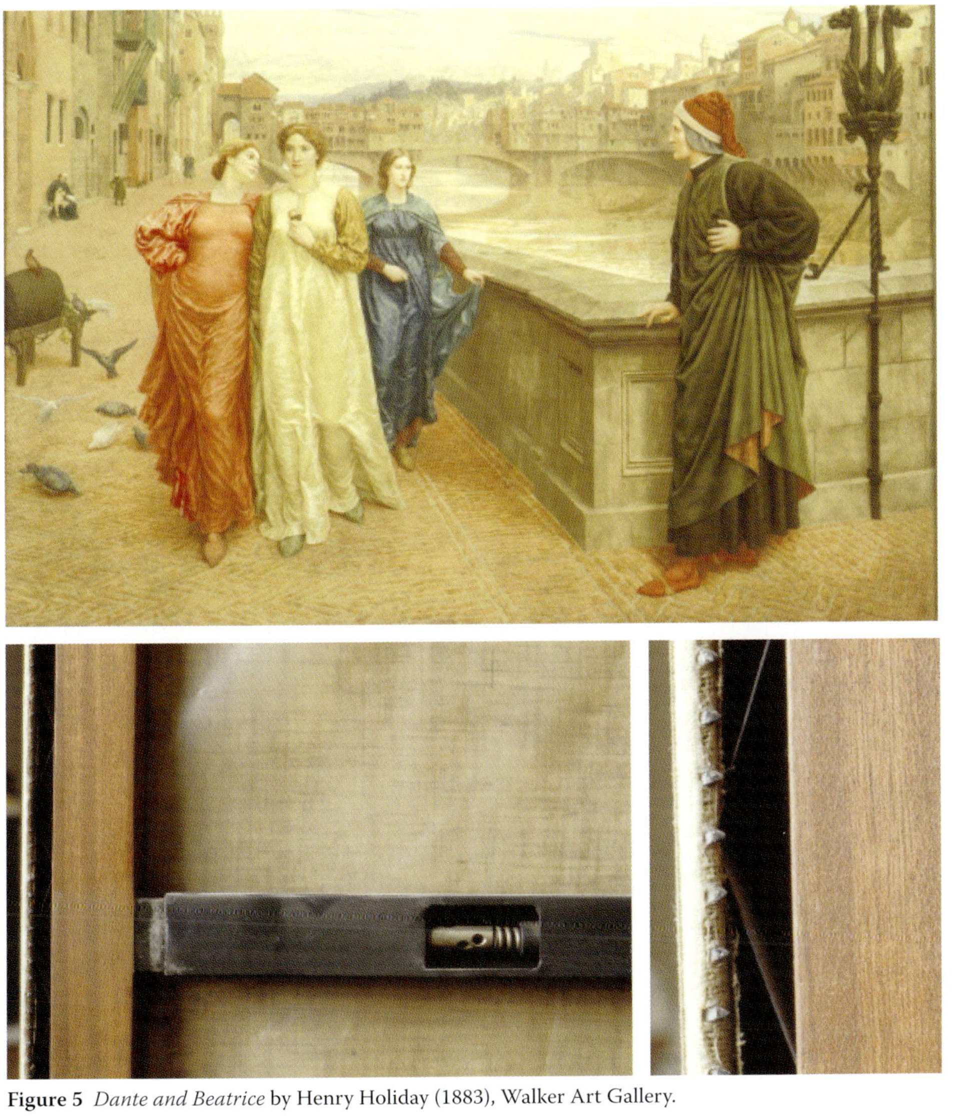

Figure 5 *Dante and Beatrice* by Henry Holiday (1883), Walker Art Gallery.

Gassed *by John Singer Sargent (1919) (Fig. 6)*

Imperial War Museum, London. 2.3 × 6.1m five-member aluminium stretcher, not original (1970s). Aluminium box-section with an additional 'fin' – perhaps to add extra rigidity. Mortise and tenon joints from mahogany inserts, screwed in place. Keyable with wood keys. Canvas attached to wood edge strips. This structure proved light and rigid. The wood keys were moderately effective at tensioning, but contact with the metal caused some crushing.

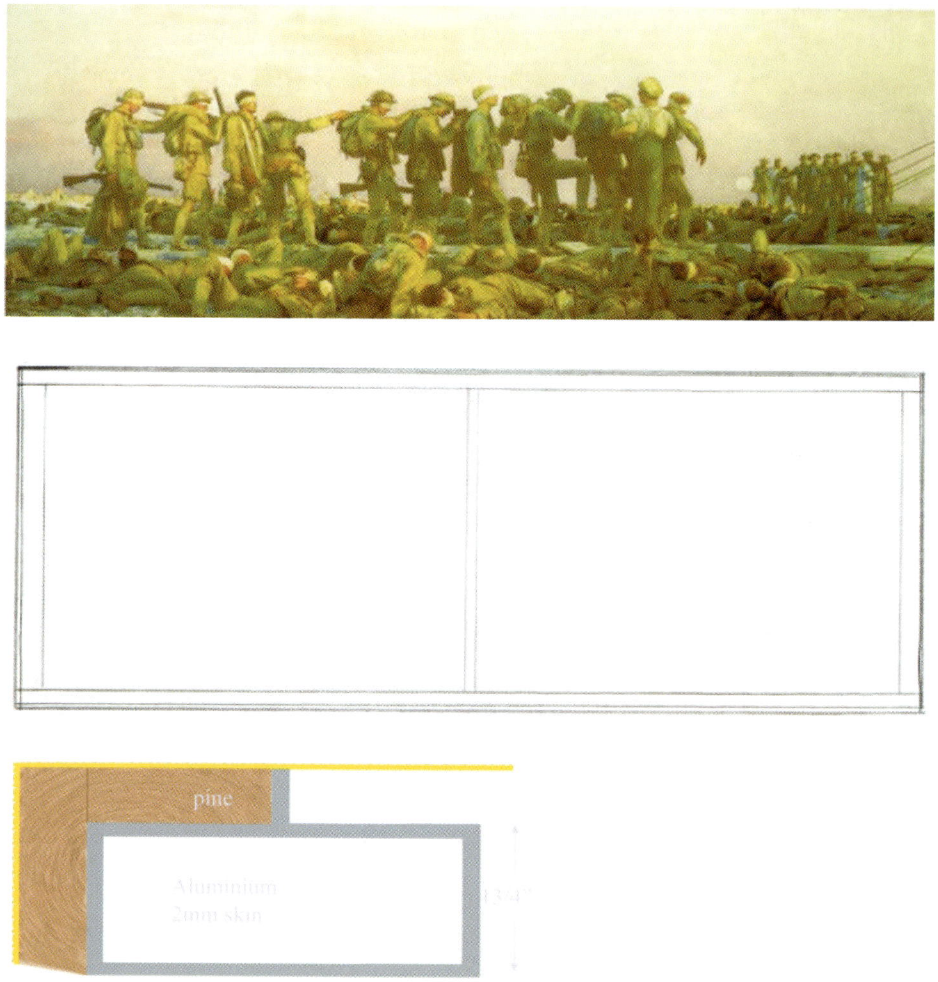

Figure 6 *Gassed* by John Singer Sargent (1919), Imperial War Museum, London.

Norwegian Sight *by Federle (1998) (Fig. 7)*

Tate. 3.3 × 4.9m. 15-member aluminium stretcher, original. This is made from two square stretchers joined, with bolts, vertically down the middle. The outer and inner members are two different complex extrusions (internal structure not known). The verticals are continuous. Channelling allows the members and tensioning system to be interlocked. The outer members are attached to a two-component wood frame providing the desired profile edge and the surface for canvas attachment. The cross-member pattern and spacing is as for our standard wood stretchers. The structure is light but lacks torsional rigidity for handling. There is no sign of stretcher distortion from canvas stretching. When moved in a transit frame the rigidity of the structure is acceptable.

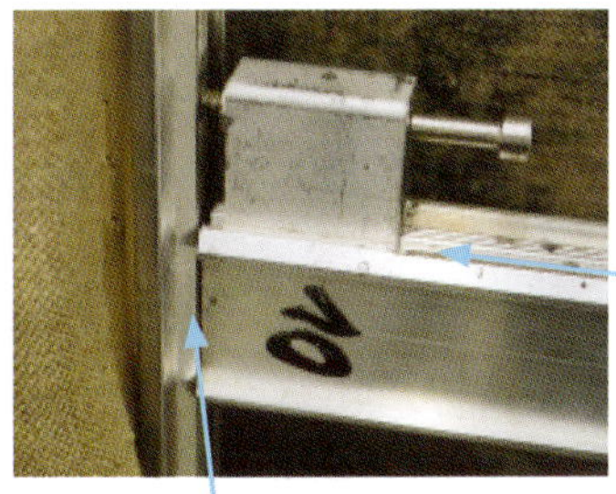

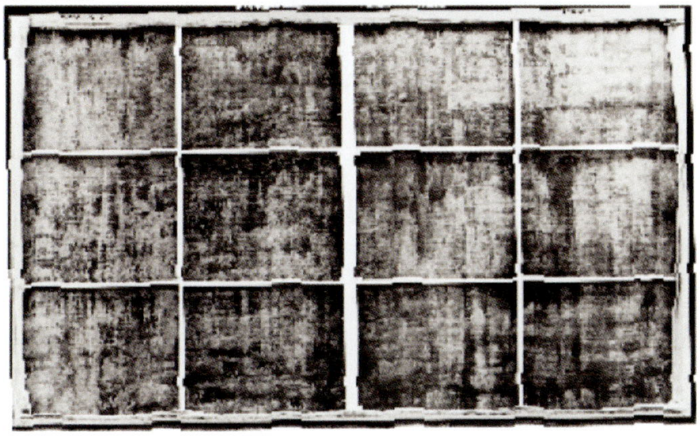

Figure 7 *Norwegian Sight* by Federle (1998), Tate.

Exposed Painting, Cadmium Orange on White *by Callum Innes (1997) (Fig. 8)*

National Museums and Galleries on Merseyside. 2.2 × 2m seven-member aluminium stretcher, original. Again the artist has exploited the ability of aluminium to hold channelling into which members and tensioning mechanisms can be slotted. The vertical member is continuous. Canvas is stapled to the reverse of the

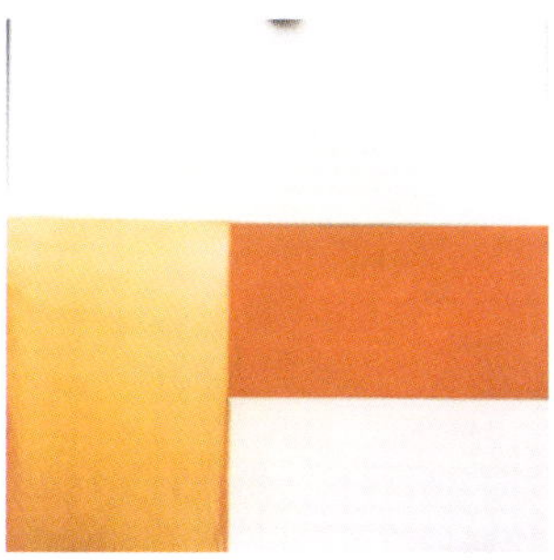

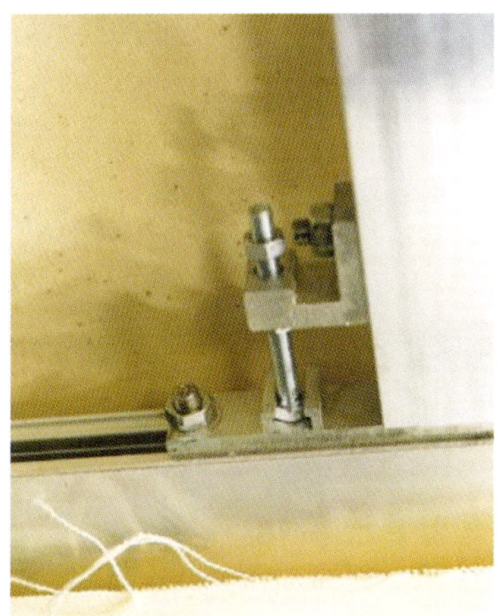

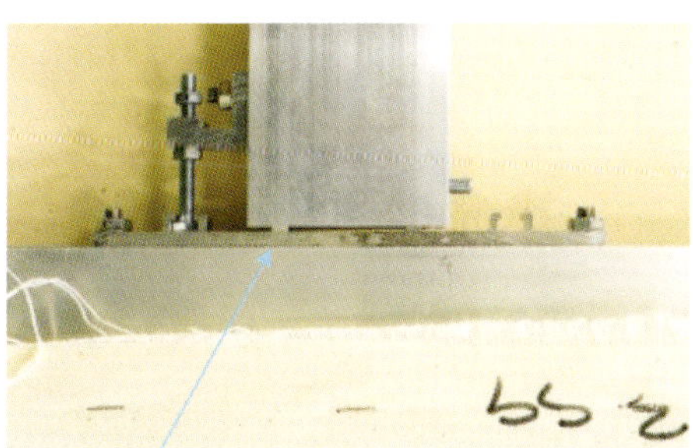

Figure 8 *Exposed Painting, Cadmium Orange on White,* by Callum Innes (1997) Walker Art Gallery.

wood profile edge. The structure is rigid but not overly light for its size. The cross-member pattern and spacing is as for our standard wood stretchers.

Aluminium/wood stretcher produced by an artists' supplier (Fig. 9)

This stretcher for large works was produced in response to the fact that artists found that suppliers' standard designs twisted during stretching of canvas. The outer members comprise aluminium box-section edged with wood. The corners, profile edge and cross-members are tulipwood. The same wood cross-section is used for both small and large stretchers. The screw tensioning mechanism braces the corners. The wood corners are held in place by metal straps. The structure aims to provide the desired torsional rigidity but is heavy. The cost is approximately double that of the same manufacturer's wooden stretcher.

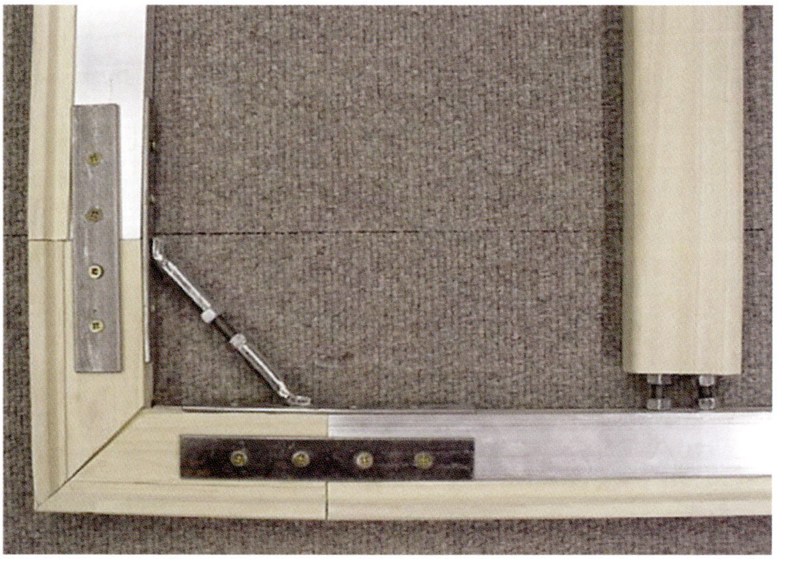

Figure 9 Detail of aluminium/wood stretcher produced by an artists' supplier. (Reproduced courtesy of John Jones Art Centre.)

Issues arising

- Do big pictures pose a special problem for stretcher design?
- How big is big? We defined 'big' as any work needing cross-members in our traditional stretcher design, but small enough to be moved across Tate sites.
- What aspects of traditional wood stretchers are inadequate? Is changing the design or materials the best way to deal with these?
- Are conservators' criteria at odds with those of the artist?
- Weight: if our 'big' pictures are required to be moved, then weight is a significant handling issue. Heavy works make handling difficult and the risk of damage higher. Is the stretcher the more significant weight component for both framed and unframed works? Can structures be too light? How will this impact on shock and vibration?
- Rigidity: the stretcher must be able to withstand, without distorting, the stresses exerted during canvas stretching and during handling. When on the wall, the rigidity is less important. During handling, traditional works are made more rigid by their frames. Unframed works are generally transported in transit frames.
- Cross-members: introduced to gain rigidity they are also the cause of the most common disfigurement of the painting surface. Attachment of stretcher

bar linings, loose linings and foam inserts can help to reduce this problem, but if the cross-members could be avoided, this would be even better. Perhaps conservators should be looking to wider outer members, greater chamfers and more robust corner joints and corner braces where the canvas flap issue is less important.

Acknowledgements

Thanks should go to Christopher Holden for allowing his treatment of the Cruikshank to be the guinea pig; Christina Young for help with the mathematics and general discussion; Helen Brett for lengthy discussions and helpful comment; Ron White for PhotoShop assistance; David Crombie (NMGM) and to all in the Paintings Section at Tate for throwing in their ideas.

Bibliography

Green, L. and Thickett, D. (1993) 'Modern metals in museum collections', in *Saving the Twentieth Century: The Conservation of Modern Materials*, Proceedings of the Conference Symposium 1991, D.W. Grattan (ed.), pp. 261–72. Ottawa: Canadian Conservation Institute.

Hallam, D. and Adams, C. (1993) 'Finishes on aluminium: a conservation perspective', in *Saving the Twentieth Century: The Conservation of Modern Materials*, Proceedings of the Conference Symposium 1991, D.W. Grattan (ed.), pp. 273–86. Ottawa: Canadian Conservation Institute.

Young, C. and Hibberd, R. (1999) 'Biaxial tensile testing of paintings on canvas', *Studies in Conservation* 44(2): 129–35.

Useful websites

- www.bacometalcentre.com
- www.creativealuminium.com
- www.worcester-aluminium.com
- www. eltherington.co.uk

The authors

Jacqueline Ridge is Head of Paintings Conservation, Jack Warans is Head of Conservation Technicians and Dave Jones is Senior Conservation Technician at Tate, London.

The Challenges of Storing a Collection of Theatre Backcloths

NICOLA COSTARAS AND STEPHEN KING

Introduction

When a theatrical production ends, costumes and backcloths, scenery and properties are often sold, destroyed, hired out or reused until there is little physical evidence left of the production. Theatre is a practical business that can rarely afford sentiment. Painted cloths have suffered more than costumes or props in this respect, being large and difficult to store, and it is sometimes only due to chance, or to the determination of individuals, that some of the most stunning and important cloths have survived. Even so, any collection with backdrops still faces the considerable problems of the expense of conservation and finding space for storage and display. Some long-established theatres, such as Covent Garden in London and Drottningholm in Sweden, have preserved historic cloths, but the Theatre Museum in London is probably unique in owning a collection, one of the most important in the world.

The Theatre Museum's collection

The Theatre Museum possesses a collection of over 30 cloths, ranging from three small canvas backcloths, each approximately 1.5 × 2m, painted front and back with multipurpose scenes for Victorian marionette performances of melodrama and pantomime, to the monumental 10 × 11m canvas cloths for performances by Diaghilev's innovative Ballets Russes. The collection includes designs by Utrillo, Giorgio de Chirico, Leon Bakst and Natalia Gontcharova. Most recent acquisitions include the atmospheric drop curtains painted with John Piper designs for his opera *Death in Venice,* first performed at the Aldeburgh Festival in Suffolk (UK) in 1973.

The star of the collection is undoubtedly the cloth painted by Count Schervachidzé, Diaghilev's most respected scenery painter, for Picasso's front curtain for *Le Train Bleu,* first performed by the Diaghilev Ballet in Paris in 1924 (Fig. 1). The work of this company established that every aspect of a ballet – choreography, music, design, lighting, make-up – was of equal importance and that the whole stage was seen as a work of art. *Le Train Bleu* was set on a fashionable

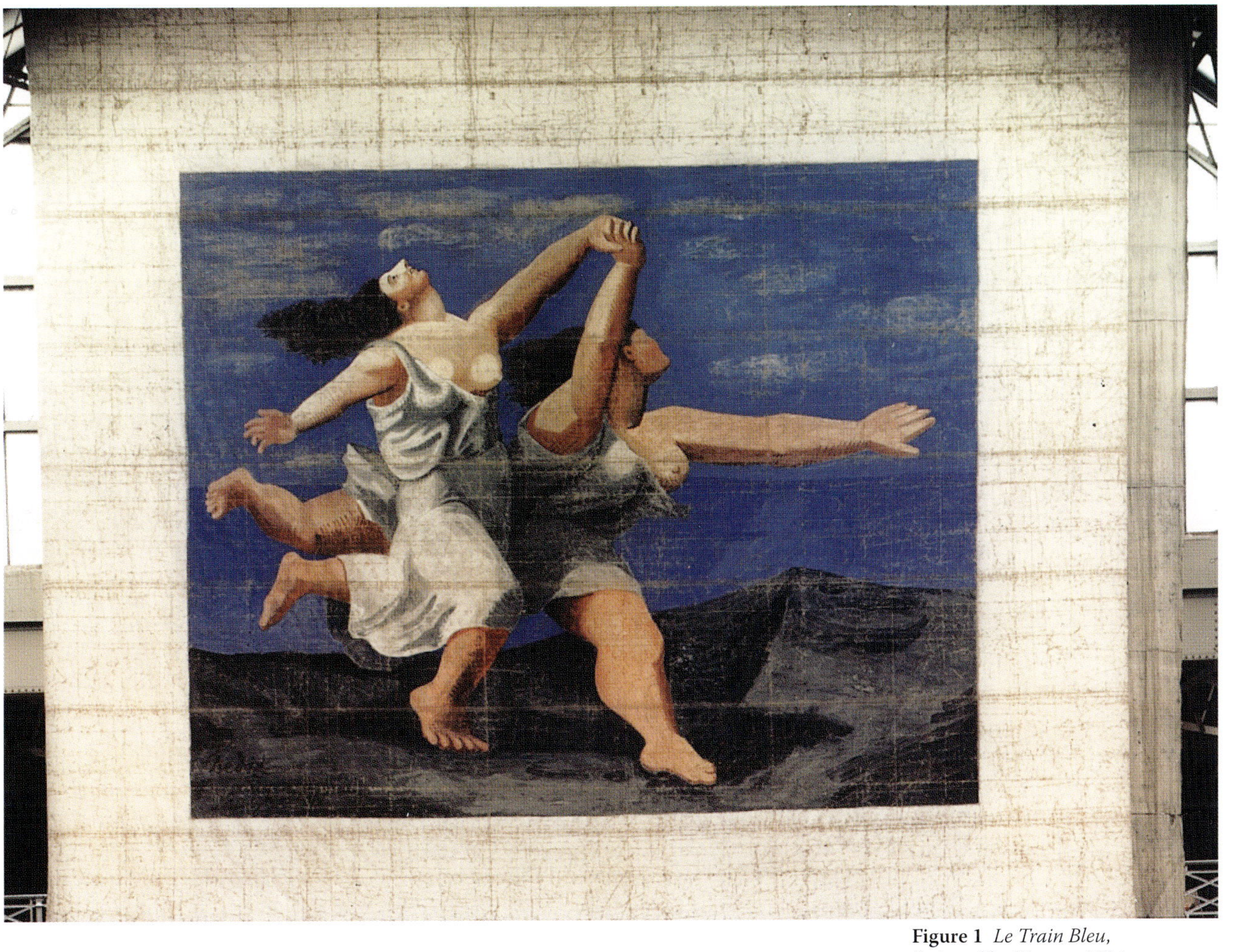

Figure 1 *Le Train Bleu*, designed by Picasso, 1924. Theatre Museum, S.310-1978. (Photograph: Cathy Haill.)

beach in the south of France, and Picasso's design was a reworking of a small work he had painted the previous year, *La Course*, representing two statuesque classical women, 'running giantesses', hand-in-hand, by the sea. The curtain was apparently painted in 14 hours and Picasso and Diaghilev were so pleased with its execution that Picasso dedicated it to Diaghilev, personally adding the dedication, signature and date. Diaghilev then decided to use this curtain as the official frontcloth for the Ballets Russes.

This cloth and others were purchased for the British nation along with a considerable number of costumes at the Sotheby's sales of the effects of the Diaghilev and de Basil Ballets Foundation in 1968 and 1969. As Richard Buckle recalls in his book *In The Wake of Diaghilev*, the purchase of these items proved to be the catalyst for the establishment of the Theatre Museum as a branch of the Victoria and Albert Museum. Once the consortium had bought them, it worked hard to secure their future as the stars of a newly amalgamated collection that, after 1974, embraced the archives of the British Theatre Museum and the V&A's important collection of theatrical memorabilia, the Enthoven Collection.

The Theatre Museum eventually opened in Covent Garden in April 1987, realising Richard Buckle's dream of a theatre museum in the heart of London's Theatreland. Although the present premises cannot accommodate displays of any but the smallest of its cloths, there is ever-increasing awareness of their rarity and a pressing need for environmentally controlled storage and facilities for public access. Given funds, and development of its premises, the Museum will work towards its ideal of allowing its collection of backcloths to be exhibited to new audiences in the twenty-first century. However much they are used to seeing images in books and on screens, people cannot fail to be amazed and impressed by the sheer scale and beauty of the remarkable images of the unrolled cloths.

Original techniques of manufacture and handling

The *Le Train Bleu* frontcloth was examined in 1998 as a result of a loan request. The frontcloth measures 10.2 × 11.7m and consists of nine horizontal strips of linen (1.23m from seam to seam). The lower edge of the cloth was sewn to form a sleeve to take a round pole across the whole width. The rigidity of the pole would keep the canvas hanging straight and the weight would keep it taut. Traditionally, theatrical cloths are attached to the fly bar, from which they are suspended, by means of cloth ties at short intervals. However, the top edge of *Le Train Bleu* was sandwiched between square battens screwed together and there was no sign of any ties. There were numerous holes close to the upper edge, suggesting that battens had been used several times. It was also obvious from the pattern of holes in the upper two metres that, at various times, a tuck had been taken at the top to reduce the height of the cloth for theatres that otherwise could not accommodate it.

The medium is distemper which was the traditional material used by theatrical cloth painters until relatively recently. Raymond White at the National Gallery in London analyzed a sample from *Le Train Bleu* in 1978 and found the paint of the border to consist of calcium carbonate bound with animal skin glue. This is consistent with the materials traditionally used for priming cloths according to Hilary Vernon-Smith, Head of the Scenic Studio at the Royal National Theatre.[1]

Originally, the cloths would have been folded if they had to be stored or if the production went on tour. The lines of paint loss along these folds can be seen clearly on the *Le Train Bleu* (Fig. 1). Folding the cloths creates lines of weakness in the textile as well as causing paint loss and is therefore not an option for their preservation in a museum.

Problems of preservation and storage

The larger backcloths vary in size from 8 to 11.5m in height and between 7 to 16m wide. Their size makes storage difficult and providing access to view the cloths unrolled is a major challenge. One of the larger cloths would cover an area of $160m^2$.

Le Train Bleu was rolled around the round pole mentioned above, which had an 80mm diameter. The battens along the upper edge were broken in several places and had pierced the canvas. These were removed to prevent further damage and the frontcloth was transferred to a roller. Although a diameter wider than 250mm would have been desirable, it was the only tube of sufficient length that could be found at short notice, and it was thought preferable to avoid having joins in the roller. The roller is made of PVC, which, although not an ideal material from the point of view of preventive conservation, was an improvement on the previous situation. The roller was first given an isolating layer of aluminium foil and then covered with acid-free tissue. The cloth was interleaved with acid-free tissue as it was rolled. At least ten people were involved with rolling the frontcloth and six people were needed to carry it to its storage place (Fig. 2).

Smaller textiles can be stored easily on rollers supported at either end but this becomes more difficult with wider cloths. So far, this type of storage has only been provided within the Museum for textiles up to 6m long; other cloths are still rolled around narrow poles. One difficulty has been identifying a suitable material for a

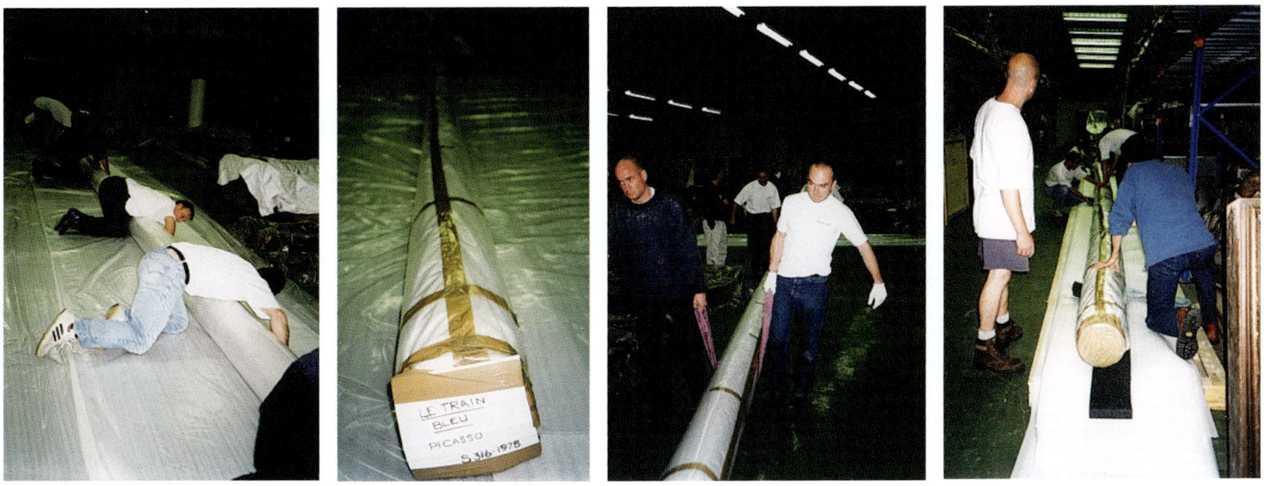

Figure 2 *Le Train Bleu* being wrapped and moved to its current storage place. (Photograph: Cathy Haill.)

roller that will be rigid over 15m, inert and not so heavy as to make it impractical, bearing in mind that the large cloths are a significant weight in themselves. The estimated weight of the *Le Train Bleu* is 300kg. To date no suitable roller has been found.

Proposed solutions

Although rolling painted textiles around a core that is then suspended at either end has been the aim until recently, theoretical models of the pressures on a rolled textile suggest that a cradle or sling system might be preferable (Fig. 3). Whether a roll is suspended or supported, the object will experience both compression and tension. With this system, the pressures would be distributed over a larger

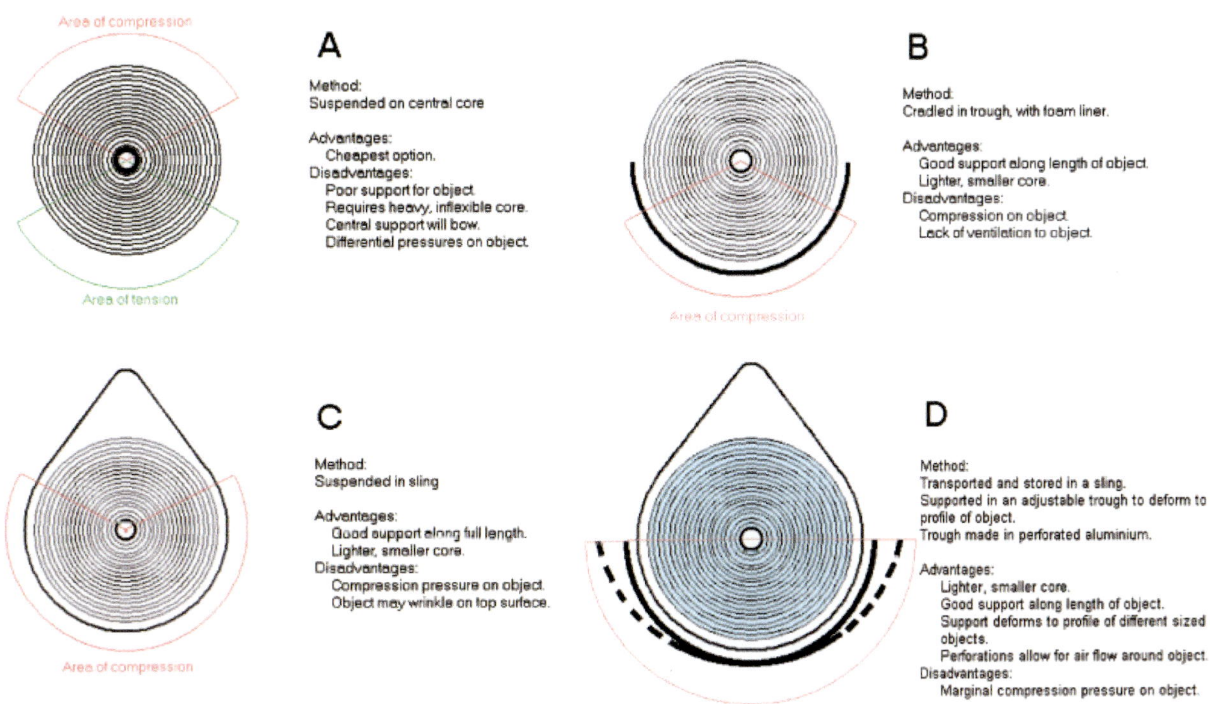

Figure 3 Diagram showing the distribution of tension and compression on a rolled textile using different methods of suspension (© Stephen King).

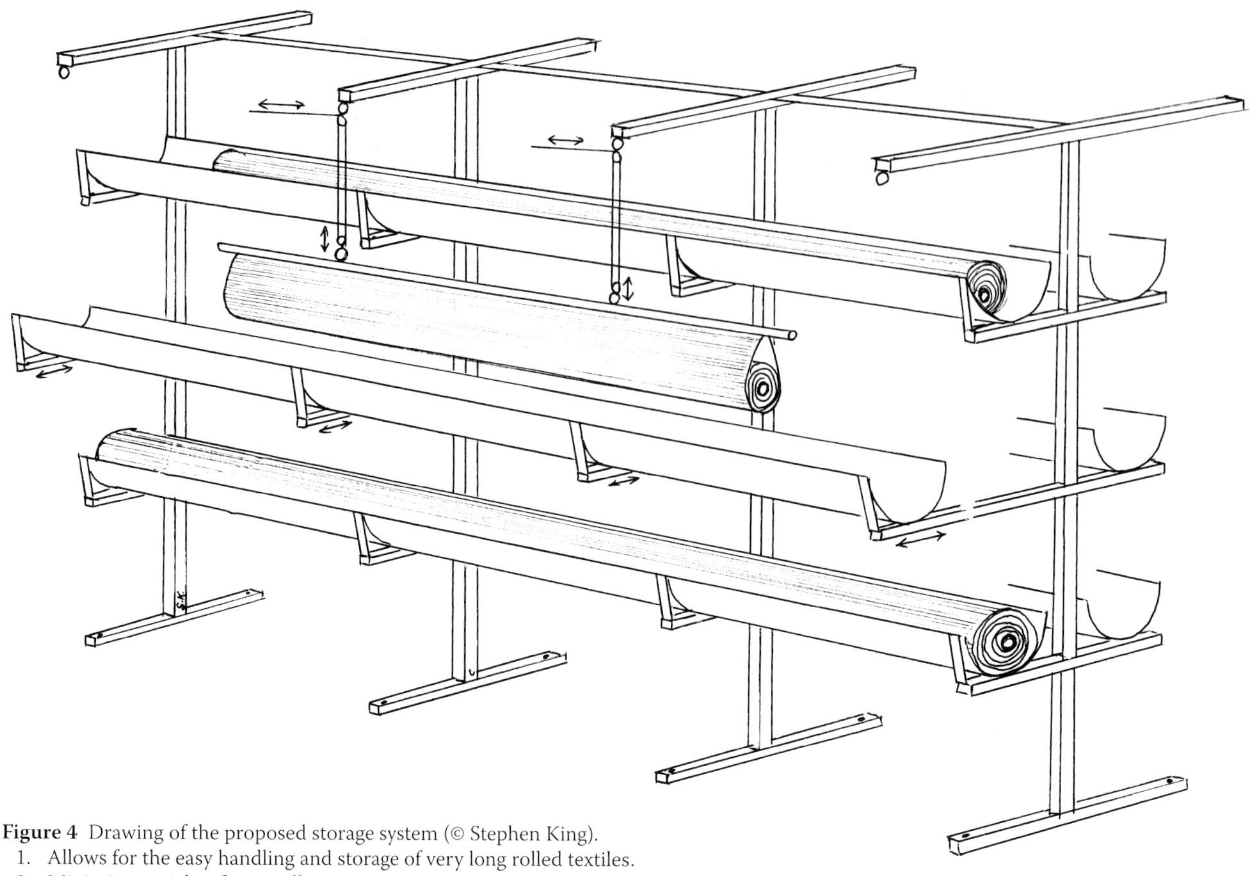

Figure 4 Drawing of the proposed storage system (© Stephen King).

1. Allows for the easy handling and storage of very long rolled textiles.
2. Minimises weight of core roller.
3. Minimises damage to fibres of rolled object.
4. Allows for a variety of core sizes for rolling objects to minimise damage to object surface.
5. Objects supported equally over total length.
6. Storage system has built-in handling system.
7. Material sling also acts as object dust cover.
8. Object lifting bar can also double as a handling and display system.
9. Perforated aluminium support trough allows for all-round air ventilation.
10. Perforations prevent the build-up of dust or moisture below object.
11. Flexible support trough moulds to profile of object during storage.
12. Quick and easy object retrieval in case of emergency.
13. Complies with manual handling regulations.
14. Reduced risk to object during handling and storage.
15. Support structure can be enclosed to maintain a microclimate.
16. Flexible and adaptable to suit different object weights, lengths and diameters.

area. Currently, the proposed design for a storage system for the backcloths is a rack with cradles (Fig. 4). This would provide support along the whole length of the object. Further work is being undertaken to design a method for lifting the backcloths into and out of such a rack with smooth, controlled movements, maintaining even support along their length.

This does not resolve the problem of public access. Ideally, a suitable structure would be constructed in order to simulate a theatre fly tower. This is the apparatus that is employed in theatres to raise and lower backcloths during a performance and is designed for objects of this size. In this way, a number of cloths could be 'flown' for a limited period, which would allow interested parties to view them as they were meant to be seen. However, achieving this within an existing building and the constraints of preventive conservation presents dilemmas. A previous public display of several backcloths was staged in the exhibition halls at Olympia.

It has been suggested that the cloths might be stored in a 'fly-tower' arrangement so that they would always be accessible. Unfortunately this would not be the best method of preserving the cloths. Storing them suspended, even if there was

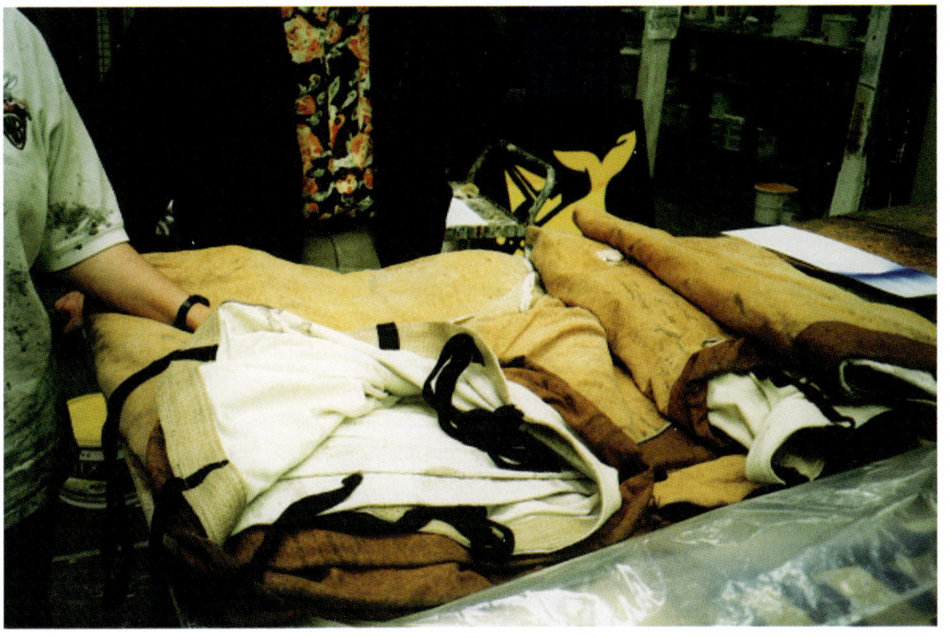

Figure 5 Folded backcloth showing cloth ties in the 'Paint Frame' at the Royal National Theatre. (Photograph: Cathy Haill.)

sufficient space, would put a great strain on the upper edges and there would be no way of protecting them from surface dirt. The traditional method of attaching the top of the cloth to the fly bar is by cloth ties roughly every 300mm (Fig. 5). This does not distribute the weight evenly across the whole width and it is therefore not considered desirable as a method for their future display. Different methods of attaching the cloths are being investigated: Velcro is common in the textile conservation field, while a clamping method was used on the Mesdag Panorama in The Hague, Netherlands. Simple mechanical hoists, which gently raise and lower one edge of an object, have been installed recently within the V&A's carpet and tapestry store to facilitate periodic inspection, and something similar could be used for the theatrical cloths.

Conclusion

Investigation is continuing by the team[2] into the paper and carpet industries to determine how they handle large, heavy, rolled objects. However, the problems revolve around the sheer size of the objects, both rolled and unrolled, and the space required to manoeuvre them safely, both for the object and the object handlers. Thus, initially, it seems sensible to concentrate on the provision of an appropriate, safe, long-term storage system and to review the periodic display of several backcloths in suitable public venues. At present there is no space of sufficient height in the Museum's stores where any apparatus could be built to fly the larger theatrical cloths.

Acknowledgements

The authors would like to thank Cathy Haill of the Theatre Museum and Amanda Ward at the V&A.

Notes

1. Ms Vernon-Smith informed us that size was the medium used for scene painting when she began her career and provided us with the following recipes:
   - 'Treble size' – dissolve 1lb of size (not pearl size) in 1 gallon of hot water.
   - For priming take 3 parts of treble size, 1½ parts water and 2 parts of whiting paste (3lb whiting in 1 pint of cold water).
   - Working size for painting – use 1 part of treble size and 8 parts of hot water. Some pigments require more treble size and less water. To test whether the pigment is sufficiently well bound, paint a sample onto paper and rub it when dry.

   Ms Vernon-Smith made a distinction between *size* and *distemper* as binding media. She considered that distemper would contain a quantity of drying oil in addition to animal glue. The confusion may be related to the introduction of commercially prepared distemper paints for use in scenery painting; see E. Kerr (1999) *Tear Repair Testing Project*, London: V&A.
2. Nicola Costaras, Conservation Department, Victoria and Albert Museum, London; Cathy Haill, Theatre Museum, London; Stephen King, previously Projects Division, Victoria and Albert Museum, London; Amanda Ward, Records and Collections, Victoria and Albert Museum, London.

The authors

Nicola Costaras is Head Paintings Conservator, Victoria and Albert Museum, London. Stephen King is Director of his own company, Project Restoration.

The Battle with Trafalgar

VALENTINE WALSH AND RICHARD PELTER

Introduction

In 1997, the Royal Naval Museum at Portsmouth commissioned the conservation of a very large painted panorama of the Battle of Trafalgar as part of the redevelopment of the Museum and in particular, the Victory Gallery. The conservation project involved considerable skills and innovations which are not normally required in the conservation of paintings of a more usual size. The particular problems associated with this project serve to exemplify the complications of conservation on this scale.

The redevelopment was a very exciting project as the Museum had been granted considerable funds by the Heritage Lottery Fund for a dramatic renovation. The Museum itself is situated within the historic area of the modern naval base at Portsmouth. The significance of the whole site is hard to exaggerate as Nelson's importance to Great Britain and the Royal Navy is legendary – on Nelson's death in 1805, the whole country went into mourning. The Panorama is housed in an annexe to a former rigging house, directly opposite Nelson's own ship, HMS *Victory*, which led the Battle of Trafalgar depicted in the painting. It was conceived and painted in 1930 by William Lionel Wyllie (1851–1931) shortly before his death at the age of 80. He had been involved in saving the *Victory* from destruction and wished to paint something to raise money for the ship's preservation. Wyllie had been impressed by seeing the panorama of the Battle of Waterloo and felt that a naval equivalent was required.

Panoramas

Panoramas have a very interesting history. The concept of a panorama was put forward and then patented by Robert Barker in 1787 as *la nature à la coup d'oeil.* The term 'panorama' was first used in 1791. Today we have such high-tech, modern illusions to impress the viewer that it is probably difficult for us to realise the impact that nineteenth-century panoramas had on the public. They were often treated as theatre rather than art. The concept is to portray a view so as to deceive viewers into the belief that they are actually present. Barker's patent included features such as a curved canvas, top lighting and a viewing platform or enclosure constructed to position a viewer so that it was not possible to see the mechanics of the painting's support or its edge. This is in contrast to a framed painting, which has visibly finite borders and so, no matter how realistically it is executed, the viewer cannot be deceived into believing it is real. Eventually, panoramas became immensely elaborate, including objects in the foreground and light and sound effects. In fact, they could justifiably be called the first installation art.

The painting's history

Wyllie's painting carried on in this tradition. He designed a semicircular glass-roofed (in order to light the painting as realistically as possible) annexe to the rigging house in which to hang his panorama. He meticulously researched the battle and how it would have looked from the stern of the French ship *Neptune* at precisely 2pm when the battle was at its height. According to his daughter Aileen, who assisted him in executing the painting, he booked a cabin at water level on a cruise ship in order to paint looking out of the porthole to depict accurately the water as seen from that point. The canvas was commissioned from Rowney and was hung in a semicircular, concave shape using the skills of the sailmakers at the dockyard, with lacing passing through brass eyelets in the canvas and then around tubular steel piping. At some stage, two pieces were added to the ends to make the painting 12.8m (42ft) long and 3.6m (12ft) high. The painting was to be viewed through a mock-up of the stern of *Neptune* and a skiff was placed in the foreground to restrict the view of the edges and lacing. The effect was so realistic that only the addition of sound and movement of the floor would have been required to make the deception total.

Wyllie's daughter Aileen records:

> The home of the panorama was growing at a great pace. The firm of George Rowney had made a 46' by 12' canvas, specially woven on a wide loom. Three big pictures, 3' by 6' each, were finished in detail by Daddy for us to work from which when joined, gave the whole composition. The stern cabin windows of the French ship from which the panorama would be viewed were growing. Two high step ladders had been made and the supporting metal frames were in position to hold the picture. When the canvas arrived the sailmaker came and made eyelets in the top and bottom and the lacing and straining began. When the canvas was ready and primed with white we ruled in the horizon. Then both the pictures and the canvas were squared and the squares numbered to aid enlarging. I started copying ships across the horizon using a pair of proportional compasses and a pencil and Daddy followed with his palette ...[1]

The painting had twice been removed from the annexe. First, during World War II, it was taken to a Portisdown hill fort for storage and safety. On its return in 1945 it was found to be flaking. However, in the aftermath of war, there were no funds for its restoration. Both the painting and its housing began to deteriorate through neglect; the glazed roof and rear wall, far from weatherproof, allowed rain to seep onto the canvas in storm conditions.

By 1965 it was pronounced beyond redemption unless urgent remedial treatment was undertaken. It was once again dismantled, removed 'on a huge roller' and sent to Robin Ashton of the Northwest Area Museum Service in Manchester which, it is recorded in the associated correspondence, had the only hot table in the country large enough to accommodate it. Following wax impregnation (it was not lined), it was returned in 1967 using the original method of fixing with the

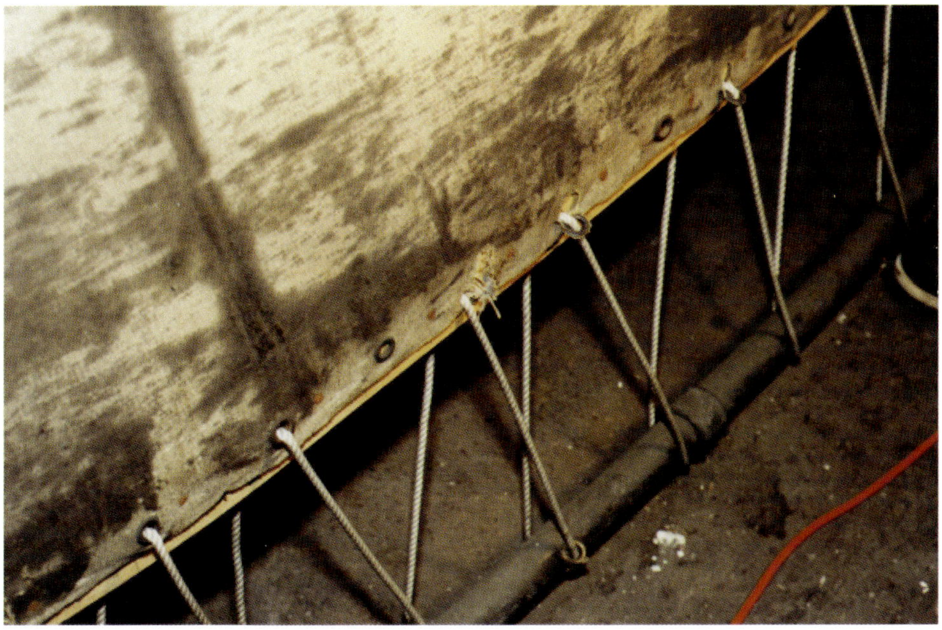

Figure 1 Condition of the Panorama. Detail of original support system, which resulted in localised tears to the canvas and large surface distortions.

possible addition of battens all around the edge of the painting at the back. The annexe was also re-roofed, improving the lighting and insulation and allowing air conditioning[2] to be installed. Nevertheless, the flaking problem continued alarmingly and in 1977 another conservator was called in to consolidate the paint *in situ*. This was carried out by ironing wax from the back with supports held up to the front, but the flaking continued.

In 1997 it was found that there were numerous areas of imminent paint loss and the legacy of rolling and unrolling was imprinted in the craquelure. There were also considerable cupped and dry, flaky areas of paint. The canvas was in a degraded condition with the eyelets pulling out and the battens misaligned. The two additions stitched to the ends were causing considerable strain in the paint layers as well as in the canvas. The canvas had also taken on an extraordinary shape. The whole painting was concave, curving away from the viewer, but the bottom third had a convex bulge all the way along, coming forward about 305mm (1ft). It was obvious that if the painting were to survive it would need to be taken down again and, this time, lined and restored (Fig. 1).

The Museum asked its paintings conservator, Valentine Walsh, to undertake this conservation. The painting required removal from the building and the expertise of a conservator with experience of consolidating and lining paintings of this size. Valentine therefore called upon International Fine Art Conservation Studios Ltd. (IFACS) to join with her in this project, and to undertake this aspect of the work. A final member of the team was the engineer, Graham Richmond who, together with Richard Pelter, was indispensable in the designing and construction of rolling, lifting, moving gear, and steel gantries and tensioning framework. Valentine oversaw the whole project and undertook the cleaning and restoration. The project spanned the period from end of October 1998 through to mid-July 1999.

The battle with Trafalgar: shipshape and Bristol fashion

Conservation and restoration treatment

The painting had considerable surface dirt which was removed with an aqueous solution of triammonium citrate 2% in deionised water. This revealed heavy and uneven yellowed varnish which was removed with isopropanol as it considerably distorted the tonal effect of the work. It was found that retouching had been carried out in numerous places during previous restoration work. This no longer matched and needed to be replaced more sensitively. The restoration was therefore also removed with acetone.

Removal and transportation

In order to transport the painting, a large diameter cylinder was constructed of fibreglass mounted onto a heavy steel turntable (Fig. 2). The turntable was carried by a steel frame which tracked along the face of the painting. Numerous architectural obstacles, such as roof trusses and concrete steps, and space constraints necessitated precision construction of this structure. Another complication was the fall or unevenness of the concrete floor. Tracking wheels attached to the support carriage were made adjustable to keep the cylinder and canvas at a constant level.

The painting was faced with bleached muslin and BEVA 371 adhesive diluted 40% with white spirit. When the facing was complete, the cylinder and steel track system was installed and removal of the canvas from its support frame took place starting from the right end of the Panorama; this involved taking out the nylon rope, which was part of the original hanging method, and fixing the canvas to the cylinder. The painting was fixed with screws through the eyelets onto the wooden top of the cylinder as rolling progressed. Contrary to normal rolling practices, the

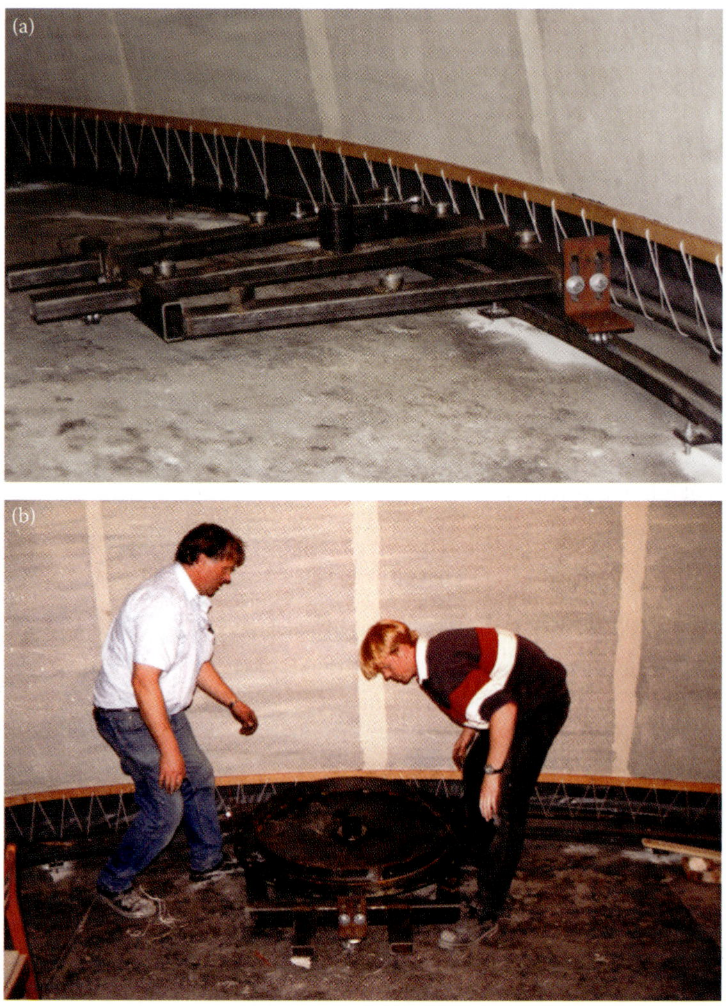

Figure 2 Tracking system. Detail showing (a) steel tracking system and (b) turntable upon which the fibreglass cylinder was situated.

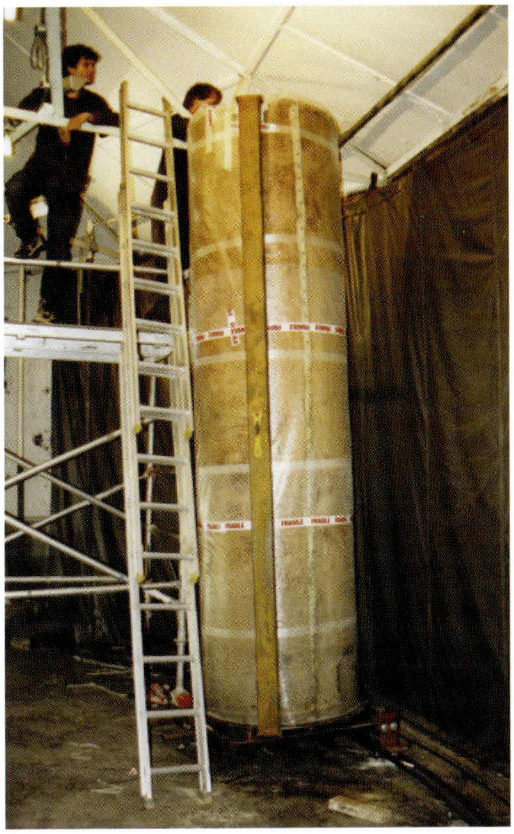

Figure 3 Transportation of the Panorama. The faced painting is rolled face-in onto a fibreglass cylinder mounted on a steel turntable, ready for transportation to IFACS' studio.

paint side was turned inwards as this was the actual painting's shape. Progression was slow due to the effort required to keep the canvas smooth and even on the cylinder. The timber battens that had been added for support were removed altogether, along with the tacks that held the wood in place (Fig. 3). A combination of cross-props, steel beams and winches was installed to lower the cylinder into a horizontal position. Once lowered, the cylinder was placed in a travelling cradle which ensured that no pressure was put on the painting itself. This was then transported to IFACS in Bristol where a crane was used to hoist the painting through the first-floor window into the studios.

Unrolling and canvas treatment

Although the canvas' dimensions had been measured *in situ*, there was a brief moment of apprehension when the Panorama was unrolled as to whether it was longer than the studio (Fig. 4). Fortunately it was not. The canvas was slowly detached from the cylinder and unrolled onto the studio floor, where vast surface distortions became apparent. There were lateral bulges caused by the weight distribution on the hanging frame and vertical ripples that had resulted from the long-term hanging system of rope and eyelets.

It was our original proposal and intention to line the canvas flat but the distortions would need to be flattened first. Initial moisture treatment tests were carried out locally, but these proved ineffective due to the BEVA 371 facing, which was holding the buckling in a fixed position, and the old wax saturating the canvas fibres. It was decided to release the facing and remove as much of the wax as possible using hot irons, and then proceed with moisture treatment (Fig. 5). The deformations were sprayed with atomised distilled water and 5% methylated spirits, gently ironed through a pad of blotting paper, and left overnight under weight. The level of buckling was greatly reduced after moisture treatment, although there

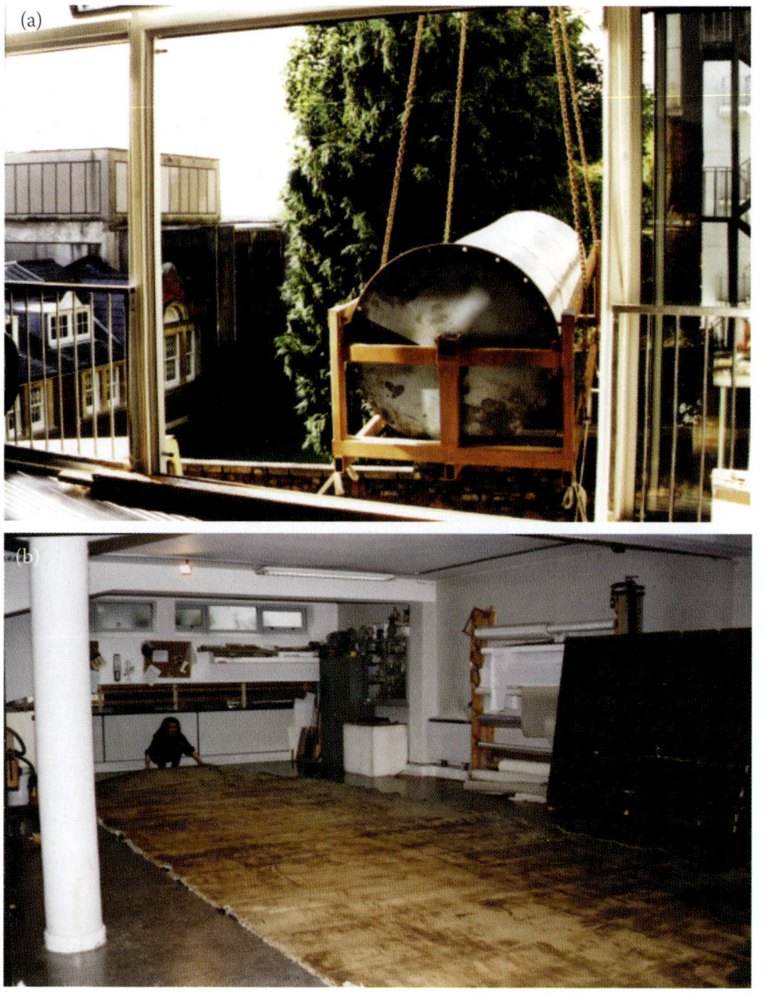

Figure 4 (a) Arrival of the Panorama at IFACS in Bristol. (b) The reverse of painting when unrolled at the studio.

remained minor bulges and ripples, which appeared permanently deformed. A vacuum envelope system was set up as an attempt to improve these deformations. This was effected using a plastic film, Bagging Film Polyester, taped around the perimeter with mastic tape, and two vacuum pumps for extraction of air. A membrane of moisture-absorbing Bleed Cloth Polyester was spread over the front of the Panorama, which had been previously moistened on the reverse, and it was then enclosed in the plastic film. Bulges still remained after this treatment. Concern over these producing creases in the canvas and disturbing the paint layer during flat lining prompted the idea of lining over a semicircular support in the shape of the Panorama's curve.

The painting was faced before lining, this time with an aqueous adhesive of glue paste (rabbit skin glue, flour and water 1:3:6) diluted 70% in water, and muslin.

Construction of a timber former and lining

Construction of a timber former was carried out in a rented warehouse. Each piece of the former was measured accurately to ensure the dimensions accorded precisely with the original canvas. When the former was complete, each wooden section was colour-coded, numbered and then dismantled and reassembled back in IFACS' studio. A linen canvas was prepared for lining, stretched onto a loom, de-crimped and impregnated with BEVA 371, of the same dilution, to fill the canvas weave sufficiently to achieve a bond. A new hanging system for the Panorama was devised at this stage due to the failing original brass eyelets. It was decided to

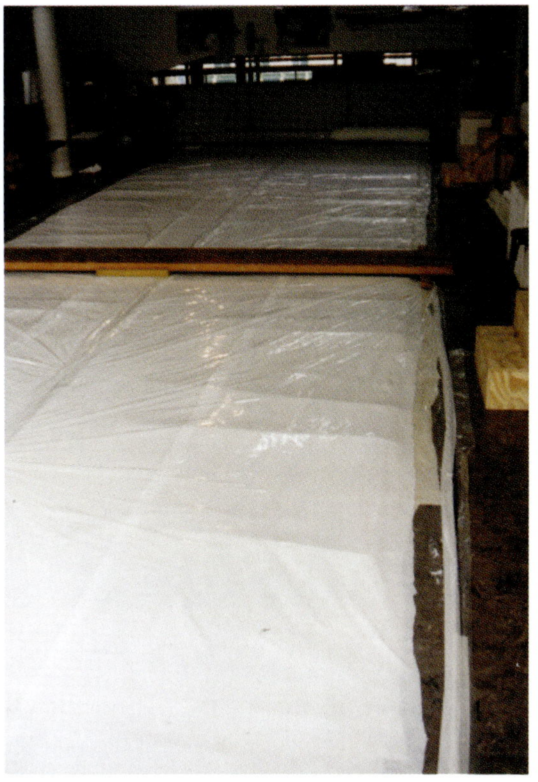

Figure 5 Moisture treatment under vacuum pressure. A vacuum extraction system was used during moisture treatment. This entailed plastic film Bagging Film Polyester, being sealed to the floor and the air being extracted using two vacuum pumps.

stitch a polyester sailcloth sleeve around the perimeter of the treated lining canvas – this was undertaken by an experienced sailmaker. This sleeve contained a nylon rope, 1.3mm in diameter, which would slide into an aluminium track frame sited in the exhibition gallery. (Fig. 6).

The painting was then pulled face down across the surface of the former, covered with silicone release paper and tensioned onto metal poles fixed to the length sides by threading rope from them back through the original eyelets. The canvas began to retain a more regular surface shape. Waste edges from the two original seam joins, which accommodated eyelets, had to be trimmed before lining. The lining canvas was then placed on the reverse of the original, stretched over the round edges of the former and stapled into position. Hand ironing commenced from the centre, working to the edges in both directions (Fig. 7). Throughout this process it was not possible to view the face of the Panorama, but various distortions could be felt during ironing and most of them were eliminated.

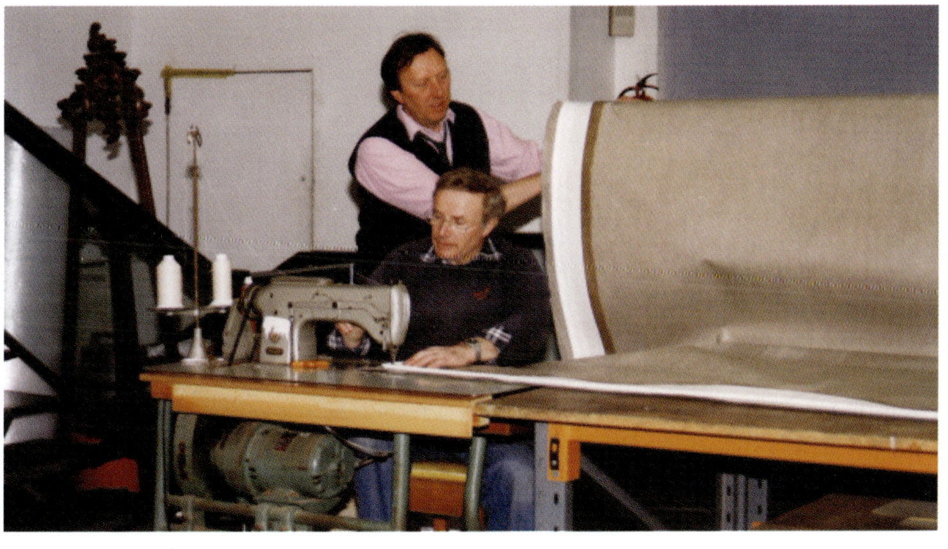

Figure 6 Preparation of the lining canvas. A sailmaker sewed over 30m of the polyester sailcloth onto the lining canvas, which was prepared with BEVA 371.

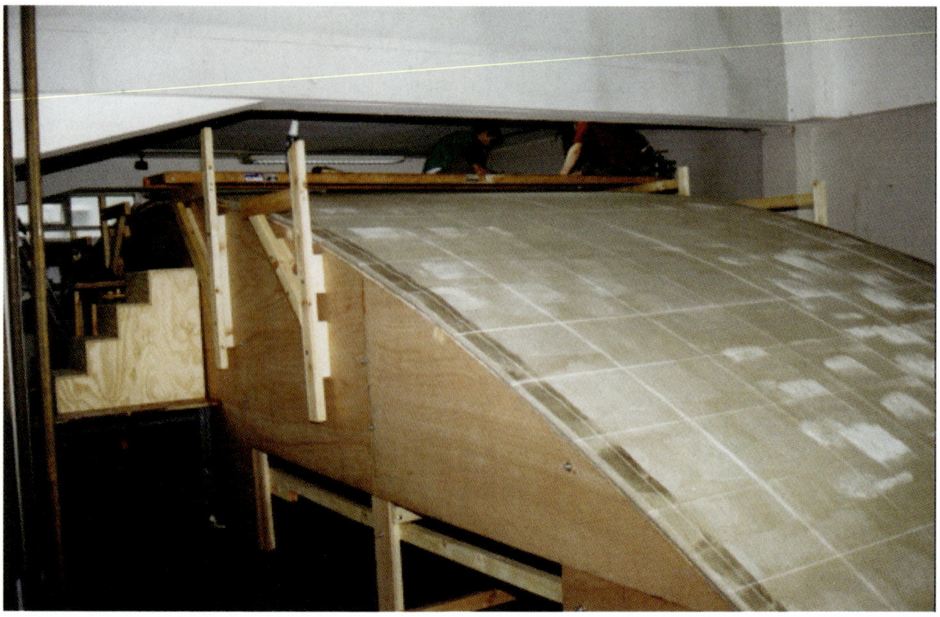

Figure 7 Lining of the Panorama. The painting was placed face down on the wooden former with the lining canvas on top. The joining surfaces had been pre-prepared with BEVA 371, 20% in white spirit.

After removing the staples and detaching the lined canvas from the former, it was possible to inspect the face of the painting. This was achieved by suspending each edge of the canvas, alternately, from the centre over a cylinder hanging on two poles. Several areas still required further ironing. The canvases were re-stretched over the former and re-ironed. With the exception of one or two areas, distortions were brought into plane. Undoubtedly treatment of the distortions would have been more successful had we been able to also work from the front of the painting on a reversed former but time and cost restraints made this impossible.

Reinstatement

The painting was to be replaced in the gallery on a metal framework supporting an aluminium track made from Luffgrove Extrusion, which is frequently used in the tent and marquee industry (Fig. 8).[3] This track was attached to the structural framework by tapped metal inserts, joined to M8 A2-70 stainless steel studding (Figs 9 and 10).[4] These were conceived to allow the painting to be tensioned once in place. The framework also included a walkway gantry approximately two-thirds up the height of the canvas to allow adjustments to tension along the top and access for the painting's ongoing care (Fig. 11). The Luffgrove Extrusion would accommodate the rope which had been sewn into the sleeve to the edges of the lining canvas. This new method of hanging the painting was particularly engaging as it used technology employed in the mounting of sails on modern boats, thus continuing the conceptual link initiated with Wyllie's original design.

The transportation cylinder was also modified with a series of aluminium support brackets which threaded onto the canvas rope sleeve, and assembled at the top to secure the canvas in place. The painting was slowly released from the former and rolled face-in onto the cylinder. This was then craned out of the studio and returned to Portsmouth (Fig. 12), where the process of removal was reversed.

The cylinder was placed upright on the turntable ready to fix the canvas into position. The aluminium track was installed along the top and bottom of the support frame and held in place by an adjustable metal bar. The painting was released from the cylinder and fed through the aluminium track. As more canvas went onto the support frame, the weight increased and the canvas warped in the track,

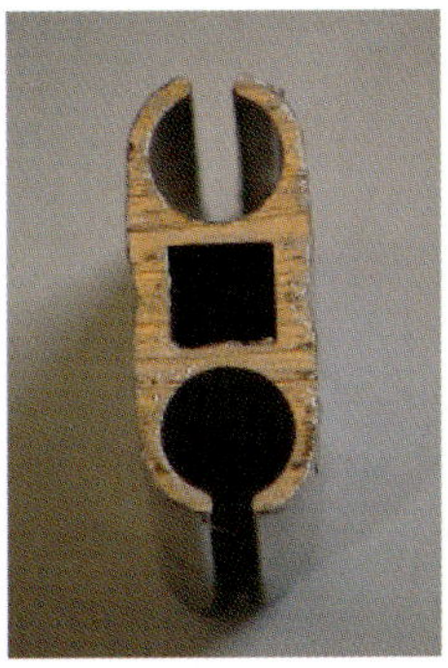

Figure 8 Cross-section of aluminium track used in the support system. The rope, inside the polyester sailcloth, fits through one of the slots in the aluminium. The tapped insert fits in the slot on the other side (see Fig. 11).

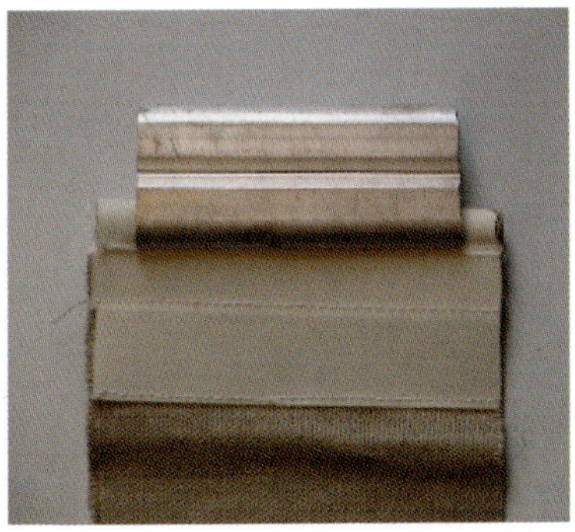

Figure 9 Support system. The canvas has a polyester sailcloth sleeve around a rope, stitched onto its edge and the aluminium extrusion slotted along the length of the rope.

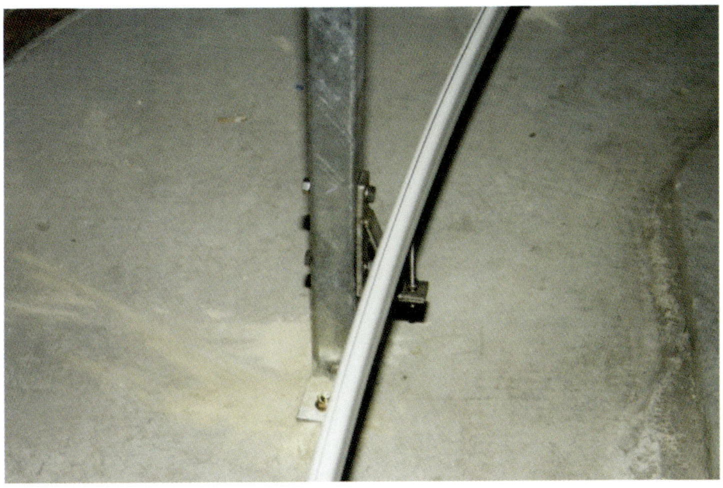

Figure 10 Support system. The aluminium track runs horizontally and is attached to the structural framework by tapped metal inserts, joined to M8 A2-70 stainless steel studding. The track runs the same convex as the original hanging system.

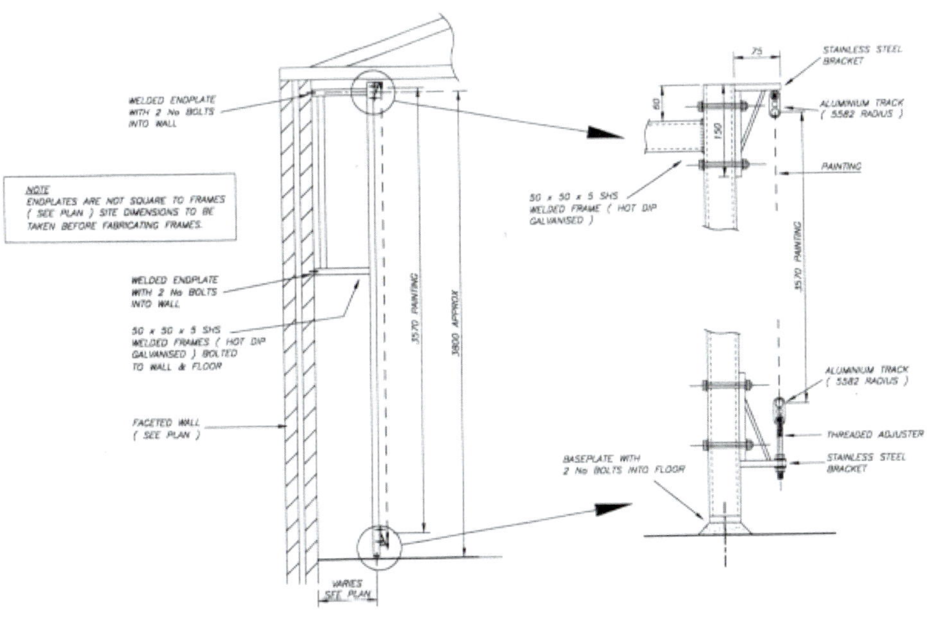

Figure 11 Diagram showing construction of the frame. The metal frame supports the curved aluminium track to which the canvas is attached. A service walkway was also designed to allow access to the top of the painting from the reverse.

causing some concern. Gradually the Panorama was eased along the length of the track and the sidetracks were fitted. Once in position the adjustable fixing bars were tensioned and in so doing, the track and the canvas straightened.

The facing, which remained in place throughout transportation, was removed with deionised water, ready for filling and retouching where necessary *in situ*.

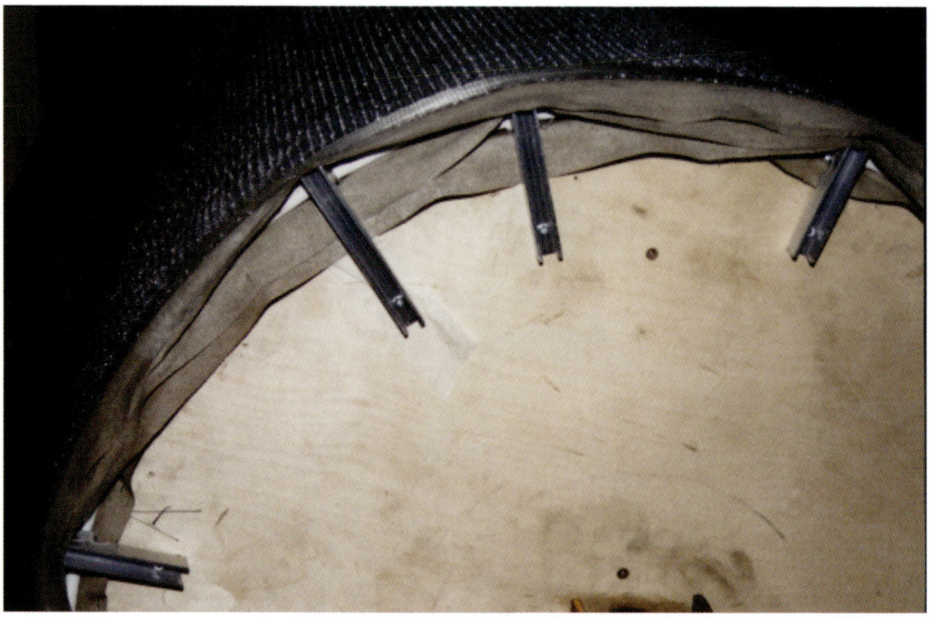

Figure 12 Transportation of the Panorama back to the Royal Naval Museum, Portsmouth. The painting was once again rolled face-in onto the fibreglass cylinder. Metal brackets were attached to the canvas rope sleeve on the edge of the painting and these were then screwed to the end of the cylinder. This prevented movement during transportation.

The battle with Trafalgar: the battle with bureaucracy

The Museum wished to contract the conservators for this painting directly and maintain day-to-day contact with them while also overseeing the larger contract for the building work and the Museum installations. This was a testament to the close working relationship the curators had with its conservators. However it caused considerable problems in the execution of the contract; the conservators were not consulted at the start of the gallery redesign with regard to environmental requirements and conservation considerations for the Panorama, nor were they consulted as to its appropriate display as part of a greater new 'Trafalgar Experience'.

Contract

Contracts for a large project of this sort necessarily call for many more elements than are required for a simple easel painting. Beyond the straight conservation plan, every possible detail must be considered at the outset. Details such as working conditions, timing, hours of access, extra equipment supplied by builders not within the conservation contract, accommodation, liability, requirement for surveyors' structural reports, etc. must be clearly stated in the contract. Schedules of work stages and payments, health and safety arrangements, insurance – both for the painting and the conservators – security and future care of the painting must also be included. All this must be costed and then spelt out very precisely for a particularly complex site project such as this. The work was painstakingly priced consulting all the team members, the quotation was accepted and a contract finalised. Although a fair method of tendering is fundamental to a job of this sort, it is always a complicated and gruelling process and should be the subject of a paper in its own right. It is often the case that once a price has been quoted, the funds are then raised to match the quote and there is little scope to go back later for more. It must be absolutely clear what is included in the quote – anything that is excluded should be expressly mentioned in correspondence additional to the contract in order to highlight it. In the case of the Panorama, for example, the client missed the fact that the contract stipulated that the scaffolding was to be supplied by the other builders on site, therefore no financial provision was made for this. Extra manpower had been requested on the day the painting was to be removed but the surveyor and the project foreman, unaware of this request, had laid the builders off that day to keep them out of the way. Furthermore, the building contractors had not budgeted for their time as copies of our requirements agreed with the Museum had not been forwarded to the main building renovation contractor. A major consideration with a redevelopment such as this is that the building work takes up all the spare financial slack in the system and conservation can easily lose out in a crisis.

It is essential to establish a clear mode of communication so that the conservator has the authority to communicate directly with the foreman of the building work. Curators and surveyors are often not at hand when they are needed. As there was a good understanding between the Museum professionals and conservators, the quote was less pedantic on the subject of communication and liaison with the other contractors than it would have been in the case of a subcontract within the overall renovation contract. The Museum had clearly considered conservation a special part of the redevelopment and wished to communicate directly. Valentine Walsh had overall responsibility for the painting's conservation; she subcontracted the lining and engineering. This appeared at the outset to be a perfectly reasonable arrangement. Complications arose, however, when the builders, their surveyor and foreman did not dovetail with the conservation project and worked to their own deadlines. The day-to-day problems of access, safety, electrical supply, etc., required the conservators to have the facility to communicate with surveyors and foremen on site. This could be tricky as aims, on a daily basis, were often conflicting.

All this might give an indication of the amount of administrative time needed by the conservator in charge of a project of this scale. About 60% of the lead conservator's time was spent in keeping track of finances, finding the foreman, attending crucial meetings with the Museum director, curator, surveyor, designers, etc., arranging a tea venue, getting security clearance and finding accommodation within the budgeted amount (when in a holiday resort in the summer). It should not be assumed that the head conservator will have much time left over for the actual work. Should the budget allow, large projects should ideally have a site administrator – probably not a conservator – to ensure that the conservators' skills are used to the best advantage.

Timing

Timing was not only dependent on the schedule of work but was further constrained by the builders' schedule. Any contract of this sort will generally contain requirements to complete stages by a particular time and will include penalties if these are not met. In an ideal world the penalties would also work the other way so that compensation would be made to conservators if the conservation work is held up because of factors outside their control. As the main conservation contractor assigning subcontracted work on a project, such penalty clauses should furthermore be reflected in this contract. The costs must also anticipate significant amounts of time taken up by meetings with the surveyors and the Museum designers. Much time was lost waiting for plans of the rebuilt building as the size of the framework was critical and there was almost no tolerance between the top of the painting and the roof struts. Changes made to the building at the last minute necessitated a redesign of the support for the canvas shortly before the painting was to be reinstated. Other timing hiccups involved getting the Panorama out before the floor was removed in the adjacent rooms. The builders had got going right away to dismantle the room leading out of the building, necessitating the engineer's genius to manoeuvre the painting out over this bombsite. The sense of grievance over this was all the greater as doors in the annexe had been requested so that the painting could be removed and replaced directly from the outside. This was considered to be a breach of naval security, but after the Panorama had been removed, it was decided to dismantle and rebuild the annexe anyway – to be fair, this was partly in order that the building would meet our stipulated environmental conditions.

Access

Access to the Museum outside normal opening hours to the general public was complicated as it is situated within a high security naval base. This required security clearance, which added considerably to the bureaucratic burden. Furthermore, access was only permitted within the normal working day as the Museum required security staff always to be on hand. This restriction can be quite tedious for conservators who are working *in situ* away from home, as there is little to do in the evening from 5pm – many conservators would prefer to work a longer day in this sort of situation. Constraints on the length of the working day may well influence the number of days allocated to complete the project. As work fell slightly behind schedule due to elements beyond our control, a request was made to be allowed to stay on in the evening but this was refused on the grounds that the budget did not allow for overtime payments to security staff.

Miraculously, when the building works were running late, work late into the night was allowed.

Health and safety

In addition to the normal health and safety measures, there are further requirements when working on a large scale. Working, as in this case, at a nuclear naval base has its own special quirks, but generally, working within a building site requires compliance with fairly stringent regulations. The leader of such a conservation project should speak to the health and safety officer in charge of the overall building site in order to discover what particular arrangements have been made. For instance, because we were in charge of our particular area, the builders did not take into consideration any solvents being used; one day they were welding very near to the outlet from which solvent vapours were being extracted. This caused some consternation. Potential problems with a building site include safe lighting and the provision of a constant supply of power at the right voltage (building sites in the UK operate on 110 volt electricity and the rest of the country is on 240 volts). This was a daily battle, along with the struggle for the provision of air – keeping out of the way of the builders' mess required elaborate arrangements to be made for access and ventilation. Fire drills and plans for the rest of the building workers did not include the conservators as they were not the contractors' responsibility – in the eventuality of a fire they may not have been informed due to the lack of awareness of their presence. Any conservators in this position should familiarise themselves with the regulations covering building sites and make their operations and presence well known to the foreman and other workers. It took some days to work out a system for this. The requirements for working on scaffolding must also be considered. Unless the conservator is armed with certificates indicating that he has the necessary training, it should be stipulated clearly in the contract that the scaffolding is to be supplied and erected by other contractors. Finally, the conservators' welfare should be considered, i.e. providing the best conditions possible and ensuring that there is somewhere to get away from the work for breaks to have tea and coffee without the damp, dust smells, cold and fumes that can make working *in situ* a misery.

Insurance

Insurance also must not be forgotten. Public liability cover, employer's liability and, finally, professional indemnity will almost certainly be a condition of a large contract. Furthermore, in this case a 10-year cover beyond the completion of the work was also stipulated in the event that any of the work failed in this time including structural failure of the new support. The Museum stipulated a longer period than is generally required by British law, which allows a client to sue for faulty workmanship at any time up to six years after completion of the work. Conservators should therefore carry insurance for at least that amount of time after completion even after they have retired.

Broader considerations

Finally it is vital that the conservator should be included in the planning meetings before things are set in stone. In the case under discussion, the Museum was planning to create a 'Trafalgar Experience' of which the Panorama was to be the last part. For example, the lighting designers had planned to use lights that did not comply with the display conditions set out for the painting as they would cause hot spots – only late in the project were we informed that they envisaged warm yellow lighting, even though the painting depicts the scene on a clear day, at precisely 2 pm, and had been intended originally to be lit by overhead daylight. Fortunately this was altered. Furthermore many conflicting demands can be stipulated by the funding providers, such as wheelchair access, numbers of visitors, etc. which can influence the conservation plans. Fitting the Panorama into the new high-tech setting meant that the original installation was deemed inadequate. The need to satisfy the access requirements meant that only children and wheelchair users would have the full effect of Wyllie's original visual intent for the Panorama and it is regrettable that Wyllie's 'installation' could not satisfy the access requirements. However, involvement in this project did allow at least some of the adult viewers to be positioned at the right angle by placing a bench at the correct height at the back of the viewing gallery to get a full visual effect. The painting is now an exciting culmination to the 'Trafalgar Experience' and therefore most viewers do not find that there is a loss of effect. It is a tribute to Wyllie that it holds its own after all the sounds and smells and movement of the 'Experience'.

Notes

1. A.J. Pack *History of the Panorama of the Battle of Trafalgar*, Friends of the Royal Naval Museum and HMS *Victory*, Yearbook 1994.
2. See note 1.
3. The Luffgrove Extrusion has a rated pull out from the slot, which is 10Kn/m with a hard core. The rate is increased or decreased by the density of the core material, i.e. a soft core will pull through the slot more easily than a harder core.
4. The M8 A2-70 stainless steel studding has a tensile strength as follows:
   - Ultimate tensile strength = 700 newtons
   - Yield strength = 450 newtons
   - Elongation @ failure minimum = 4D (4 × diameter)

   The M8 A2-70 studding is mounted off stainless steal gallow-type brackets, which are bolted to the structural framework behind the painting.

The authors

- Valentine Walsh is an independent conservator based in London.
- Richard Pelter is Director of International Fine Art Conservation Studios Ltd., Bristol.

A Cold-Lining Technique for Large-scale Paintings

KATE SEYMOUR AND JOS VAN OCH

Introduction

This paper outlines a cold-lining technique for large-scale paintings developed at the Stichting Restauratie Atelier Limburg (SRAL)[1] in Maastricht, the Netherlands, by Jos van Och. The lining method is illustrated using a nineteenth-century Dutch painting as a case study. Additional information regarding the preparation of the lining canvas and the reconstruction of the original tensioning system for this painting is also discussed.

The painting in question is a large-scale oil on canvas measuring 3380 × 4880mm, painted in 1862 by J.W. Adrian Hilverdink from the Stedelijk Museum at Alkmaar (Fig. 1). The image depicts a battle scene in which the citizens of Alkmaar, with the help of the Dutch army, free their city from Spanish rule in October 1573. The canvas consists of a low quality, roughly woven linen material. Thick ground layers, present on both sides of the canvas, have a high oil content, which has rendered the painting inflexible and brittle. Paint layers are executed in an oil medium and exhibit glazing and low impasto. There is a varnish layer, although it is unclear whether this is continuous as the surface of the painting contains both matt and glossy areas. The stretcher consisted originally of five members of which the central vertical member is missing. The joints are mortise and tenon and are expandable; all keys are missing. The lower tenon joint on both vertical members has been severed.

On arrival at the SRAL restoration studio, the Alkmaar painting exhibited a large number of tears and planar distortions within the primary support. Some tears had been repaired previously and patched using various materials and adhesives including wax resin and animal glue. Tears to the primary support were mainly located within a central horizontal band. Planar distortions were perpendicular to these and appeared to have been caused by the roller used to store the painting at the Museum. It is presumed that tears within the central band resulted from the transportation of the painting at some unknown prior date. The movement of the painting from one place to another would have been hindered by its height. The removal of the vertical stretcher bars by sawing through the tenon joint halved the height of the painting. It could then be carried 'folded', supported by the horizontal stretcher bars, from one room to another. The large number of tears in the primary support excluded mending each individually. Hence, a decision to line the painting was taken.

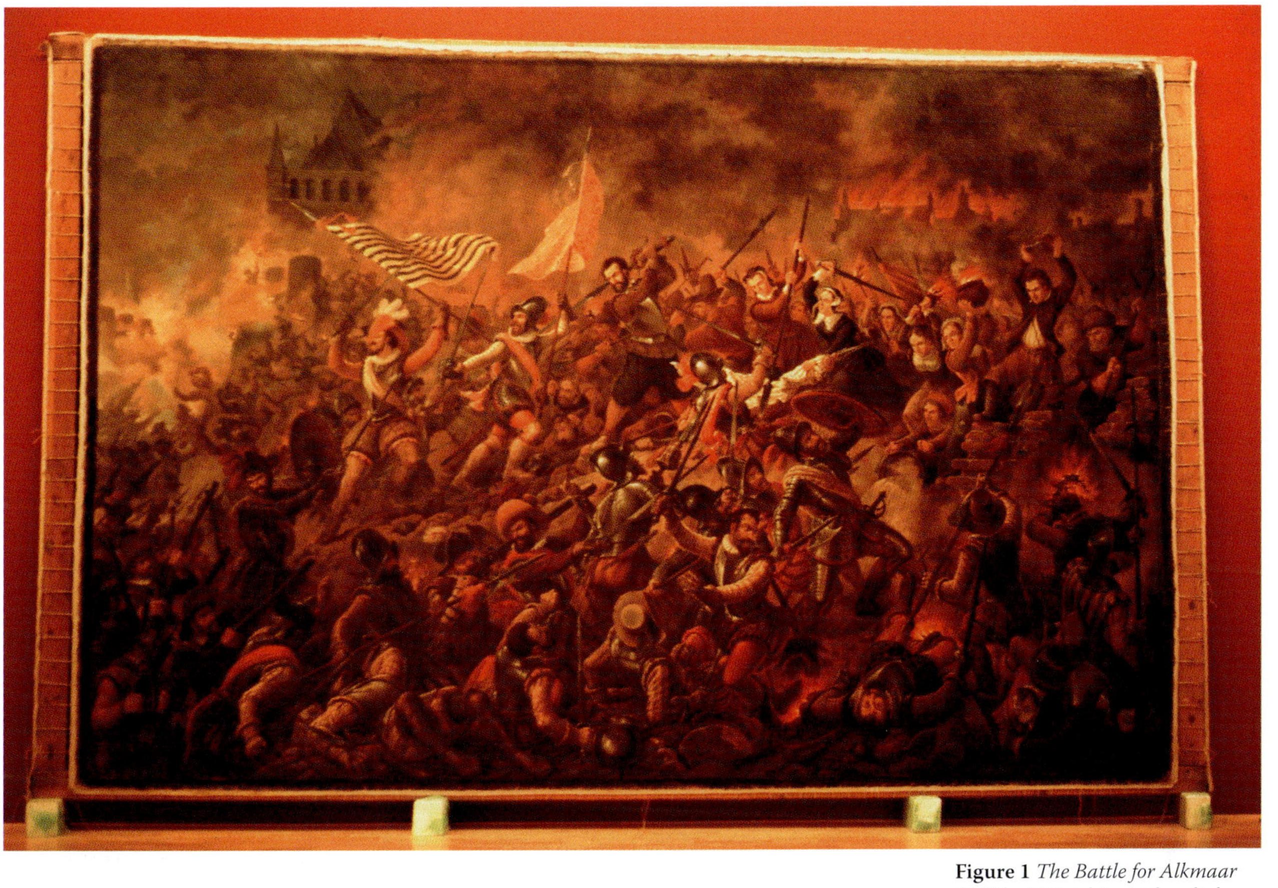

Figure 1 *The Battle for Alkmaar 1573* by J.W. Adrian Hilverdink, 1862 (Stedelijk Museum, Alkmaar). This photograph was taken after completion of treatment.

The cold-lining technique[2]

The problems of using heat, moisture and pressure during traditional glue-paste or wax-resin lining techniques are well known within the field of conservation. Alternative lining systems utilising low pressure and synthetic glues were developed and have been practised in both Denmark and the Netherlands since the early 1970s. The 'cold-lining' technique was first developed by Mehra in the mid-1970s (extensively reported elsewhere[3]).

The cold-lining technique employed in SRAL was evolved from Mehra's system by Jos van Och.[4] This system was first developed to use on large-scale objects but its versatility allows its application in various situations to remedy diverse structural problems. The core elements of the technique are:

- Minimal use of adhesive to achieve the required bond and shear strengths.
- Regeneration of the adhesive using solvent vapours.
- Elimination of moisture through the use of a dry adhesive layer.
- Application of low pressure to create the desired bond.

The original tensioning system

The painting, due to its large size, arrived in the conservation studio on a storage roll, i.e. separated from its stretcher. The painting had been stored in this manner for at least 50 years, therefore information regarding the original tensioning system was obtained through studying both the stretcher bars and the borders of the painting. Strips of a rough hessian material, commonly used to upholster furniture, remained attached to the edges of the original canvas and to the stretcher bars.

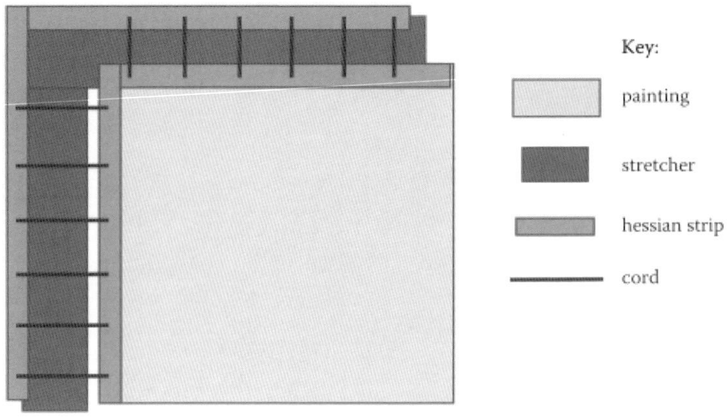

Figure 2 Diagram showing a reconstruction of the original lacing system.

Remnants of string or cord were present in the strips attached to the stretcher. It seemed that these strips and the cord functioned as part of a lacing system used to tension the canvas and attach it to its auxiliary support.[5] This supposition is supported by the fact that the dimensions of the stretcher are larger than those of the painting. The cord tensioning system involved connecting the hessian strip, nailed to the stretcher, to its opposite sewn onto the canvas border. Once pulled tight, the lacing cord kept the canvas taut. The attached hessian strips lessened the possibility of cusping occurring to the edges of the primary support during tensioning (Figure 2).

Preparation of the lining canvas

A tabby weave, linen canvas with a double thread was chosen as a lining fabric. The breadth of the canvas bolt prohibited the use of a single piece of material therefore three pieces were sewn together. The flattened seams were placed perpendicular to the main area of damage within the original support. The composite lining canvas was pre-washed and subsequently stretched. A lack of height in the studio prevented the use of an intermediary loom for this process so the canvas was stretched on the floor using a lacing technique. Nails were inserted into the floor along a straight line, leaving a gap of 100mm between the canvas and the row of nails. String was alternately threaded through the border of the canvas and around individual nails. It was then tightened until the desired tension was achieved. The canvas was re-washed and left to dry under tension. Once dry, the lining canvas was roughened using sandpaper to increase the nap surface of the material; it was to this that the lining adhesive was to be attached.

The adhesive was applied while the lining canvas was under tension on the original stretcher. To facilitate stretching the lining canvas, a replication of the original tensioning system was employed. As the original hessian strips attached to the primary support were retained, the lining canvas had to extend beyond these. A stiff border on the lining canvas was needed to substitute for the degraded hessian strips. The stiffness of this border would also prevent cusping occurring during tensioning. Cusping may lead to the lining adhesive delaminating at tension points, therefore the edges of the lining canvas were folded over twice and adhered with a thickened mixture of Plextol D360 and D541. To achieve additional stiffness, a nylon cord was inserted into the outer edge of the border prior to adhesion. Lengths of linen canvas were stapled to the stretcher bars to replace the degraded hessian strips. A lacing cord was passed alternately through holes punched in the canvas strip attached to the stretcher and through the stiffened border of the lining canvas (these holes were re-employed when re-hanging the painting in the Museum).

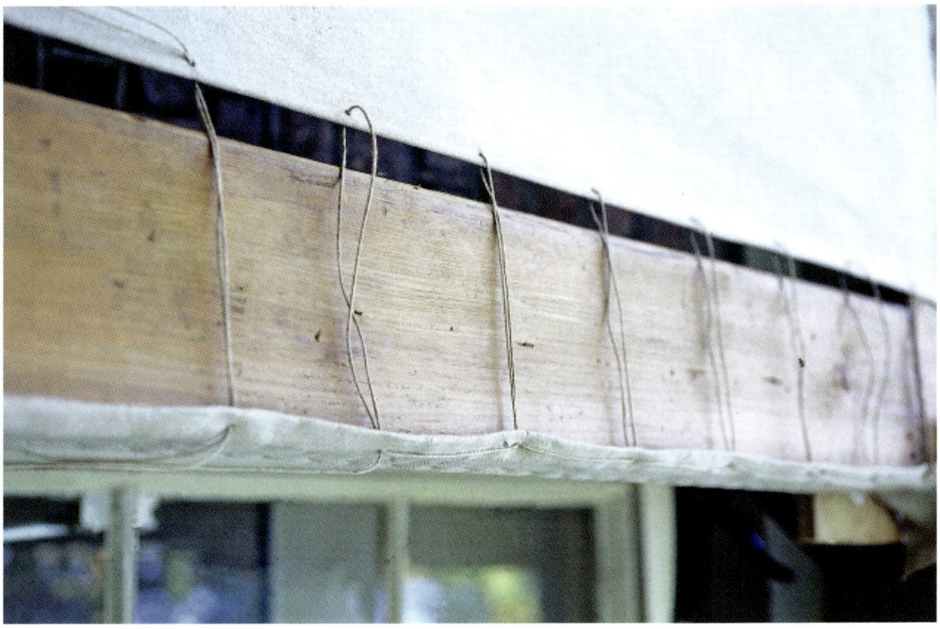

Figure 3 This photograph shows the lacing system used to tension the lining canvas on its stretcher. (Photograph: Kate Seymour, SRAL.)

To tension the lining canvas (both for the application of the adhesive and the final mounting of the painting), the upper horizontal border was first laced to its corresponding stretcher bar. The assembled stretcher was swung into an upright position, with the canvas hanging freely between the bars, before the remaining three sides of the lining canvas were secured and tensioning commenced. The extra width between the painting and the stretcher in the horizontal direction allowed the canvas to reach a vertical position without touching the stretcher's side members. As the canvas was tensioned, the lacing cord was passed from back to front through the hole in the strip attached to the stretcher, threaded through the border of the lining canvas and then back through the same hole in the initial strip. The cord then ran to the next hole on the strip attached to the stretcher and the process was repeated (Figure 3).

Choice and application of lining adhesive

Plextol[6] is an aqueous emulsion of a thermoplastic acrylic polymer for washproof finishing, coating and laminating textiles. It is obtained from the polymerisation of acrylic derivatives, chiefly from the esters of acrylic acid CH_2:CH·COOH (ethyl acrylate) and methacrylic acid CH_2:C(OH_3)·COOH (methylacrylate), consisting of n-butyl methacrylate and methacrylate.[7] It is soluble in organic solvents with the exception of aliphatic hydrocarbons. The physical properties of a synthetic resin are highly influenced by its molecular weight, consequently by increasing the molecular weight of the polymer, properties such as tensile strength and elasticity can be augmented. On its own, the copolymer Plextol D360 is considered too flexible and plastic to achieve an optimum bond for lining purposes. The desired plasticity may be obtained by mixing it with a second copolymer of a higher molecular weight, Plextol D541. The lining adhesive mixture used for the Alkmaar painting contained 70% Plextol D360 (61% concentration) and 30% Plextol D541 (40% concentration),[8] emulsified (thickened) with 1.5% Rohagit SD15 (a polymethacrylic acid). The resulting copolymeric film remains soft and elastic when dry, however it is stiff enough so that creep does not occur. The application of *either* gentle heat *or* solvent regeneration of the dried film is sufficient for the creation of a nap bond. The film is chemically stable and non-responsive to fluctuations in

Figure 4 The sprayed Plextol adhesive viewed under magnification: the weave of the canvas is still visible between the flocked tendrils of the adhesive. (Photograph Kate Seymour, SRAL.)

relative humidity. As acrylic emulsions have a high surface tension, penetration into the lining canvas during application is minimal, therefore nap bonds can be achieved. This will facilitate the removal of the lining canvas, if required, at a later date by either peeling or by regenerating the adhesive with solvents.

The adhesive was applied to the stretched, sand-papered lining canvas in three coats using a pressurised spray gun. In Mehra's cold-lining technique, the amount of Plextol adhesive spread onto the lining canvas could be regulated by varying the mesh in the application screen.[9] However, by applying the adhesive in a spray mist, an open, flocked layer coat can be attached only to the nap surface of the lining fabric. The final spray coat of Plextol contained 25% (by volume) of the solvent iso-octane. The evaporation of this solvent from the adhesive layer creates a more open texture. When viewed under magnification, the unsaturated weave of the lining canvas is still visible between the flocked adhesive layers (Fig. 4). Due to the open texture of these layers, the reactivation of the adhesive, via solvent vapours, could be carried out from the reverse of the lining canvas; this would not be possible if a closed adhesive film were used. The adhesive was left to dry until all moisture and solvent content had evaporated before lining commenced.

Pre-lining procedures

Before the lining process was carried out, various pre-treatments were implemented. Although a detailed description of these treatments is not the main emphasis of this paper, a brief outline follows. All treatments were carried out with the painting lying flat on a large table. A bridge was constructed over the table to enable the central section of the painting to be reached. Consolidation of flaking paint surrounding the tear areas was undertaken before dirt from the surface of the painting was removed. Subsequently, the tears were individually faced with Japanese non-woven paper before a complete facing consisting of Japanese *gampi* paper was applied with the adhesive methyl cellulose over the whole surface of the painting. This action was carried out with the painting under tension. To tension the painting, thin wooden plates were clamped to the vertical borders. A cord was passed through holes in the plates and tensioned onto nails situated underneath the table rim. This stretched the painting in a horizontal direction and helped to alleviate the vertical planar distortions present in the primary support caused by its storage on a roller. The existing thin varnish layer was not removed. At this point the painting was turned face down using a wide diameter tube to enable treatment of the reverse of the canvas and to facilitate the lining procedure. Distortions were further flattened using moisture and locally applied pressure. Old patches and remnants of adhesive were removed and surface dirt was cleaned from the reverse of the painting. Lacunae in the paint surface were filled with a flexible BEVA 371 and kaolin mixture before the painting was lined.

The lining system

The Alkmaar painting was lined on a smooth, flat table in a sealed envelope capable of realising low pressures rather than a vacuum. In this instance, the painting was lined face down on the table to allow the lining canvas to be positioned precisely before lining commenced. The lining adhesive was regenerated using ethanol vapours before air was extracted from the envelope to aid bond formation. The construction of this envelope and the procedural steps were as follows:

- A sheet of cheesecloth material was placed over the table surface. This porous material aids the air flow between the envelope and the table surface, ensuring that there is no contact during the lining process.
- Above this, a layer of thick plastic was stretched over the table and secured with clamps. The thick plastic sheet functions as the lower membrane and bestows some rigidity to the envelope. Thus, while minor deformations in the original canvas may be eliminated through the pressure exerted by this sheet, its rigidity prevents any distortions in the original support from being transferred to the lining canvas.
- Polyester sailcloth was placed between the lower membrane of the envelope and the painting. This material cushions the paint surface from potentially adverse pressure during lining and its porosity aids the extraction of air from beneath the painting as low pressure is effected.
- At this stage, the painting was rolled out over the table face down. The lining canvas was positioned over the original painting. Both were left unrestrained.
- Plastic electrical tubes (20mm diameter), with holes drilled in one side at 250mm intervals, were used to assist the extraction of air from the envelope. These were placed in a ring around the painting and connected using a 'T' joint to a centrifugal pump. The polyester material was wrapped around these tubes to help seal the envelope.
- The envelope was completed with a thin, solvent-resistant, polyethylene foil which extended around the outer edges of the plastic tubing (Fig. 5). This malleable foil conforms to the surface topography of the lining canvas when low pressure is exerted. Due to its thinness and flexibility, it will not exert unwanted pressure onto the reverse of the lining canvas.
- The dry lining adhesive was reactivated using solvent vapours. This eliminated the use of liquid solvents. Ethanol vapours, contained within the envelope, were used to swell the Plextol adhesive. A cloth, cut to slightly larger dimensions than the lining canvas, was used to deliver ethanol vapours to the adhesive layer through the lining canvas. This cloth was rolled and enclosed in a sealed bag into which a predetermined amount (1250ml) of ethanol was injected.[10] The dampened cloth was rolled out over the reverse of the lining canvas and immediately covered with the upper membrane of the lining envelope. Excess air was extracted from the envelope to ensure maximum contact and effect. Tests carried out on the reverse of the original support indicated that the ethanol vapours regenerated the lining adhesive sufficiently after a contact time of 20 minutes to create the desired bond.[11] After this time elapsed the cloth was removed before pressure was applied to achieve adhesion.

- Air was extracted from the envelope using a Willard Induction Motor.[12] In this way, low pressure was created within the envelope to effect the desired bond between the two canvases. Pressure levels reached 100 mbars for a period of 10 minutes; the level was gradually dropped over a period of 20 minutes until 60 mbars were reached and then maintained for a further 30 minutes. A valve was used to regulate and measure the pressure exerted.

This concluded the lining process. To complete the treatment of the Alkmaar painting, a thin isolating dammar varnish was applied and lacunae in the paint layers were retouched. The painting was returned to the Museum rolled on a wide tube, separate from its auxiliary support. Re-tensioning the painting *in situ* on its original stretcher followed the lacing system outlined previously. The reconstruction of the tensioning system permitted the original stretcher to be retained and facilitated the re-tensioning of the large canvas.

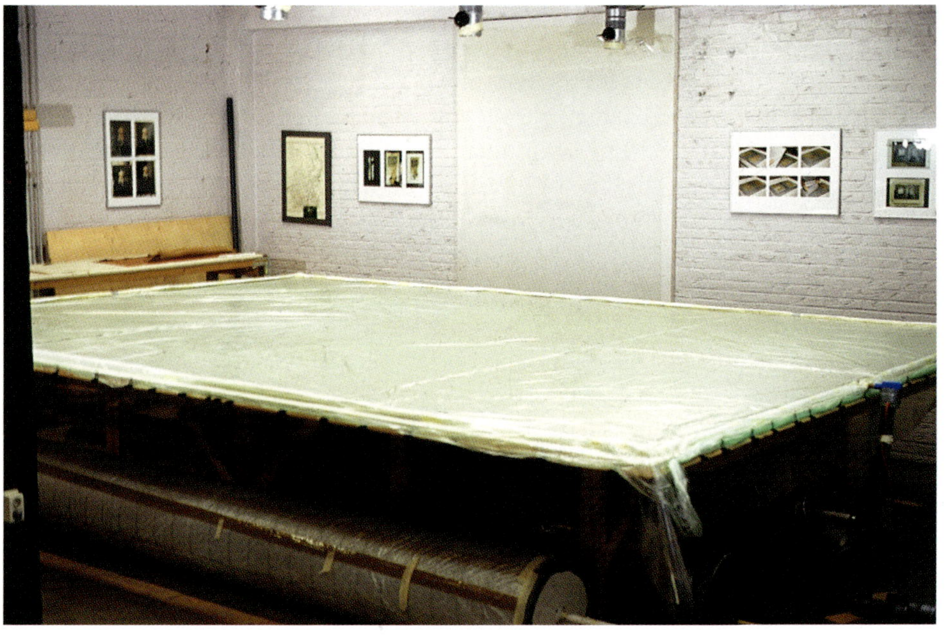

Figure 5 The lining envelope. (Photograph: Kate Seymour, SRAL.)

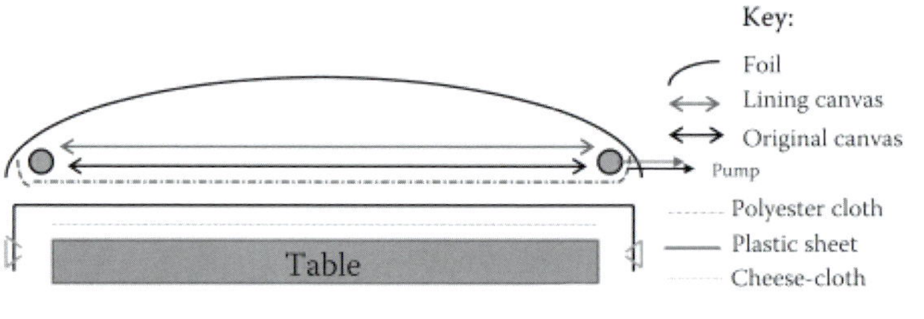

Figure 6 Diagram showing the envelope set-up.

Conclusion

In conclusion, the cold-lining approach used by Jos van Och at the Stichting Restauratie Atelier Limburg remedies some of the initial disadvantages of previous cold-lining systems. The spray application of the Plextol adhesive produces a flocked, open coat attached to the nap surface of the lining fabric, thereby restricting the lining process to a reinforcement of the original support. By spraying Plextol, the minimal amount of adhesive needed to obtain the optimum bond strength can be achieved. This aids the reversibility of the lining process, should this ever be required. The use of an open, flocked coat of Plextol, rather than a closed film, enables the adhesive to be reactivated via the delivery of solvent vapours through the reverse of the lining canvas. In this manner, the minimal amount of solvent needed to reactivate the adhesive can be calculated, thereby allowing greater control over the adhesive bond formed and also avoiding spraying free solvents. The regenerative property of Plextol in organic solvents, in combination with the use of a dry layer of Plextol, permits the elimination of potentially damaging effects resulting from heat, moisture and/or pressure associated with traditional lining methods. The positioning of the lining canvas over the original, before reactivating the adhesive, eliminates damage caused by repositioning the canvases. The simplicity and the versatility of the envelope construction, in conjunction with the use of low pressure, allows the system's use in various circumstances and situations where traditional lining techniques would not be appropriate.

Acknowledgements

The authors would like to thank the following for their advice and assistance: the Stedelijk Museum Alkmaar; Helene Dubois and Tineke Oostendorp at the Stichting Restauratie Atelier Limburg and the students at SRAL for their help during the restoration of the Alkmaar painting.

Notes

1. SRAL is a teaching institute and regional conservation centre for easel paintings, polychrome sculpture, historic interiors, modern art and paper objects.
2. A detailed outline of the lining technique developed by Jos van Och has been published under the title 'Mist lining and low-pressure envelopes: an alternative lining method for the reinforcement of canvas paintings', *Zeitschrift für Kunsttechnologie und Konservierung* (2003), 17(1): 116–28; further research regarding the relining of wax-resin lined paintings with acrylic resins is described by Ulrike Fischer in her diploma *Theoretisches Thema (Band II)* 'Doublierung von Wachs-Harz-behandelten Gemälden mit Acrylharz-Eine Versuchsreihe', *Hochschule für Bildende Künste, Dresden* (2002), unpublished.
3. V.R. Mehra (1975) 'Further developments in cold-lining (nap bond system)', in *ICOM Committee for Conservation, 4th Triennial Meeting*, Venice; A. Phenix (1995) 'Lining of paintings: traditions, principles and developments', in *Lining and Backing*, UKIC, London; S. Bjarnhof and M. Scharff (1991) *Survey of Structural Stabilization Techniques on Canvas Paintings*, Royal Danish Academy of Fine Arts; V.R. Mehra (1974) 'A low-pressure cold-relining table', in *Conference on Comparative Lining Techniques*, National Maritime Museum, London (published in 2003 as *Lining Paintings*, edited by Caroline Villers, by Archetype Publications, London); V.R. Mehra (1984) 'Dispersion as lining adhesive and its scope', in *Adhesives and Consolidants*, IIC Preprints, Paris Congress.
4. The technique developed by Jos van Och was first used to line Chinese wallpaper *in situ*, measuring 8500 × 3500mm, at Kasteel Heeswijk, 's Hertogenbosch, The Netherlands (unpublished SRAL Project Report).
5. Since the introduction of canvas as a painting support, the tensioning of fabric using lacing systems has been commonplace. Traditionally, canvases were first stretched, then primed on a strainer (a wooden framework larger than the canvas) using a cord passed through holes in the border of the canvas and, alternately, around or through the battens of the strainer. Once the priming layers were dry, the canvas would be re-stretched before painting commenced, either by using a similar lacing system or by folding the edges of the canvas around a wooden framework and securing with nails or wooden pins. See E. van de Wetering, E. (1997) *Rembrandt: The Painter at Work*. Amsterdam: Amsterdam University Press, pp. 111–23.
6. Product information from Rohm GmbH Chemische Fabrik, Postfach 42, Kirschenallee, D-6100 Darrnstadt 1, Germany.
7. J.L. Down, M.A. MacDonald, J. Tétreault and S.R. Williams (1996) 'Adhesive testing at the Canadian Conservation Institute: an evaluation of selected poly(vinylacetate) and acrylic adhesives', *Studies in Conservation* 41: 19–43.
8. Concentrations obtained from E. De Witte, S. Florquin and M. Goessens-Landrie (1984) 'Influence of the modification of dispersions on film properties', in *Adhesives and Consolidants*, IIC Preprints, Paris Congress.

9. V.R. Mehra (1981) 'The cold-lining of paintings', *The Conservator* 5.
10. The amount of ethanol vapour necessary to regenerate the adhesive is minimal, however experimentation showed that 60–70ml ethanol per square metre is needed to evenly dampen the cheesecloth. The cheesecloth was rolled into a tight bundle and wrapped in clingfilm before the calculated amount of ethanol was injected into the packet. Some hours were allowed before use to ensure an even distribution of the solvent throughout the cloth.
11. The strength of the bond created can be augmented by increasing the time the solvent vapours are in contact with the lining adhesive.
12. Willard Developments Limited, Leigh Road, Terminus Industrial Estate, Chichester, W. Sussex PO19 8TS.

The authors

Kate Seymour and Jos van Och are paintings conservators at the Stichting Restauratie Atelier Limburg, Maastricht.

The Structural Treatment of a Series of Large Dynastic Portraits of Louis XIV and Family on-site at Chateau de Balleroy, Normandy

JIM DIMOND WITH WARWICK MACCALLUM

Introduction

In 1994, Warwick MacCallum was asked to restore eight seventeenth-century paintings in the Grand Salon of the Chateau de Balleroy, not far from Bayeux in Normandy, and I was asked to carry out the structural work on the paintings.

Figure 1 Chateau de Balleroy.

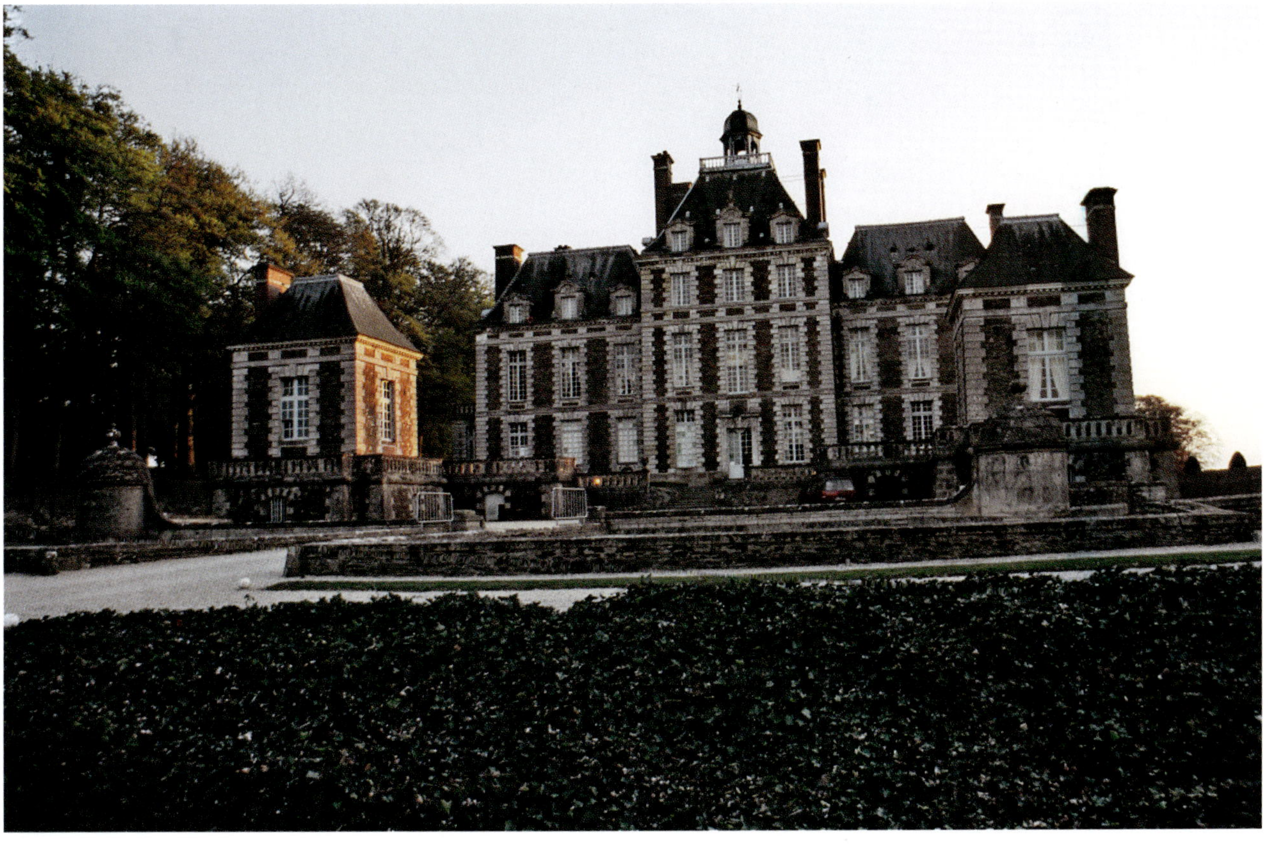

The subjects of the paintings are:

- Ann d'Austriche, Regent, boy king Louis XIV and his brother the Duc d'Anjou, 2275 × 3035mm
- Marguerite de Lorraine, second wife of Gaston d'Orleans, and their four children, 2275 × 3035mm
- The Grand Conde (oval), 1735 × 1320mm
- The Grande Mademoiselle, 2285 × 1325mm
- Marie de Medicis (posthumous portrait), 2295 × 1325mm
- Gaston d'Orleans, 2275 × 1825mm
- Louis XIII (posthumous portrait), 965 × 1305mm
- Unidentified lady, possibly the Duchesse de Longueville, 965 × 1305mm

These portraits had been painted originally for the Palace of Luxembourg in Paris in 1652 and transported to Balleroy, probably 25 years later. All the paintings had been extended, possibly to adapt them to the new decorative scheme, and therefore had a number of joins in the canvases. In addition, the nineteenth-century linings were coming away from the original canvas along joins and the upper edges. One of the largest paintings, *Marguerite de Lorraine,* had ballooning blistering all over the surface and most of the paint on the other large portrait, *Anne d'Austriche,* was flaking. *Marie de Medicis* had the largest paint losses and loose paint, which was just at the point of falling to the floor when treatment commenced.

The size of the paintings and their location in rural France meant that all restoration had to be carried out at the Chateau. A working space was provided in the disused seventeenth-century greenhouse, although seasonal weather variations allowed work to take place only in spring and autumn. The total restoration, including all structural work and restoration, took four and a half years, working two months each spring and autumn between 1994 and 1998.

Figure 2 *Marguerite de Lorraine* before treatment.

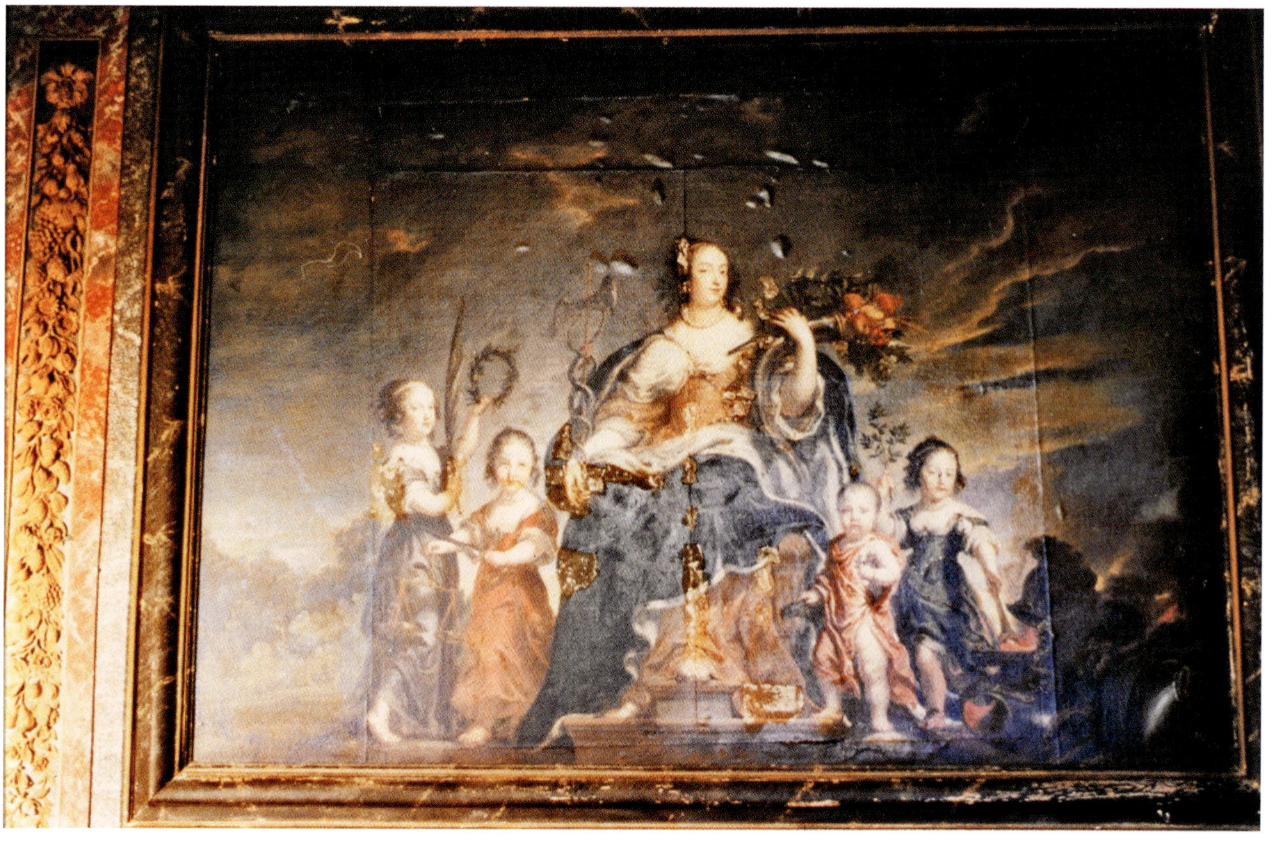

What system was used and why?

BEVA lining was chosen, mainly because that is what I do – I don't have any experience in paste lining and I was confident that I could adapt studio methods to suit the large scale and on-site working conditions. BEVA lining also seemed appropriate for these paintings. The original paste linings had '1878' inscribed in pencil on the reverse of the stretcher – 116 years is a relatively long time for a paste lining to survive, but the problems presented by these paintings were very severe, and there is no knowing how long these symptoms of deterioration took to appear. As described above, even the smallest paintings had been extended to fit the decorative scheme in the Grand Salon.

The walls behind the paintings were composed of bare brickwork and were damp; this had certainly been a major factor in their structural problems. The picture in the worst condition, *Marie de Medicis*, which had large areas of paint loss in the main body of the painting, and a great deal of further flaking, had been hung on an outside wall with several gaps in the external brickwork. Given these less than perfect environmental conditions, I felt justified in ruling out paste lining in favour of using BEVA for these paintings. I did not believe that wax lining, the old standby for very damp conditions, could be made sufficiently stiff to hold down all the joins between canvas pieces. In addition, it would have made the paintings enormously heavy and possibly prone to sagging, and was even further from the French paste lining tradition than the nap-bond BEVA canvas lining that I proposed. A solvent-activated BEVA lining was considered but to experiment with a method of which I had no experience while working onsite would have been fraught with problems. Other cold-lining methods could have been used, but again, my experience was limited to small easel paintings and treatments carried out in the safety of the studio.

There were a number of problems posed by BEVA lining large paintings on-site. I don't have a huge hot table available that can evenly deliver a measurable amount of heat to the whole painting. Falling back on hand lining, I decided that an envelope system would certainly be helpful in preventing the buckling caused by heating and cooling local areas, as well as providing most of the pressure required for the nap bond. Putting an envelope around the loomed lining fabric and painting also gives access to both sides of the painting during the lining to enable me to monitor the effect of the heat on the paint surface. In hand lining, the lining fabrics are uppermost, and with BEVA, unlike wax, there is no visual indication that an area has reached the required temperature as the back of the lining is heated. To some extent, therefore, the treatment is carried out blind. The only way to overcome this problem is to use irons to heat methodically a marked-out area for a time predetermined by experimentation, and then to cold-set each area.

I carried out tests in the studio using a Willard iron to determine the area I should work over at one time and the optimum time. I intended to use double lining and to size the fabrics with Paraloid B72 to give the kind of stiffness that could hold down the many joins in the original canvas.

For the trial, I used a test painting (inherited from my previous post at Kenwood House), placing temperature strips across its surface. Two B72-impregnated canvases were loomed up and prepared with coats of BEVA. Once complete, these were laid onto the test painting, with the painting face down. I marked out an area of 25cm^2, representing a reasonable area to heat at one time, and used the Willard iron set at 120°C to heat the marked area as evenly as possible. The time taken to reach 55°C, 60°C and 65°C at the paint surface was measured. This very crude experimentation gave a safety margin within which to work that would not cause any damage to the paint layer. Of course, my nineteenth-century test piece bears little relation to the heat conductivity of a seventeenth-century painting, and a balance between achieving an adequate bond and protecting the paint layer would have to be reached during the actual work. In experiments in the studio, 65°C was achieved after heating the 25cm^2 area for 1 minute and 15 seconds. In practice, the paint layers on the largest of the paintings were thick and stiff, and the difficulty of achieving a good strong and even bond across the entire painting meant that the heating time was increased to between 1 minute 30 seconds and 1 minute 45 seconds, with no perceptible change in the paint surface.

Practice according to the plan

The two largest paintings, and a number of the smaller ones, required urgent consolidation across large areas of the paint surface before delining could commence. The paintings were therefore moved in a tractor trailer to the greenhouse studio. The studio had been prepared with a wooden stage at about knee height, where the lining procedures could be carried out. The stage did have a join in the middle, which had to be avoided during delining and relining.

The paint surface around areas of flaking had been faced with small pieces of eltoline tissue and cold wax-resin adhesive (easily removed before flake laying) to hold the paint in place as each painting was removed from the wall. The first painting to be treated was *Marie de Medicis*, described more fully below. Isinglass was tried first of all to consolidate the flaking, but I was unable to get adequate penetration with the aqueous consolidant – the adhesive appeared just to sink away, leaving the paint down but not adhered. I then reverted to wax resin applied through the tissue to act as both consolidant and facing. Having learned this lesson from *Marie de Medicis*, I used a wax resin and eltoline tissue to act as both consolidant for the paint layer and facing to protect the paint during lining removal, for the two largest paintings. The flaking was so widespread on *Anne d'Austriche* that the type of blanket consolidation given by an application of wax resin through tissue was the most effective way to approach the problem. The facing was applied with the painting still on its stretcher and large boards were placed between the openings to support the painting as the wax was applied. Wax resin was applied gently through the tissue using large spatulas to heat no more than was necessary to allow the wax to flow and the entire surface of the painting to be faced.

Once removed from its stretcher, the painting was attached to large wooden looms using temporary polyester strip linings and BEVA film attached to the underside of the edge of the paintings and stapled to the loom (there were no original tacking margins). The looming was essential for handling the paintings. Once off the stretcher they proved to be very heavy and, at the same time, brittle. Without looming, moving them even a little way would have been impossible. While still lined the painting could support its own weight, but it was obvious that once the lining and glue had been removed the additions would separate but for the facing.

Glue and the upper lining were removed using sharpened hacksaw blades. It is quite easy to use a grinder to create an edge on the smooth side of a hacksaw blade or a packing case strap, and this is a very efficient glue remover if the original fabric is fairly strong and not prone to turning into dust at the slightest touch. The toothed side of the blade is also very good for abrading lining which refuses to come away from the original. The additions had been supported or held in place during the paste lining procedure by 20cm-wide strips of a thin open weave fabric or scrim-type cloth. This had broken at the butt join of the additions in many places but was extremely tough to remove.

Blisters in *Marguerite de Lorraine* had left depressions in the canvas and these were flattened by the application of a small amount of heat and moisture through blotting paper and then weighting. All joins and seams were first weighted and then joined using epoxy resin. Something was needed that would stand a chance of holding them down flat after lining and hence the adhesive had to be sufficiently stiff to transfer the loading as though the join was not present. Epoxy is extremely stiff and, supported by the lining, made good structural sense. Once all seams were secure, some further consolidation of the lifting paint was carried out before the facing was removed with white spirit.

Preparation of fabrics for lining was essentially the same as would be carried out in the studio. Linen canvas was stapled to two fabric looms, larger than the painting by 30cm on each side. Canvases were soaked to pull out the considerable amount of crimp in this Belgian fabric and then re-tensioned on the loom. Two coats of Paraloid B72 in acetone were applied to each one. Acetone was used simply to avoid putting an enormous amount of xylene into the air while we worked. Each coat of B72 used up 1.5 litres; we worked quickly and then left the building after application. Six coats of BEVA (2:1 in white spirit) were applied to one surface of each canvas. Solvent work was carried out last thing each evening and allowed to dry overnight. Fortunately the greenhouse studio was some distance from other buildings and well away from the public.

The envelope was set up as follows. The two prepared lining fabrics were re-stretched over a single loom and keyed out to a reasonable tension. The bottom layer of the Melinex envelope was put together (two sheets of Melinex taped together) and laid on the wooden staging. The upper layer of Melinex was also prepared. The painting was placed face down on the Melinex, the polyester strip margins were released and the painting loom removed. Canvas strips were placed to act as breathers all round the painting and led breathers from this ring to the position of each of the eight vacuum sites on the lining loom. The lining fabric loom was placed onto the painting and the breathers taped on the vacuum sites at the corners and centres of loom members.

The pre-prepared upper Melinex layer was then put over the back of the lining fabrics and taped onto the lower Melinex layer on top of the loom. Melinex is available in 150cm widths at a thickness of 12μm, so for the larger paintings, a Melinex join had to be placed on the paint surface. Concerned about the risk of imprinting, I carried out a heat test over a Melinex edge on top of the painting with no damage to the paint surface.

I have a vacuum system combining shower tap nozzles and plastic tubing, which allows eight vacuum 'suckers' to branch from one main tube and be run from an old flatbed hot table pump. These suckers were attached to each of the corners and the centre of each loom member after cutting the Melinex through to the breathers below. In establishing a vacuum, the feel of the envelope is as important as the pressure indicated by the pump itself. I regulate the pressure until the Melinex can only just be moved across the painting with manual pressure.

A grid was marked out in marker pen on top of the envelope in 25cm squares. Two of us worked from the centre, one square at a time, moving the iron methodically over the square for the predetermined time, then cold-setting with a cold hand iron before moving on to the next square. In practice, rather than relying on the bond provided by the envelope, cold-setting was found to be necessary. We gained access to the centre of the painting using mobile platforms made by resting two large loom pieces across the lining loom and placing a stiff board on top of those on which to sit. We tried to carry out each adhesion process in a single session so that the painting was not allowed to cool down completely and set up slight buckling when the next session was started. We also found that if the vacuum was released it became progressively more difficult to re-establish. In addition, reworking a local area can lead to slight 'doming' of that area.

The paintings were stretched back onto the stretchers utilising both layers of the lining canvases as tacking edges, using copper tacks. When working at a larger scale everything becomes more difficult – even cleaning the old stretch-

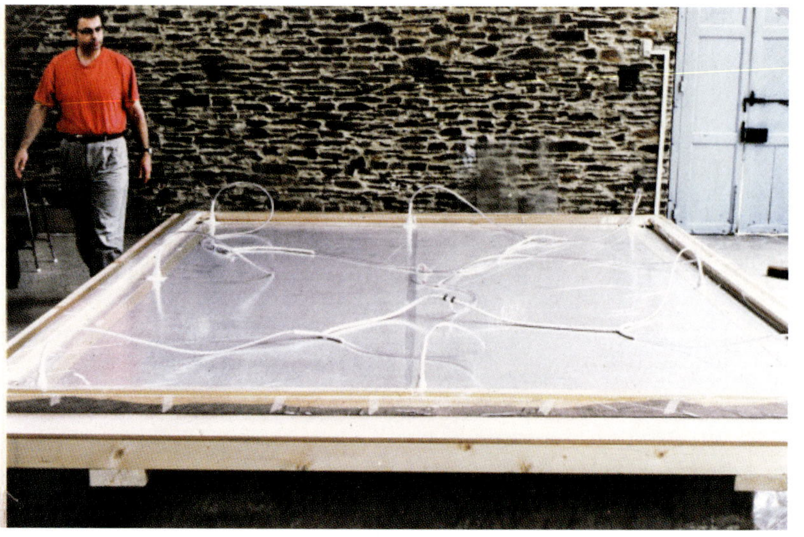

Figure 3 Envelope lining in progress.

ers of rusted tacks was a long process. We also found to our cost that hand-lined Melinex seals well to exposed BEVA-coated canvas and is extremely laborious to remove.

Treatment of *Marie de Medicis*

The first painting tackled was *Marie de Medicis* simply because it was in the worst condition. The flaking was extreme and the lifting paint very vulnerable. As described above, areas of flaking were faced with eltoline tissue and cold wax-resin adhesive while the painting was removed from the wall (easily removed before consolidation). Flake laying was carried out as described above and took place in the Grand Salon since the greenhouse had not been made ready at this time. The floor of the room was uneven, so delining was carried out with the painting off its stretcher, loomed and supported underneath by boards. Then things started to get difficult. I removed the first lining as above only to find a glue layer and another, thinner fabric, but no sign of the joins between the additions. At this point I recalled the very lumpy surface and the extreme lack of adhesion of the paint layer and started to get suspicious. The flaking had revealed a red layer with a canvas weave print that I had taken to be the original canvas somewhat stained by the red ground. I made a small window in the back of the new lining and found a lake of dried glue. Cutting through the glue revealed only paint, showing this to be a transfer. I was left with a faced paint layer supported by a very thin fabric and an old degraded glue layer, and a difficult decision to make. I had already ruled out the use of glue paste for these paintings. Removing the second lining seemed impossible, so some form of impregnation through the fabric and the glue layer seemed the only course open to me. There was a risk that BEVA might not have penetrated the glue layer, so the only option left was wax impregnation. This can be carried out using the minimum of wax, heating the wax until the fabric is uniformly saturated and then using a hot air blower to allow all excess wax to flow and then be removed with paper towels. In a sense, all ethics about impregnating the original are irrelevant here. There is no original fabric and should someone choose to transfer the paint layer once more using glue paste, this could still be achieved. After wax impregnation, a BEVA canvas lining was carried out as above.

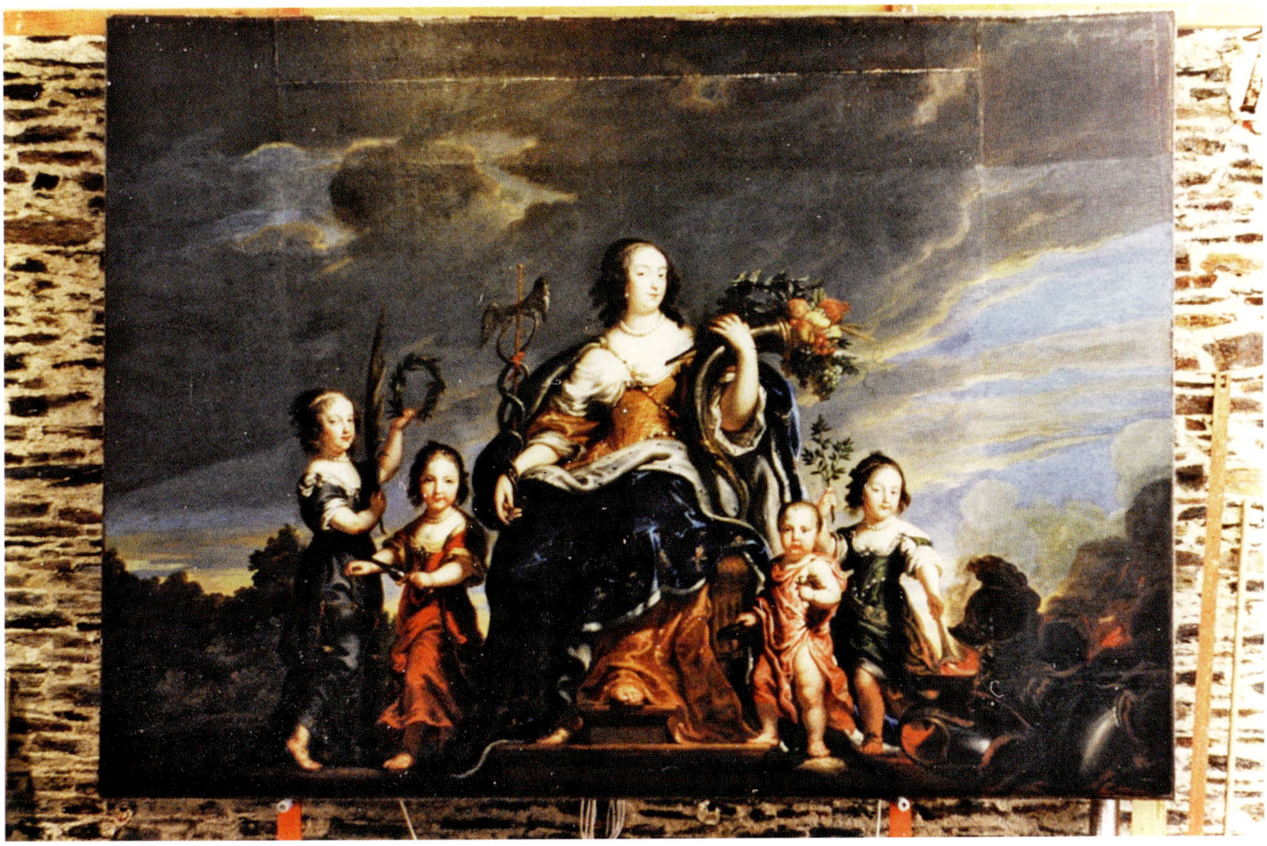

Figure 4 *Marguerite de Lorraine* during retouching.

Pre-planning

I felt a great deal of empathy with the planners of the D-Day landings once I had transported everything that definitely would, and possibly could, be needed for the work, across on the ferry to Normandy. The 3.6m (12ft) looms had to be taken separately.

The largest paintings were in such a precarious state that no cleaning could be carried out before the structural work and consolidation, but some of the others could be cleaned. With a mixed team of structural workers and restorers, the logistics of carrying out all procedures in the right order while allowing everybody to maximise their time and not stand around waiting was one of the most difficult problems. Broadly, we worked on one large painting and on an additional full-length portrait in one 3-week visit. Certainly, when we all worked together, watching a BEVA lined painting being cleaned with generous applications of propanol and white spirit was a heart-stopping experience. The pressure of getting the linings right was enormous. Warwick carried out huge amounts of restoration on the additions and having to adjust linings or reseal after restoration would have been unthinkable. These are not linings of 'least intervention' but, given what was at stake, I needed to be reassured that the lining system could be made to work on-site and that the linings could have a good long-term future.

The authors

Jim Dimond and Warwick MacCallum are independent paintings conservators based in London and Paris, respectively.

The Restoration of Caravaggio's *The Beheading of Saint John the Baptist*

MARCO CIATTI

Introduction

In 1607 Caravaggio escaped to Malta to avoid being punished for the murder he had committed while in Rome. He went under the protection of the powerful Order of the Knights Hospitallers of St John and hoped to begin a new life and to obtain, through the Grandmaster of the Order, a pardon from the Pope. Among Caravaggio's Maltese paintings, *The Beheading of Saint John the Baptist* was the most significant, not only because of its large dimensions (3600 × 5200mm) but

Figure 1 Caravaggio, *The Beheading of Saint John the Baptist*, Valletta, Malta (1608), after conservation.

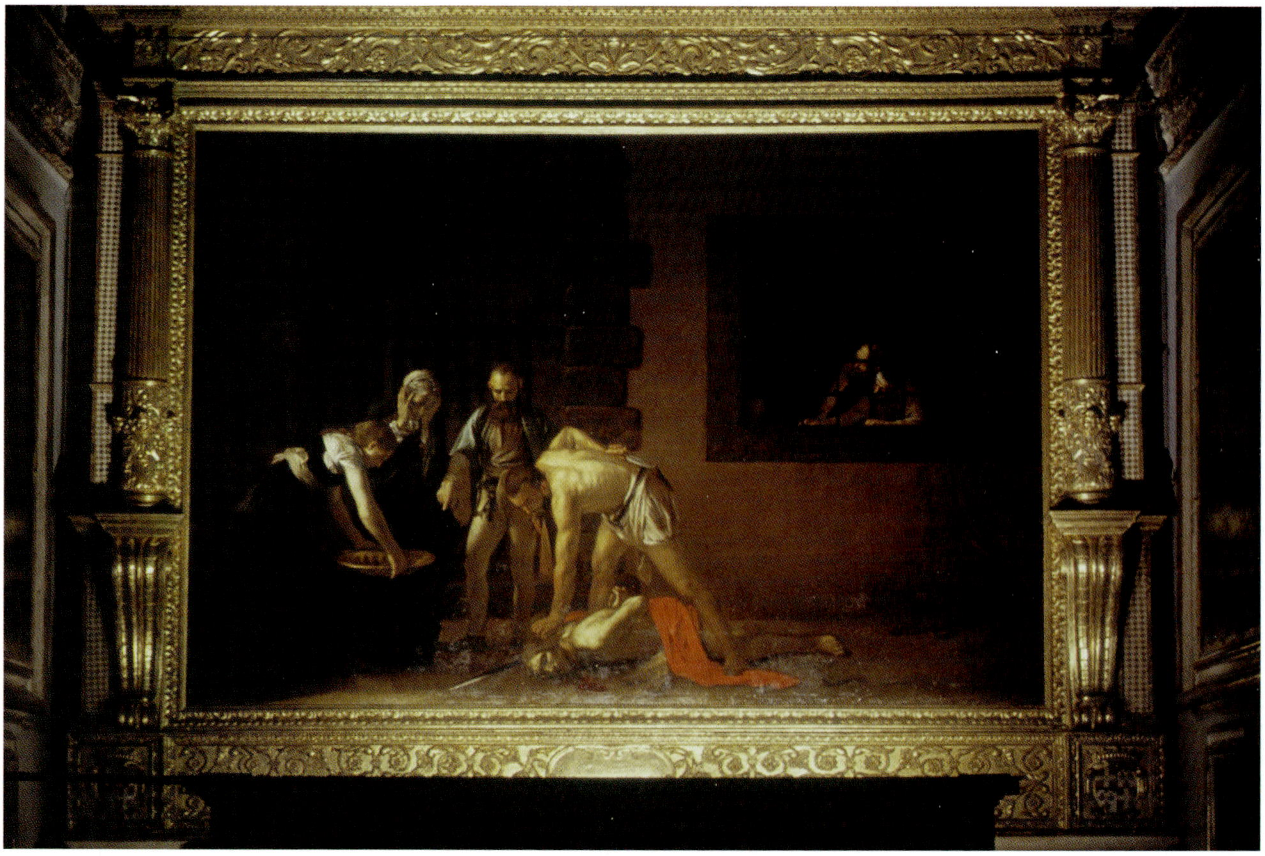

also for its location in the Oratory of Saint John, which was also used as an assembly hall for novices and was next to the cathedral in the centre of Valletta (Fig. 1). The painting was finished during the summer of 1608 and Caravaggio signed the work as if he had dipped his brush into the pool of blood under the saint's slashed neck. The painting has always been located in the Oratory but, due to many factors, it has been restored several times during the centuries.

In 1991 the painting was seriously damaged by vandals, causing a long tear along part of the lower edge. When, in 1996, the Painting Restoration Laboratory of the Opificio delle Pietre Dure in Florence was faced with the restoration of this large canvas by Caravaggio, we were confronted with several problems: principally the importance of the painting, which is the only work signed by the artist. In addition, there was the difficulty of its large dimensions and a whole series of problems regarding its transportation and the different phases of restoration. Also of concern was the painting's state of conservation, which on first inspection appeared to be of certain gravity and posed complex challenges in terms of interpretation and treatment. Finally, there had already been an earlier restoration of the work between 1955 and 1957 by the Istituto Centrale di Restauro di Roma, which had comprised one of the Institute's most interesting interventions at that time.

All these considerations informed the approach to the project, which took into account the wider aspects of the painting's conservation rather than being solely concerned with restoration. This followed the current principal methodology of the Laboratory and meant not only treating the painting during its stay in the Laboratory, but also addressing other aspects that would influence its state of preservation post-treatment. In practice, this comprised several aspects: removal from the original location and transportation (which in this case was particularly significant); the need to correlate the intervention phase with future preventive and maintenance measures; and an understanding of the environmental microclimate within the Oratory, which helped to develop procedures for the painting's relocation and treatment. In order to go beyond merely superficial activity with rapid but ephemeral results, it was necessary to understand the complex relationships between these phases and to seek to harmonise them with the decisions taken in the course of the restoration work. The solution to the problems involved in the conservation of a work of art on this scale cannot be sought in some miraculous material or extremely sophisticated treatments, but in the balancing of all these perspectives within an overall plan.

The Laboratory formulated a conservation plan in collaboration with the Maltese authorities, who always demonstrated particular sensitivity to the undertaking. All the operations were studied and planned by the Institute, beginning with the removal and protection of the canvas, and its packing and transportation by sea to Italy. In the Oratory, where the painting is displayed, a study was made of the environmental conditions over a period of one year, and provision was also made to enable access to the back of the canvas for future conservation interventions.

Once in the Laboratory, the canvas underwent a preliminary technical examination conducted with the most up-to-date procedures. This aimed to investigate artistic techniques and also to identify any problems associated with the state of preservation of the painting. The initial investigation conducted in the Oratory suggested that the condition of the painting raised serious concerns. There was a large tear in the lower part that had been caused by vandalism. In addition, there were symptoms of other physical deterioration, principally a loss of adhesion of the paint layers and a succession of repaintings, which appeared to conceal the original paint and prohibited a proper reading of the painting's aesthetic values. A plan of intervention was therefore proposed to be completed within two years, including the secondary procedures mentioned above regarding the frame and the environmental conditions in the Oratory.

Certain central considerations merit some explanation. First, the choice to proceed with a thorough cleaning of the paint surface which had been avoided during the restoration of 1955–57. Various substances from previous restorations and repaintings lay over the original paint surface and concealed the paint losses and the deteriorated condition of the original paintwork. The removal of this material allowed a better reading of the painting. The clarity of the figures and of the surrounding space, within which the dramatic scene is placed, has been revealed. The dark background that once engulfed the figures has gone, thus revealing a new articulation of space and details such as the brickwork of the arch and the gate at the entrance to the yard.

Of a less spectacular nature, although fundamental to the conservation of the painting, was the structural consolidation and the lining of the canvas. The process was carried out in light of previous experience with similarly large canvases, using an innovative method, discussed below, with the aim of minimising changes to the surface. In addition, a complex system of tensioning the stretched canvas was devised, similar to the system used during the intervention of the Istituto Centrale di Restauro in Rome in 1955–57. The Laboratory's treatment will permit the future monitoring of the painting; it was important to interrelate the restoration campaign and the painting's subsequent long-term conservation.

X-ray analysis was carried out using a procedure that permits large areas to be photographed with a single X-ray exposure. The resulting clarity and legibility has revealed new information, such as initial brushstrokes outlining the figures and the identification of an earlier stretcher frame of a slightly different size from that which we see today. On the basis of this, it would appear that the painting has been reduced in size by 180–200mm. This was probably carried out when Mattia Preti restructured the Oratory at the end of the seventeenth century. The issue of the outlining of the figures is significant in the current debate about how Caravaggio organised his compositions without the use of preparatory drawings. In this canvas there is no evidence of the incised lines that have dominated recent discussion of Caravaggio's working methods. The practice of building up the work directly, using paint to sketch in the composition, corresponds to the evidence shown by the technical examination of this canvas.

The initial part of our work was carried out *in situ*, starting with the removal of the work of art and providing adequate protection for transportation. Based on the initial examination, which revealed the bad state of conservation, particularly with regard to the poor stability of the paint layer, it was decided to transport the canvas mounted on its frame rather than rolled up, which is the usual practice with works of similar dimensions. The analysis also revealed the extreme sensitivity of the painting to humidity. The painting was therefore protected by the application of a coating of acrylic resin (Plexisol P550). This film was a temporary measure and permitted only a partial strengthening of the paint layer. Once the film had dried, the surface was carefully protected with a film of silicon polyester. The crate, specially designed by a member of the Laboratory's Environmental Control Section, was built in Malta. Non-flammable and waterproof, it protected the painting from damage caused by shocks and ensured a stable environment.

The original canvas was made out of four horizontal pieces, sewn together with whip-stitch. All four have a 'canvas' weave, although the lowest part can be distinguished by its own particular weave, by its shrinkage and by the thickness of the fabric. The height of each of the upper three pieces is 1050mm, with the lowest measuring 550mm including the folded edges.

It appears that the whole canvas was sized with a solution of animal glue because no trace of the ground preparation was found on the reverse during the removal of the adhesive (*colla-pasta*) from the previous lining. Regarding the preparatory ground, the stratigraphic examinations conducted by the scientific laboratory revealed two layers, both with an oily binding medium, with a thickness of 125–175μm. The first, of an orange-red colour, consists of a red ochre with a small amount of yellow earth. The second, of a dark brown colour, consists of a large amount of particularly porous black charcoal with the same red ochre. When observing the painter's technique it appears that the artist made full use of the reddish-brown colour of the preparatory ground, not only to achieve the effect of transparency, but even using it directly instead of paint, especially along the outlines of the figures, as is the case in the extended leg of the executioner.

The paint layer has an oily binding medium and seems to be applied rapidly, with confidence, forming a fine layer that appears denser in the light-coloured parts, where white lead is employed more frequently. The outline of certain figures is also made more evident by black, linear brushstrokes, which increase the contrast and definition of the form. 'Resurfacing' of colour, now visible as a result of the increased transparency of the upper layer, suggests that in this case Caravaggio had drafted the painting not with direct brushstrokes, as found in other work of his, but with a brief sketch in light colours. X-radiography and infrared reflectography reveal that in some parts this sketch did not correspond exactly to the final version. This was confirmed when reading the radiographic image, which indicated that this first sketch had been carried out with radio-opaque material, even where it might not be detected with the naked eye.

X-ray fluorescence, chemical and stratigraphic analyses and direct observation, indicate the great number of colours used by the artist. The pigments present are red ochre, yellow ochre, burnt ochre, green earth, brown earth, dark earth, black charcoal, white lead, carmine lacquer, vermilion, transparent verdigris, malachite and azurite. As an example, examination of a detail such as the dress of the young maid reveals a first layer of green earth, white lead and yellow ochre, and a second layer of transparent verdigris, some malachite and white lead. The executioner's girdle is the result of a background painted in azurite and white lead. The Baptist's red drapery is built up in the lighter coloured areas with vermilion, some white lead and carmine lake with an oily binding medium, and in the dark areas a layer of carmine lake. The highlights, as in the case of the young maid's white shirt, are executed in a few brushstrokes of white lead. The flesh colours on the other hand are executed in white lead with traces of black charcoal. The stratigraphic examination also revealed a layer of old varnish, although in a fragmentary and deteriorated state.

State of conservation

The state of conservation of the painting has been determined in part by the artist's methods and techniques, and in part by the previous restoration interventions, mainly the one carried out by the Istituto Centrale di Restauro during 1955–57, and of course by the damage caused by vandals in 1991.

The large tear caused by the vandals penetrated both canvases, but fortunately the edges of the tear had not deformed excessively nor had the tear enlarged. From the first assessments of the painting, carried out during the initial inspection of 1996, it appeared that there was a more insidious conservation problem in the loss of adhesion between the various paint layers. This problem had been exacerbated by a slight, but dangerous, detachment of the paint from the ground layer. This phenomenon had not only been caused by the different characteristics of the paint in the thickly and thinly painted areas, but also by the differences in the original cohesion of the binding medium and pigment between the lighter coloured brushstrokes and the darker ones. This caused a difference in the craquelure and consequently the canvas behaved differently from one area to another. This is verifiable even in the passages containing white lead, for example in the green garment of the young maid, and to a lesser degree, and with different morphological characteristics, in the browns.

Observation in ultraviolet fluorescence revealed the deteriorated aesthetic values of the painting caused by the obscuring effects of a succession of repaintings concealing and altering the original paint layer. The upper layer was also affected by the blooming of the varnish. This had been applied during the previous restoration with a particularly negative effect on the dark chromatic values of the painting.

The stretcher was considerably deformed and micro-measurements showed that it reacted noticeably to fluctuations in humidity. The system of springs applied in the 1955–57 treatment showed signs of ageing and the influence of the climate: several were rusted, some were warped and others completely slack. Limited access to the back of the painting had prevented suitable conservation treatment from being carried out, therefore large amounts of dust and debris had accumulated and had infiltrated between the stretcher and the canvas, causing further deformations.

Restoration

The initial undertaking in the Laboratory consisted of the removal of the protective coating of Plexisol from the paint surface. All altered, non-original material was also removed in order to reveal the true physical condition and aesthetic values of the painting. In accordance with the policy of the Laboratory, this was executed by a gradual and differentiated removal of the various layers. The reduction of the varnish revealed a succession of small retouchings that covered not only the losses, but almost the entire background, the garments of the young maid and the old woman, and the lower part of the floor. These repaintings covered other small losses that had been overpainted with a light-coloured coating of pigment mixed with varnish. This overpaint was not only intended to conceal the tiny losses of colour, which were evident in infrared examination, but also the blooming of the varnish and the erosion of colour caused by the paint 'sinking' into the preparatory ground.

The cleaning was divided into phases: the removal of the varnish layer dating from the restoration of the Laboratorio Centrale di Restauro, which had altered as a result of the high levels of humidity, the removal of the retouchings and, finally, the thinning of the older varnish, which had also altered slightly. During this last phase, traces of adhesives from earlier interventions became apparent. These were of a proteinaceous and polysaccharide nature. Since in some parts these adhesives had bonded to the original paint, it was not possible to remove them completely. It was therefore necessary to carry out the cleaning with different solvents appropriate to the substances to be removed (ethyl-alcohol and acetone in a neutral combination; solvent gel). After cleaning, the paint layer was varnished and a layer of Plexisol was applied, with the aim of protecting the painting from humidity.

Once off the stretcher, the old relining and its adhesives were removed. This was followed by consolidation of the back of the painting with Plexisol resin by placing it in a controlled low-pressure bag. Having successfully fixed the paint layer, it was possible to proceed with the repair of the canvas, particularly the large tear. This was joined appropriately using the torn threads of the canvas, reinforced with a thin polyester canvas fixed with *pasta* to strengthen the join at the edges and allow it to be subsequently filled. The canvas was then stretched on a temporary frame using a polyester canvas strip lining, adhered with BEVA 371.

After this initial treatment, it was possible to proceed with relining. This was carried out using a method pioneered by the Laboratory, which has proved to be especially effective in the case of large paintings, minimising the risk of alteration of the surface. This technique is based on the principle of stretching the painting and the two canvases to be used for the relining over a slightly curved plane to ensure optimal contact between the canvases without the usual application of pressure with heat. The adhesive used here is a variation of the traditional *pasta*, with a base of animal glue and flour, which becomes elastic and effective even at room temperature. This was applied to the back of the stretched relining canvas, exploiting the permeable texture of the weave of the 'pattina'-type canvas, chosen because it was the only type available in such large dimensions (Fig. 2).[1] Where the edges of the canvas were laid over the stretcher, BEVA 371 was used to give the lining a greater flexibility. The outermost edges of the lining canvas were folded over and sewn to form channels through which brass rods were inserted in order to distribute tension equally. The entire system is based on the principle of applying constant and controlled tension, achieved by means of a firmly fixed, solid wooden stretcher and a series of springs, uniformly calibrated (Fig. 3). It was necessary to replace the stretcher used in the previous restoration because of its excessive deformation and the extreme deterioration of the metal parts.

The new stretcher, built by the Woodwork Section of the Laboratory, is constructed of composite wood to prevent it from deforming. For aesthetic reasons this was covered by two strips of silver fir (Fig. 4). The outer edge of the stretcher was constructed separately in oak hardwood. It has a curved profile and

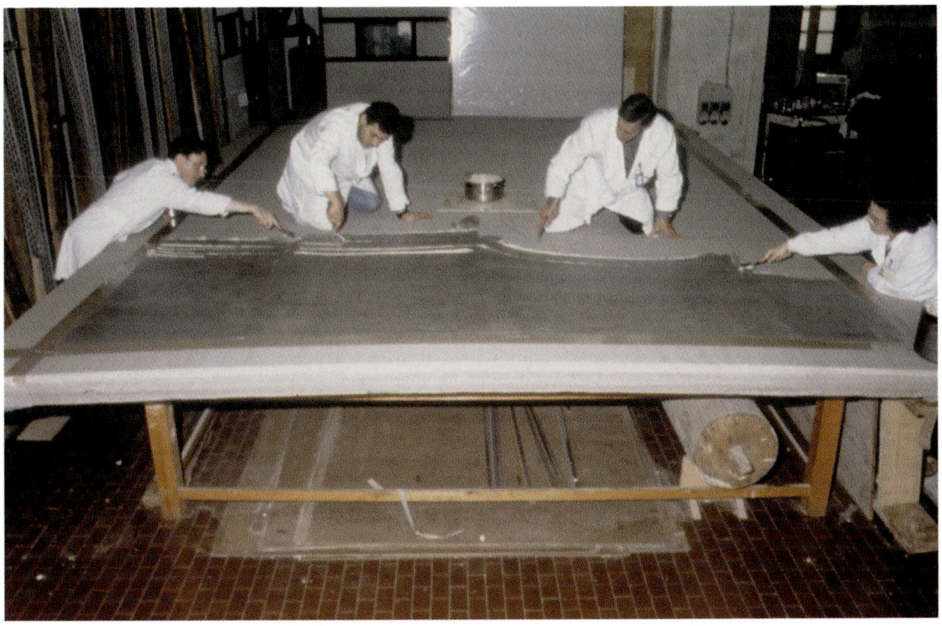

Figure 2 Lining adhesive applied to the reverse of the lining canvas stretched over a slightly curved surface.

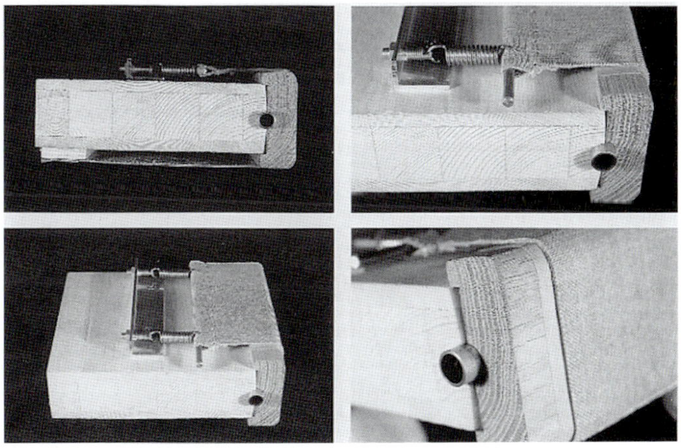

Figure 3 Four views of the model for the stretcher tensioning system.

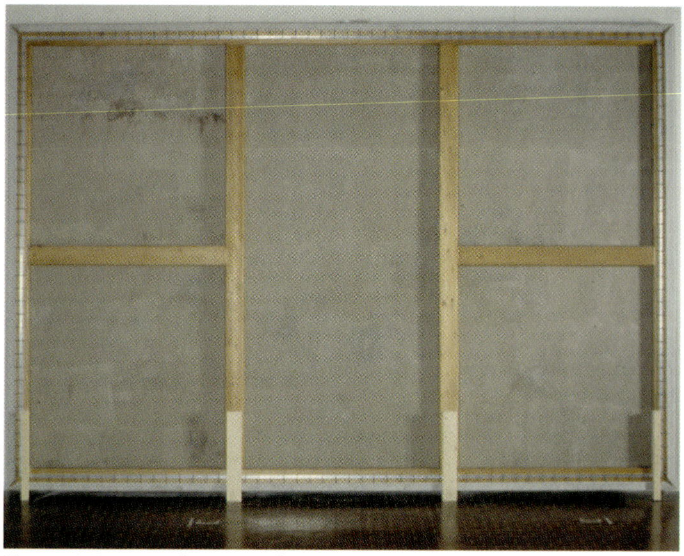

Figure 4 Reverse of new stretcher.

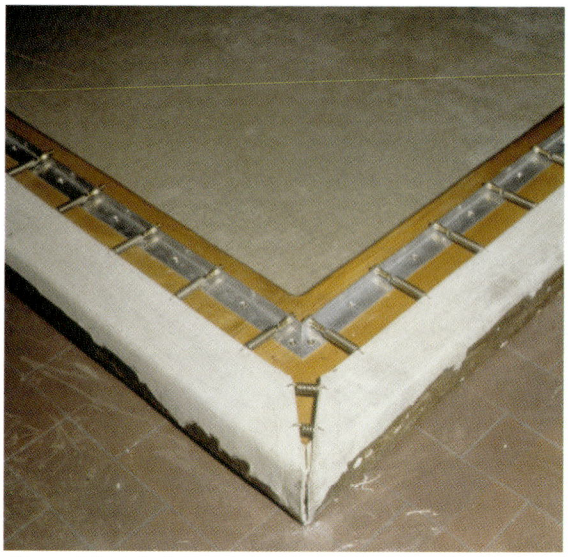

Figure 5 Detail of reverse showing tensioning system.

is attached to the composite wood stretcher via a brass rod, which acts as a pivot, allowing slight movement (Fig. 3). As a result of its width being slightly greater than that of the inner stretcher, this additional edging also serves to regulate the distance between the back of the canvas and the stretcher. The curved edge is covered with a Teflon fabric to allow the canvas to slide against it with the minimum of restriction. The canvas is tensioned by means of purpose-built stainless steel springs, each individually calibrated. These are attached at one end to the brass rod passing through the tacking margin of the lining canvas and at the other end to an L-shaped aluminium strip screwed to the reverse of the wooden stretcher, with joints that allow it to pivot (Fig. 5). The springs can be tightened or released by a nut on the other side of the aluminium strip and were calibrated using a dynamometer to give each spring the same load, measurable in kilograms. In order to minimise the invasive nature of this system, components of small dimensions were used, with each spring being placed 10cm apart. Earlier experience in this field enabled us to establish the correct amount of tension required, and this subsequently could be adapted to the needs of the painting in its final location. It is clear that such a system, which permits an optimal conservation of the canvas, requires careful consideration during the relocation of the work of art. To ensure that the system functions fully, it is necessary to offload the weight by means of flanges that can be adjusted, always leaving the edges of the canvas free.

Once the structural work was complete and the protective layers were removed from the paint surface, the cleaning process was improved further by removing the disturbing blooming caused by residues of substances from previous treatments (this was achieved using cyclohexanone, butyl-acetate and methyl-ethyl-ketone mixed with F6).[2] The next procedure was to fill the losses, paying particular attention to the surface in order to obtain good coherence with the surrounding colour. Red earth was added to the mixture of gypsum and glue to relate it to the colour of the original preparatory ground, thereby obtaining an appropriate chromatic base for the retouching. The significance and gravity of the paint losses led to the choice of *selezione cromatica* (chromatic selection) as the most appropriate method of retouching so that none of these losses caused a substantial and untreatable loss of formal values. This was executed with varnish colours over a chromatic tempera base.

Of particular complexity was the pictorial restoration of the lower part with regard to the signature that had been disfigured by the tear and which had been completed again by an accurate *tratteggio* (hatching lines) restoration. A close study of the composition and of existing indications in the work has enabled the resolution of some lacunae of particular significance, such as those present in the shoulder of the young maid, on the back of the executioner and in the pool of blood. Ultimately this has permitted a better reading of the formal and expressive values of the work.

A final sprayed varnish was applied in two different phases: the first was a mastic resin with white spirit and the second a ketone resin and petroleum spirit. This latter type was chosen to avoid any possible alteration of the surface, a common phenomenon in natural resins exposed to a high level of humidity. The final varnish is also intended to diminish the uneven absorption caused by the porosity of the paint layers, which had been observed in the preceding intermediate varnish layer consisting only of mastic resin.

After the conclusion of the exhibition of the painting in Florence and its return to the Cathedral of Malta, the treatment and the preventive measures were considered together in the context of the total conservation plan. The architectonic space on the back of the painting was cleaned accurately and the upper part was closed with a wooden ceiling. The back of the frame was covered with Gore-tex fabric fixed with Velcro to protect the canvas from dust and humidity. Finally, three humidity and temperature sensors were sited: the first in the Oratory, the second behind the painting and the third between the canvas and the Gore-tex (Fig. 6). The condition has been checked every six months, and from June 1999 onwards the evidence shows that the climatic changes have had less effect in the protected area than outside.

Our conservation project will hopefully contribute to the future conservation of this masterpiece by Caravaggio.[3]

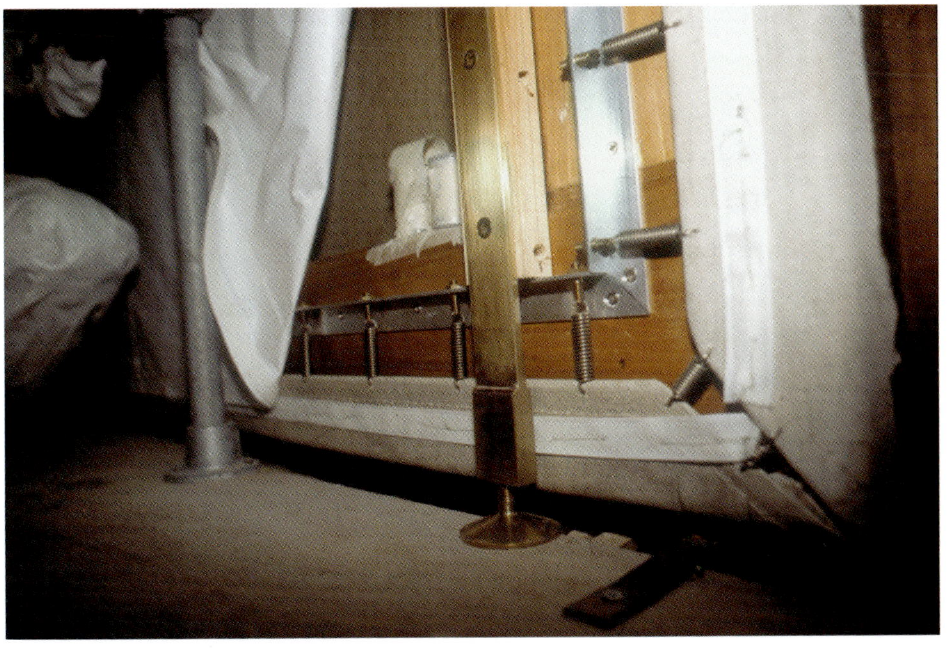

Figure 6 Detail of reverse *in situ* showing Gore-tex back protection, and humidity and temperature sensor between the canvas and Gore-tex.

Notes

1. 'Pattina' is the canvas typically used for traditional lining in Italy.
2. F6 according to Richard Feller's solubility test.
3. This English text is based on the translation of our conservation report by Theresa M. Vella from the National Museum of Fine Arts in Malta.

Bibliography

Conservation of works by Caravaggio

Bonsanti, G. and Gregori, M. (eds) 1996. *Caravaggio da Malta a Firenze*, catalogue of the exhibition, Milan.

Ciatti, M. 1999. 'La "Decollazione del Battista" di Caravaggio: storia di un progetto di conservazione (e qualche novitá)', *OPD Restauro* 11: 290–306.

Ciatti, M. and Silla, C. (eds) 1999. *Caravaggio al Carmine. Il restauro della Decollazione del Battista di Malta*, Milan.

Vella, T.M. (ed.) 1999. *The Return of Caravaggio's* The Beheading of the Baptist *to Malta*. Valletta: National Museum of Fine Arts.

X-ray investigation

Adrovandi, A. and Ciappi, O. 1995. 'La radiografia di grande formato: problemi e soluzioni tecniche', *OPD Restauro* 7: 163–8.

Relining of large canvases

Ciappi, O. and Ciatti, M. 1996. 'La conservazione dei dipinti su tela: esperienze e innovazioni per dipinti di grandi dimensioni', *OPD Restauro* 8: 159–64.

The author

Marco Ciatti is Director of the Easel Paintings Conservation Laboratory in the Opificio delle Pietre Dure, Florence.

The Battle of Meanee by Edward Armitage, 1847

CLAIRE CHORLEY

Introduction

The Battle of Meanee was a key moment in the British campaign in modern-day Pakistan. The heroic defence of the northern territories drew admiration from the British generals, even as they gained ground. A competition was announced to commemorate the battle in 1845 with a prize of £400 which was won by Armitage. The resulting painting was greatly admired by all (except perhaps General Napier who is rather alarmingly portrayed in the upper left quadrant and was displeased not to have been more prominently placed) and travelled to Dublin and Paris on

Figure 1 *The Battle of Meanee* by Edward Armitage (1847).

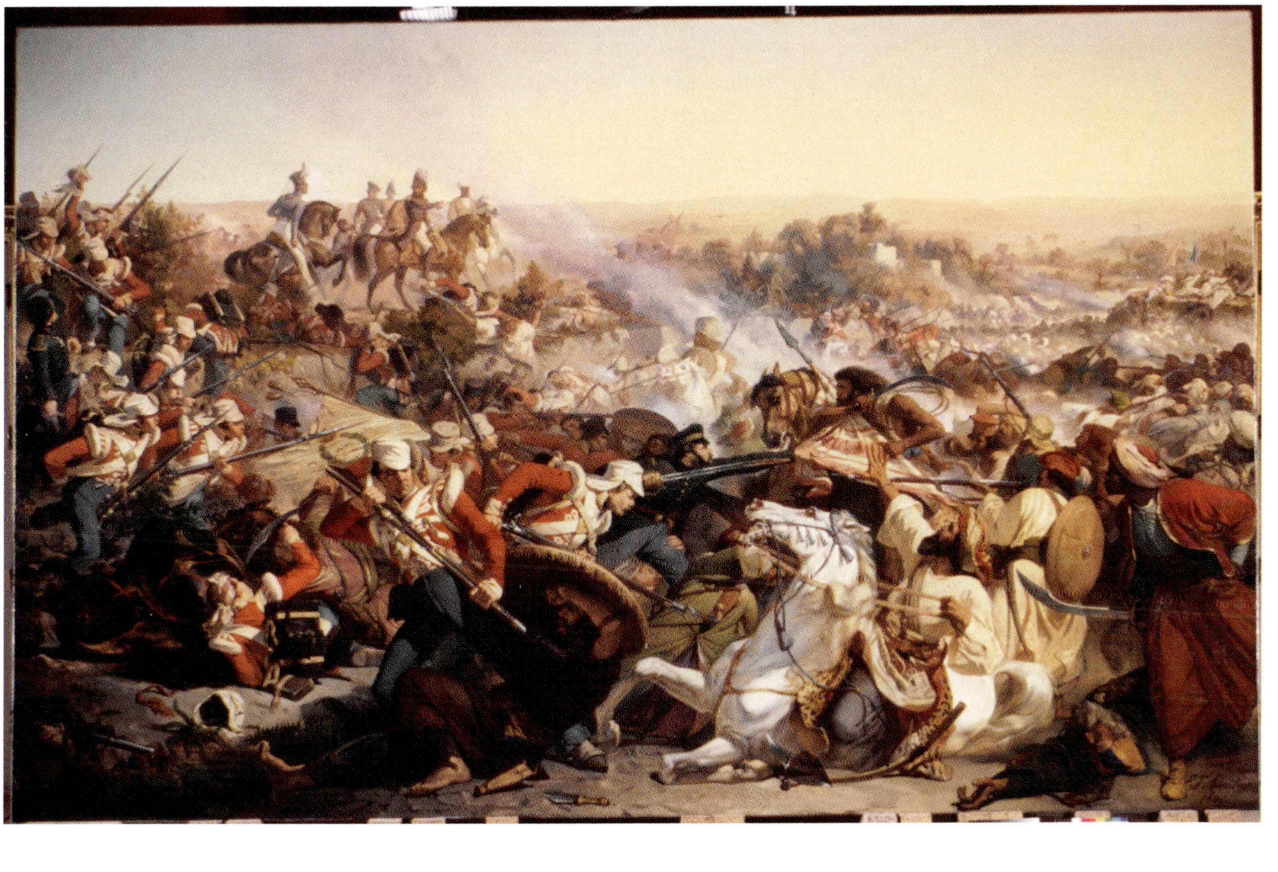

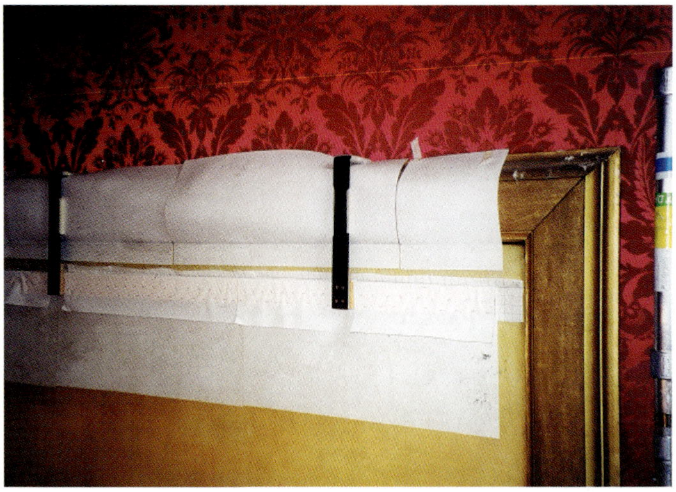

Figure 2 BEVA 371, non-woven polyester and Bondina were used together with steel brackets and wooden beams to construct a support system for securing the unattached tacking edge while the painting was moved down from the wall.

exhibition before returning to London following its purchase by Queen Victoria and Prince Albert. A folding stretcher was devised for the purpose of travelling (Fig. 11).

This large painting, 3.9 × 6m (13 × 20ft) was treated at St James's Palace, London, to rectify large deformations in the canvas that had formed over several years. Last surface-cleaned and re-varnished in 1962 by W. Freeman, it was discovered to be completely detached from the upper stretcher bar, causing the deformations which were particularly noticeable during periods of high humidity. There were also a number of old damages, at least one of which was dramatic in scale. The framing of the painting also presented problems as the frame was being supported by the stretcher.

As the painting required structural treatment with some urgency it was decided that it would be appropriate to carry out a full treatment at this time, i.e. cleaning and restoration. While this was not necessarily out of the ordinary in terms of treatment, logistically it presented some interesting problems, mainly as a result of the fact that due to its size it had to be treated *in situ*. Although it had travelled loosely folded when first painted, it was of course undesirable to roll an aged painting unless absolutely necessary.

Treatment[1]

Felt-covered boards, protected with Melinex, were used to provide a resistant surface on which to iron the strip lining as the room in which the painting was being treated was carpeted. These were easily moved from in and out of the front of the painting. A linoleum flooring was considered but dismissed as being no more effective than moveable boards.

BEVA 371, non-woven polyester and Bondina were used together with steel brackets and wooden beams to construct a support system for securing the unattached tacking edge while the painting was moved from the wall (Fig. 2). Scaffolding towers and hydraulic lifts were used to remove the painting from the wall (Figs 3–6).

A wooden jig was constructed to enable both sides of the tears to be treated at any one time, treating the tears from the reverse while the painting was supported vertically from the front (Fig. 7). The largest tear, 27.7cm long, was repaired using canvas threads and Resin W adhesive (Fig. 8). In areas where canvas was missing, inserts were made from new canvas and bonded with Resin W; canvas threads

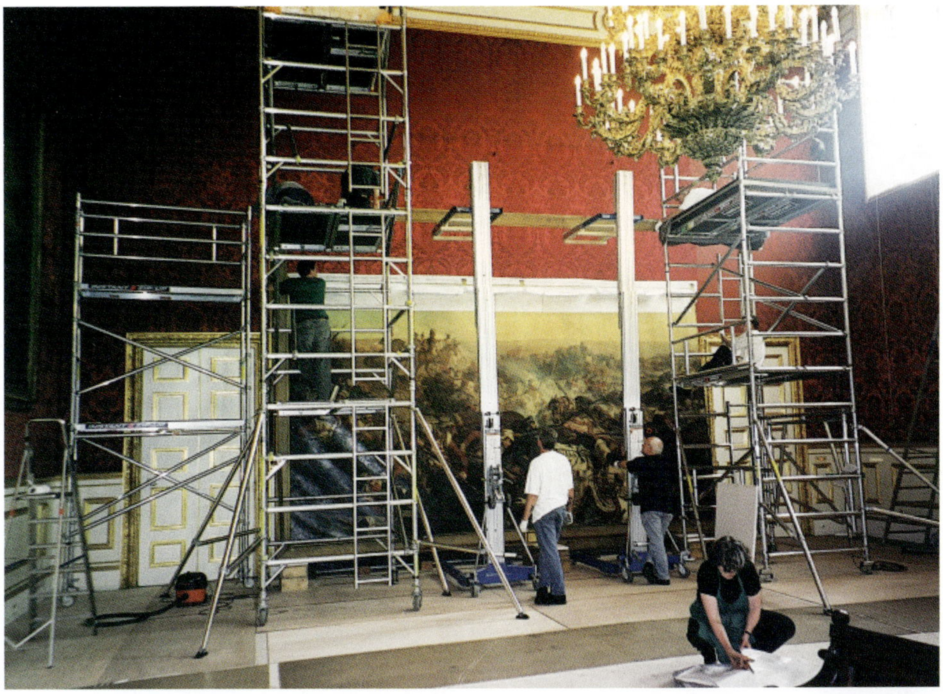

Figures 3–6 Scaffolding towers and hydraulic lifts were used to remove the painting from the wall.

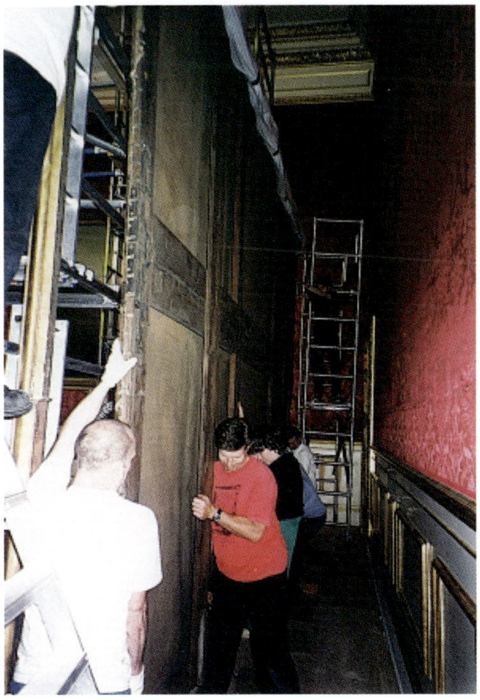

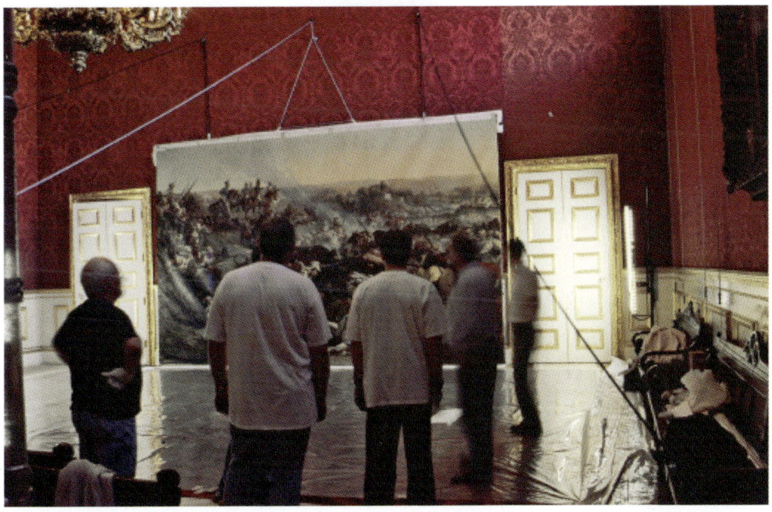

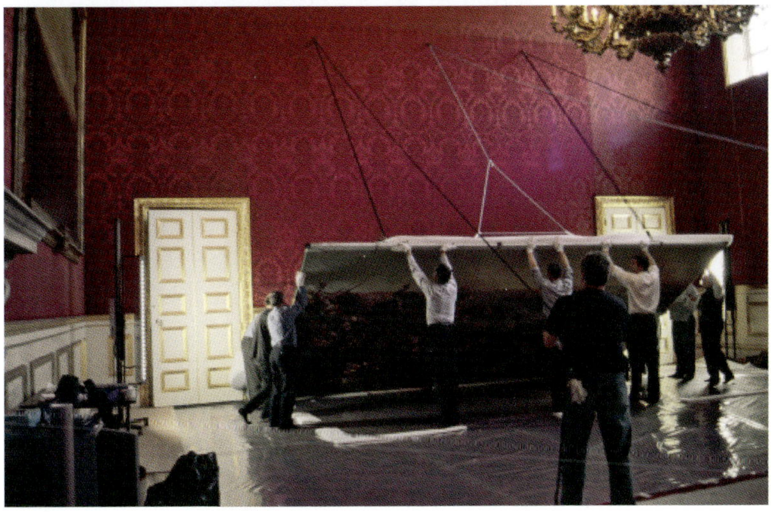

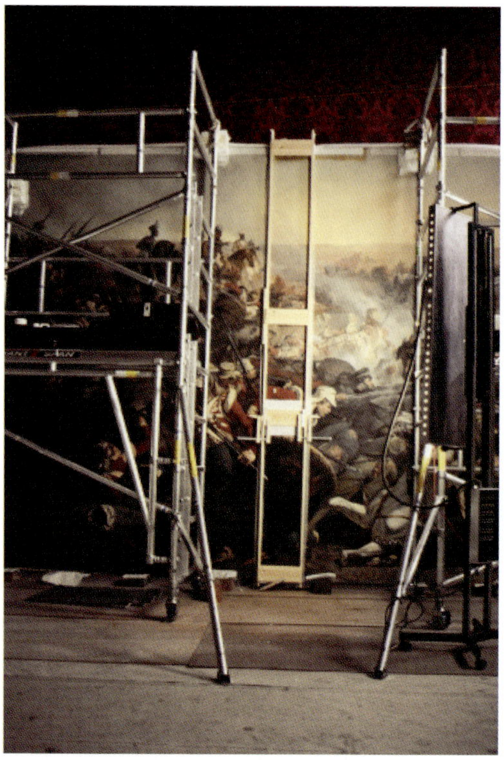

Figure 7 A wooden jig was constructed in order to treat the tears from the reverse while the painting was supported vertically from the front.

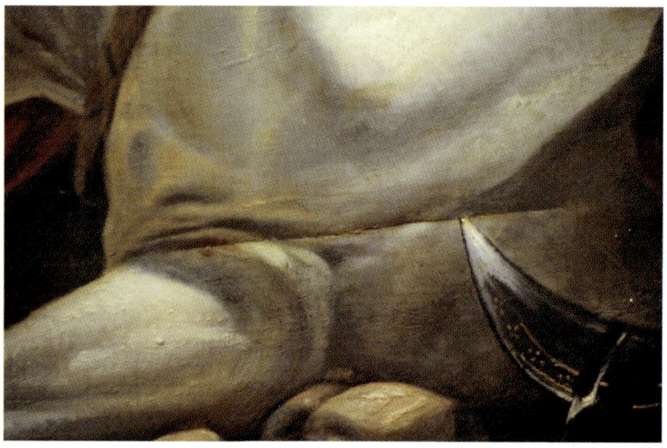

Figure 8 The largest tear, 27.7cm long, was repaired using canvas threads and Resin W adhesive. In areas where canvas was missing, inserts were made from new canvas and bonded with Resin W; canvas threads were used to bridge where necessary.

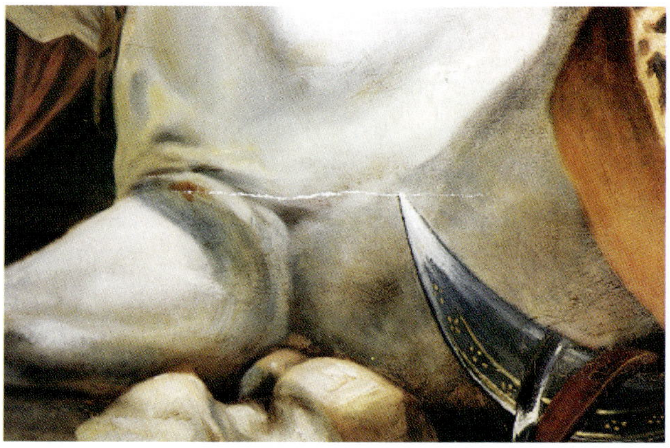

Figure 9 After structural treatment.

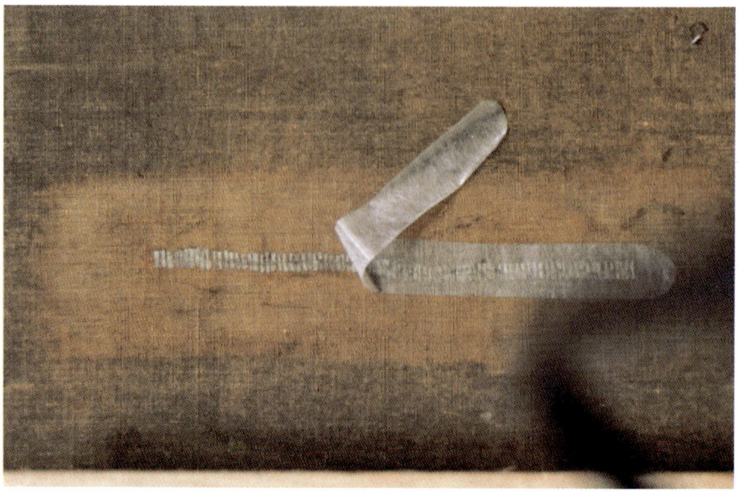

Figure 10 Reverse. Original threads were butt-joined as far as possible. Non-woven polyester patches were adhered using BEVA 371 to provide additional support.

were used to bridge where necessary. On the reverse, original threads were butt-joined as far as possible (Fig. 10). Non-woven polyester patches were adhered using BEVA 371 to provide additional support.

The stretcher was originally able to fold in half for travel and was held in place by iron shutter bars (Fig. 11). The hinges have two pivot axes to prevent a sharp fold in the painting. The stretcher was stabilised in-plane with steel plates. After an interleaf of non-woven polyester and BEVA 371 was inserted to support any

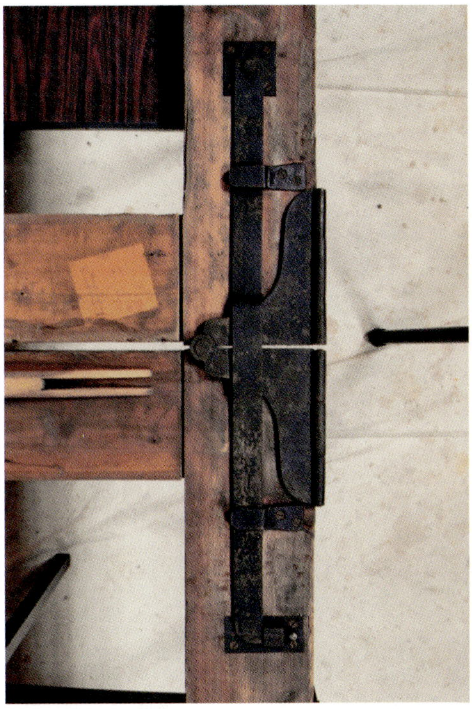

Figure 11 The stretcher was originally able to fold in half for travel and held in place by iron shutter bars. The hinges have two pivot axes to prevent a sharp fold in the painting. The stretcher was stabilised in-plane with steel plates.

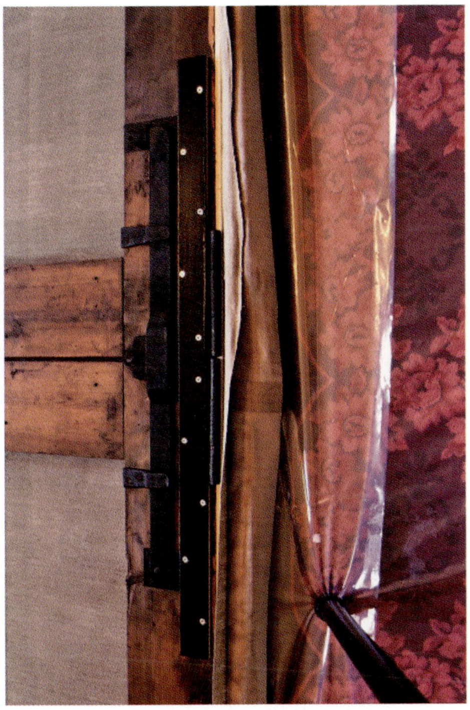

Figure 12 After an interleaf of non-woven polyester and BEVA 371 was inserted to support any vulnerable areas of tacking edge, the canvas strip lining was ironed in place. This had been previously coated with liquid BEVA. As the original canvas was very brittle, the strip lining was applied 18cm into the painting as it was feared that there might be failure along the line of craquelure indicating the edge of the stretcher bar.

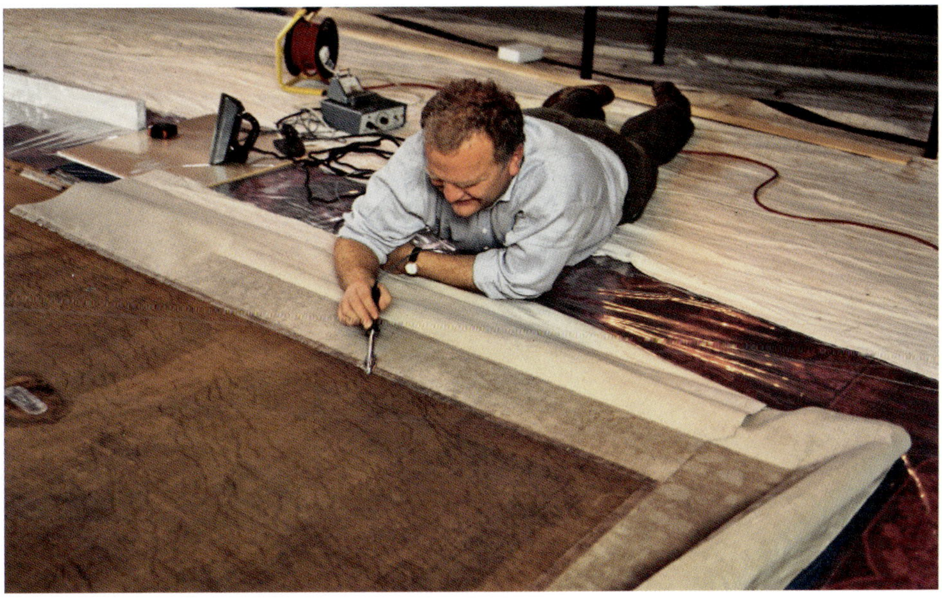

Figure 13 The feathered edge of the strip lining was tacked separately in position to prevent distortion and achieve an optimum bond.

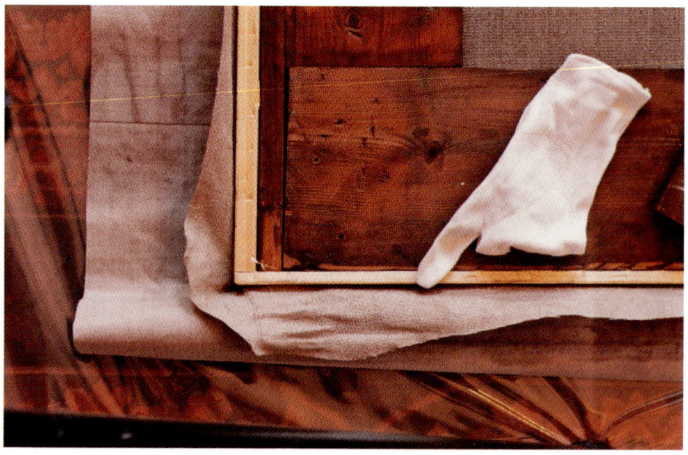

Figure 14 An extra strip of wood was added around the original stretcher to provide a new edge for tacking. Loose lining (indicated by the pointing glove) and strip lining are visible.

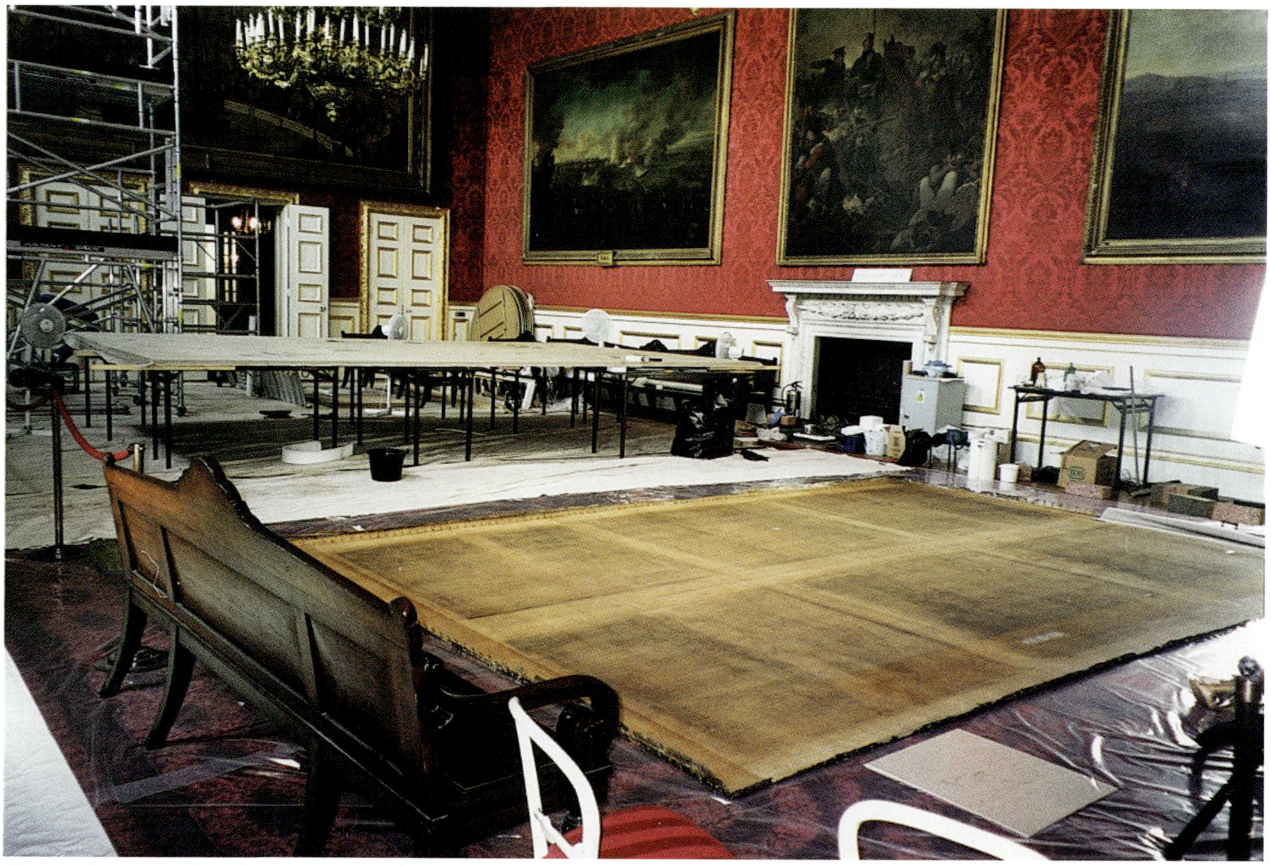

Figure 15 A canvas loose lining was prepared. It was stretched on the original stretcher, wetted to shrink and re-stretched three times. Two priming coats of Plextol B500 were applied to the loose lining. It was then removed from the stretcher and reversed in the hope that this would help to mitigate the effects on the painting of the occasional high humidity in the room.

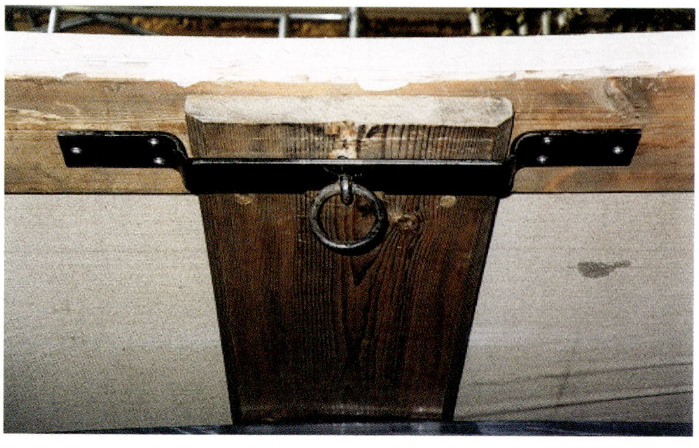

Figure 16 Metal plates were added to the supporting members of the stretcher to prevent the original screw eye from bending upwards.

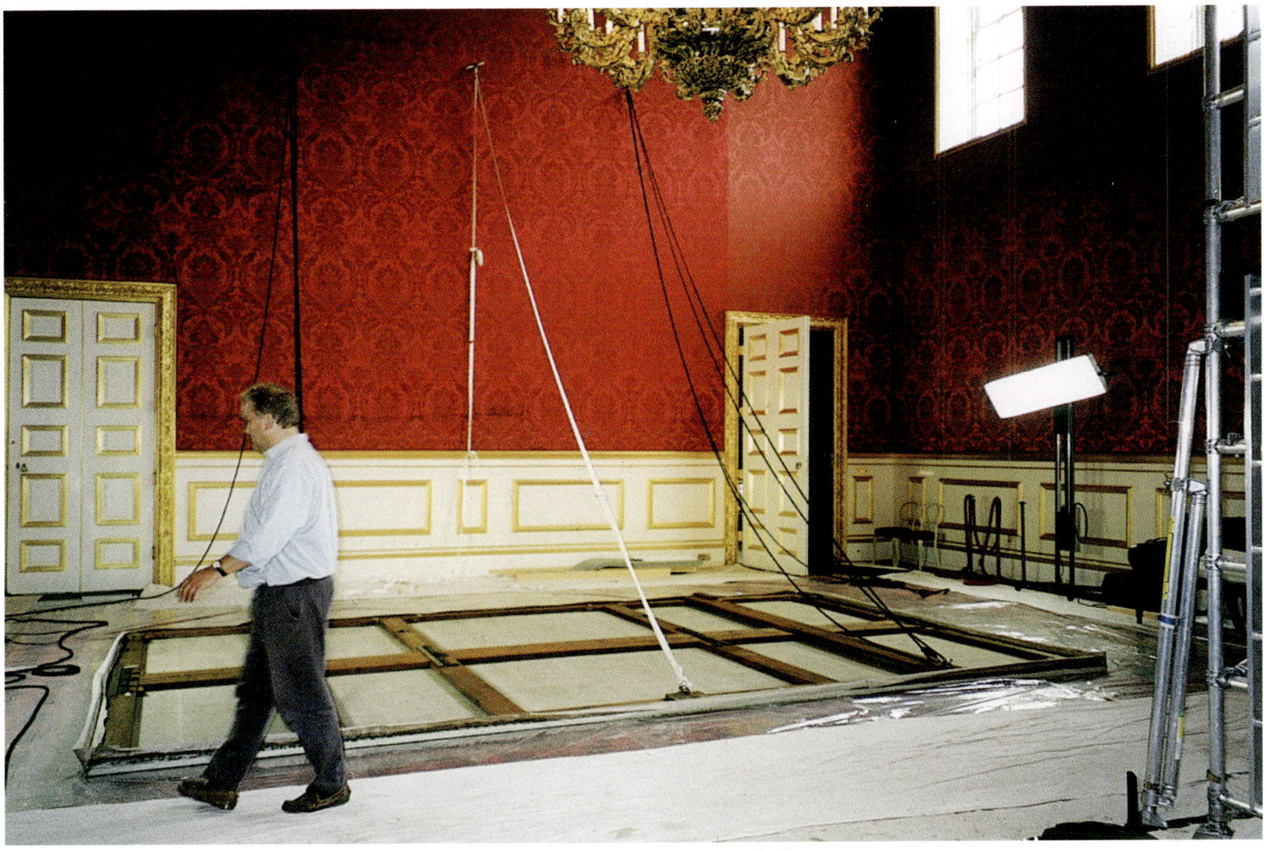

Figure 17 The stretcher was lowered into position. The original canvas was re-stretched.

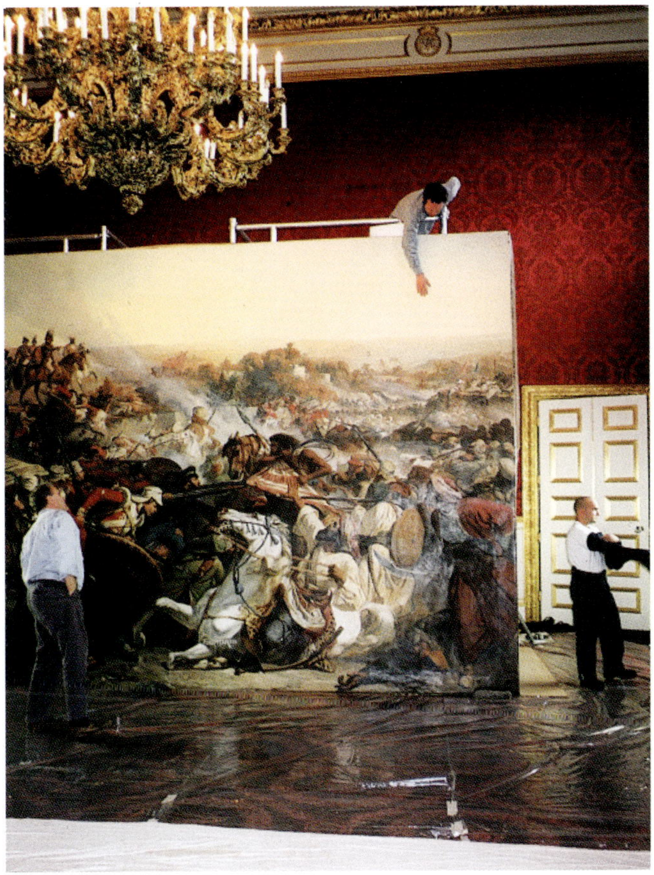

Figure 18 The painting was raised and tension adjusted.

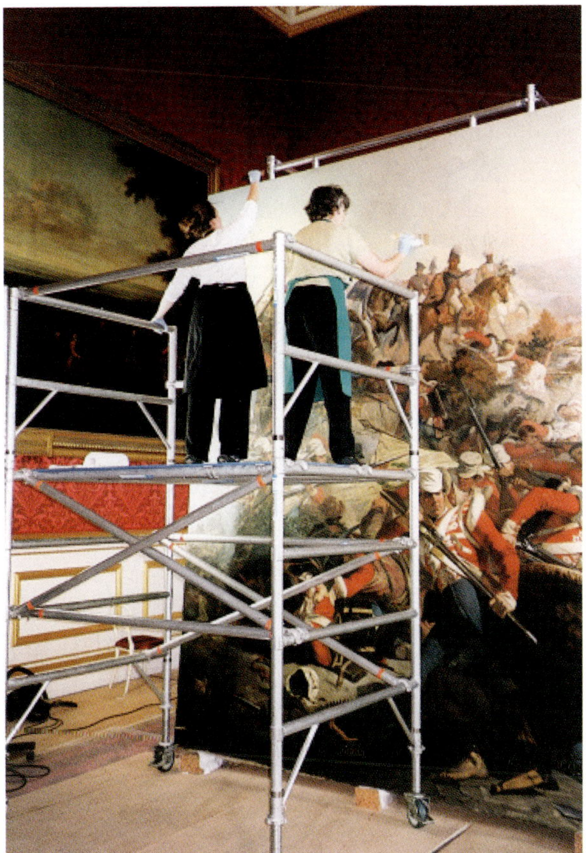

Figure 19 The painting was brush-varnished using MS2A resin. Losses were filled using a sturgeon glue, chalk and linseed oil putty. Retouchings were carried out using egg tempera with MS2A glazes.

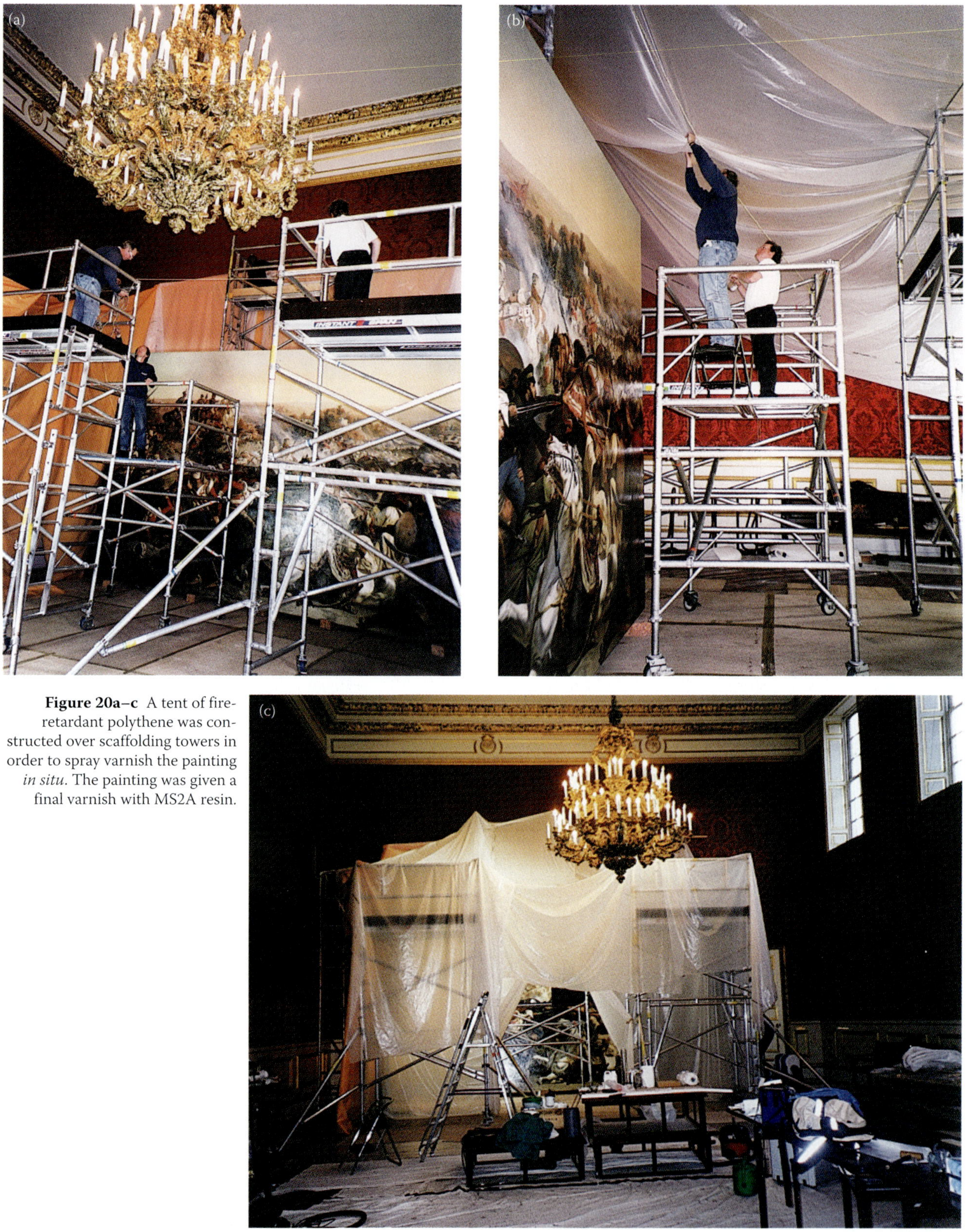

Figure 20a–c A tent of fire-retardant polythene was constructed over scaffolding towers in order to spray varnish the painting *in situ*. The painting was given a final varnish with MS2A resin.

vulnerable areas of tacking edge, the canvas strip lining was ironed in place (Fig. 12); this had been previously coated with liquid BEVA. As the original canvas was very brittle, the strip lining was applied 18cm into the painting as it was feared that there might be failure along the line of craquelure indicating the edge of the stretcher bar. The feathered edge of the strip lining was tacked separately in position to prevent distortion and to achieve an optimum bond (Fig. 13).

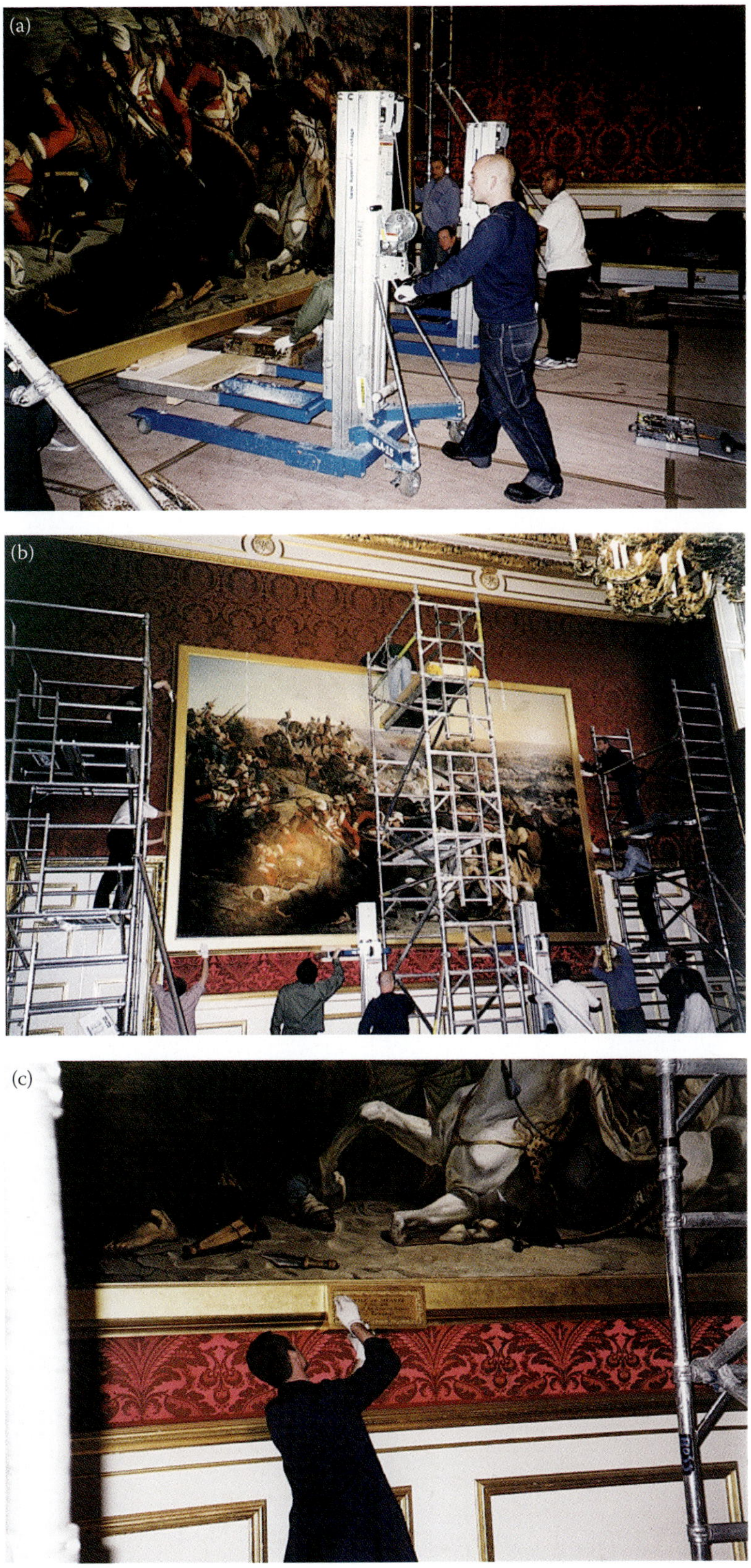

Figure 21a–c After re-framing, the painting was re-hung using hydraulic lifts to raise it into position. The hooks were then fixed to their original rings.

An extra strip of wood was added around the original stretcher to provide a new edge for tacking. Loose lining (indicated by a pointing glove) and strip lining are visible in Figure 13. A canvas loose lining was prepared. It was stretched on the original stretcher, wetted to shrink and re-stretched three times. Two priming coats of Plextol B500 were applied to the loose lining. It was then removed from the stretcher and reversed in the hope that this would help to mitigate the effects on the painting of the occasional high humidity in the room in which it hangs.

Metal plates were added to the supporting members of the stretcher to prevent the original screw eye from bending upwards (Fig. 16). The stretcher was lowered into position (Fig. 17) and the original canvas was re-stretched. The painting was then raised and the tension adjusted (Fig. 18).

The painting was brush-varnished using MS2A resin (Fig. 19) and losses were filled using a sturgeon glue, chalk and linseed oil putty. Retouchings were carried out using egg tempera with MS2A glazes. A tent of fire-retardant polythene was constructed over scaffolding towers in order to spray varnish the painting *in situ* (Fig. 20a–c). The painting was given a final varnish with MS2A resin. After re-framing, the painting was re-hung using hydraulic lifts to raise it into position. The hooks were then fixed to their original rings (Fig. 21a–c).

Acknowledgements

Conservation was carried out by Royal Collection staff: Al Brewer, Claire Chorley, Rupert Featherstone, Viola Pemberton-Pigott and Rosanna de Sancha, with assistance from Geraldine van Heemstra, Christopher Lloyd, the Royal Collection Furniture Conservation staff and St James's Palace staff, Simon Bobak Conservation, Pippa Balch, Michael Field (Royal Collection) and MOMART.

Note

1. Most of the materials mentioned in the text are available from Preservation Equipment Ltd, Vinces Road, Diss, Norfolk IP22 4HQ.

The author

Claire Chorley is a paintings conservator at the Royal Collection, Windsor.

The Defeat of the Floating Batteries off Gibraltar by John Singleton Copley: History and Display

GERRY ALABONE WITH LOUISE DANDY

Introduction

This paper chronicles one of the largest oil paintings in Britain. Its scale has produced major problems for its accommodation and indeed survival since its creation in the late eighteenth century. Coming perilously close to destruction during World War II, it has only recently been returned to display. Restored after a long period of neglect, the painting and its original frame were hung using an unconventional system in the new Guildhall Art Gallery.

The Corporation of London's Guildhall Art Gallery includes a painting by the American artist, John Singleton Copley (1738–1815), commissioned in 1784 by

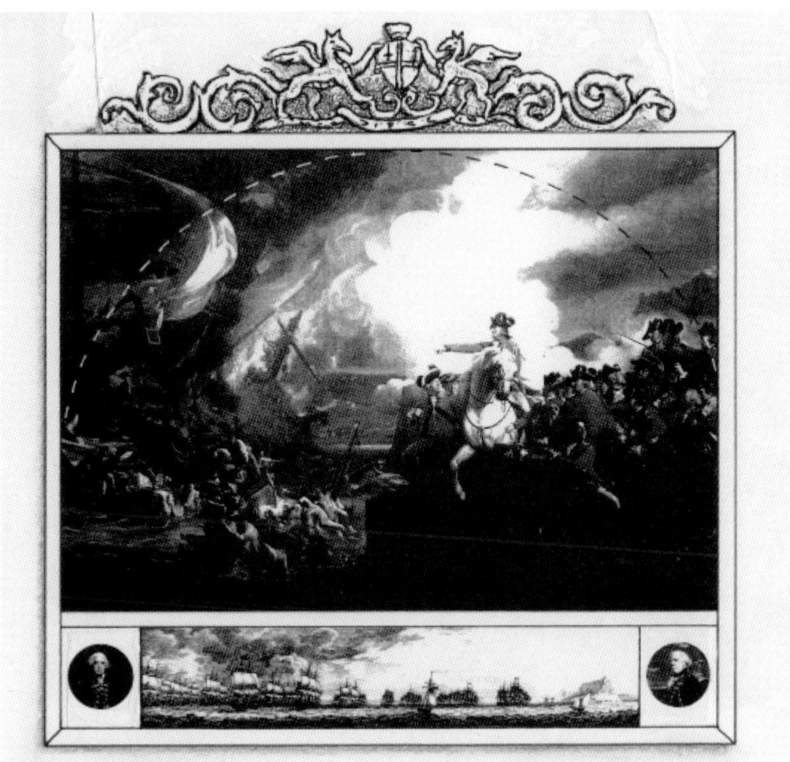

Figure 1 *The Defeat of the Floating Batteries off Gibraltar* and its pendant, *The Relief of Gibraltar*, flanked by the portraits of Admirals Howe and Barrington, arranged as they were intended by Copley within a conjectural diagram of the frame as it may have been first designed. The hatched line indicates the spandrels in Copley's initial composition. (Guildhall Art Gallery, Corporation of London.)

the Corporation in recognition of a popular patriotic victory two years before. It was designed to illustrate two successive events: the destruction of the specially designed battering ships that bombarded the British garrison on Gibraltar, and the Royal Navy's lifting of the four-year siege by the Spanish and French. Copley's canvas at Guildhall measures 5464 × 7635mm and is displayed within the original frame commissioned by the Corporation. However, the canvas initially had three pendants. The painting of one, depicting *The Relief of Gibraltar*, was subcontracted by Copley to the marine painter Dominic Serres (1722–1793). Either side of this were two portraits by Copley, one of which, the portrait of Admiral Howe, is now in the collection of the National Maritime Museum, London, and the other, of Admiral Barrington, is untraced (Fig. 1).

Copley initially painted both the siege and relief as one image, with spandrels at the top corners, on the extant canvas, a single piece of linen. Spandrels appear in the oil sketch for the picture, now belonging to the Coram Foundation in London. Copley reluctantly altered the format after complaints from the army officers depicted that they were too small. Together, this multiple image was known as *The Siege of Gibraltar*. The painting took eight years to complete, rather than the two Copley had estimated to gain the commission. A visitor to his studio reported: 'The picture was immense; and it was managed by means of a roller, so that any portion of it, at any time, might be easily seen or executed. The artist himself was raised on a platform.'[1] Before delivering them to the Guildhall, Copley exhibited the whole group of canvases as a paying attraction in a tent in Green Park and took orders for an engraving (Fig. 2).

This was the first recorded one-picture exhibition in London and was very well attended. Copley hoped to turn a healthy profit on his huge investment of time, but this proved beyond him. Complaints by local residents about the tent led to the king advising: 'Push it up nearer to my Wife's house [Buckingham Palace] – she won't complain.'[2] The frame shown on the admission ticket was only temporary but surrounded the whole scheme of paintings. The Guildhall Committee, when it realised that the square picture would not fit into the intended position in their Common Council Chamber, which had a vaulted ceiling, had the room altered. The Corporation's new frame was also made to accommodate the four

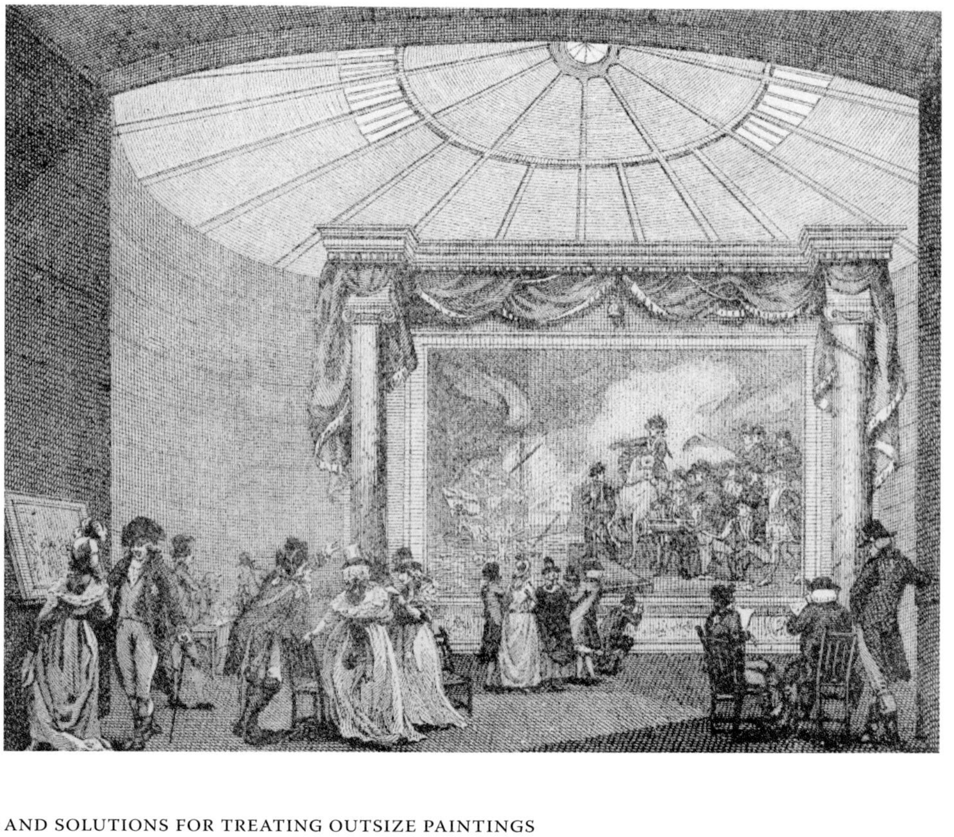

Figure 2 'Mr. Copley's Picture of the Siege of Gibraltar, as exhibited in the Green Park near St. James's Palace, engraved by F. Bartolozzi.' Facsimile of the admission ticket to the 1791 exhibition of The Siege of Gibraltar (© British Museum.)

canvases, but was found to be still too large for the, by now, altered room, so the pendants were removed from the main canvas and never exhibited with it again. The pendants' central depiction of the *Relief* was destroyed in storage in the mid-nineteenth century.

The *Carlo Maratta* style frame was designed by George Dance the Younger, Clerk of the City's Works, and made by James Brewer, a local carver and gilder of the city. The frame was surmounted by the city's heraldic device. There is no evidence of precisely how the pendant canvases were originally to be accommodated within the frame. On 27 June 1793, the Corporation's General Purposes Committee noted that:

> Mr James Brewer laid before this Committee pursuant to the order of the seventeenth of May last a Drawing of a Gilt Frame for the Picture of the Relief and Defence [i.e. *The Siege of Gibraltar*] of Gibraltar together with an Estimate: ... Gentm. Having made an Estimate with the greatest attention – find the frame ornament &c. will come to £130 – Executed in the Best Manner – yr most obt servt Jas Brewer 126 Newgate Street June 27/93.

In six months it was ready. On 18 December 1794 it was noted that:

> Mr James Brewer acquainted this Committee he had Pursuant to the Drawing and Agreement made on the 27th of June 1793 completed the frame for the picture of Gibraltar but since that the Common Council Room had been altered from a Circular to a Square Form which would not admit the Frame and Picture being placed at the West End of the said Room. Ordered that the small scale of the Defence and Relief of Gibraltar [sic] be detached from the Picture and that Mr Brewer do alter the Frame accordingly.

By 4 June 1795:

> ... the Relief and Defence [sic] of Gibraltar executed by Mr Copley, which is now fixed at the West End of the Common Council Room [see Fig. 3] in an Elegant Gilt Frame made by Mr James Brewer, whose Bill for the same and some unavoidable additions made thereto occasioned by the great Alteration at the end of the said Council Room, we have received amounting to the sum of £178.5s.6d ... and likewise a Bill of £5.5s.0d, of Mr Dance's for making drawings for mouldings and design for the frame.'[3]

The frame was rumoured in the *Oracle* (9 July 1794) to have cost £400.00, '... a greater sum, we believe than was ever given before for a similar article'.[4] There has been no evidence found at Guildhall of this, but James Brewer had become an Alderman of the City in 1782 and so in some part helped oversee works that were contracted to himself.

The frame's crest was removed in about 1815 when the picture was rehung at the other end of the Chamber. Its fate is unknown but it must have been spectacular when first displayed. The top member of the existing frame contains what are surely the mortises and screw holes to receive and secure the crest. It would have been heavy, being carved timber, and, if deteriorated, it might have compromised the safe function of the frame, necessitating its removal. The Chamber was noted as being very damp and other pictures displayed there suffered.

The picture was moved to the newly opened Guildhall Art Gallery in 1886 and remained at Guildhall until being taken down and stored just prior to the destruction of the Gallery in 1941 (Fig. 4). The frame was reduced again at some stage, being cut down by 250mm from each of its side members. This was perhaps done on the occasion of the new hang in 1886 to hide damage along the top edge of the

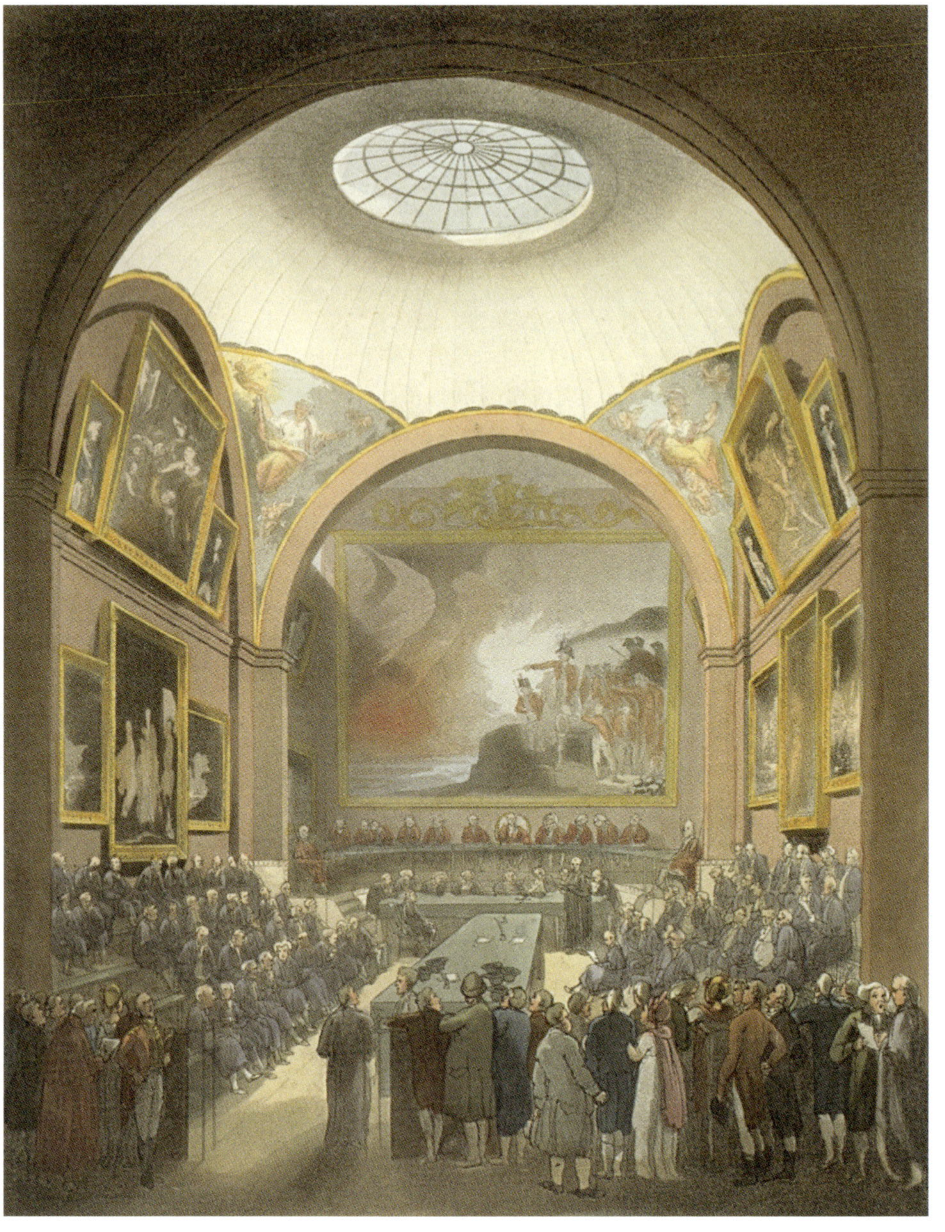

Figure 3 The Common Council Chamber, 1808, coloured etching and aquatint by Rowlandson and Pugin for Rudolf Ackermann's *Microcosm of London*, volume 2. Reproduced from an original in the Prints and Maps Section of the Guildhall Library, Corporation of London.

canvas where the tacking edge had split and the painted surface was nailed onto the stretcher to provide support. The original stretcher, which still survives in storage, was reduced by the same amount as the frame. The frame's inherently weak rebates had split along entire members and were filled in with wooden blocks. When one of the side members was reduced in length, its severed rebate had one end sawn off, but at the opposite end than the rest of the member. It was therefore reattached with the wood fibres misaligned. The painting was then fitted onto the back of the rejoined frame. The redundant rebates had the 38mm gap from sight edge to canvas spanned with black battens.

In 1915 the painting was rolled, crated and placed in the crypt beneath the Great Hall for safety throughout World War I, being rehung in the Gallery in 1923. During the next war, in 1940, it was discussed whether to protect the painting from 'concussion' by boarding it up where it hung or by rolling it and storing it in the crypt as before. The latter was presumably not undertaken as the Great Hall was gutted later that year and works stored in its crypt badly damaged by water. In 1941 the painting was rolled, crated and sent for safe storage at Swallowfield Park in Berkshire. The Director reported to the Library Committee that '... the removal of this huge canvas with its valuable frame was not an easy matter and was indeed

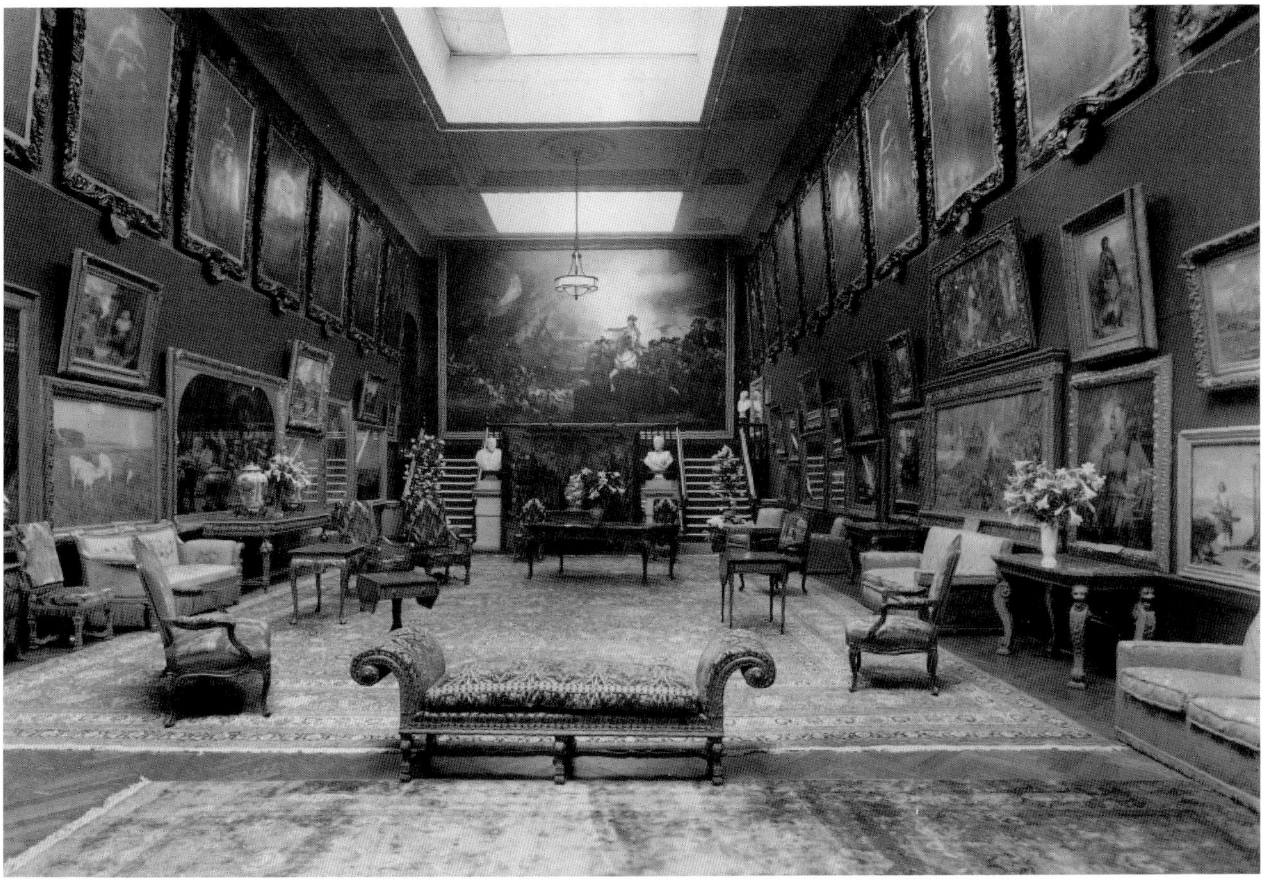

Figure 4 Gallery 1, Guildhall Art Gallery, *c.* 1917. Reproduced from an anonymous photograph in the collection of the Prints and Maps Section of the Guildhall Library, Corporation of London.

attended with some risk but it has been accomplished without injury'. The canvas was rolled with a layer of Kraft paper reinforced with bitumen and muslin. It was put in a crate of 1070mm width. Only one month after the picture's removal, the Guildhall Art Gallery was destroyed in an air raid.

Post-war the painting was stored in a barn, rented by the Corporation as a picture store and, on a rare inspection in 1953, damage to the painting by damp and rats was noted, as were numerous tears. The Corporation had no suitable area to display the painting and many institutions in Britain and abroad were approached as possible homes, but all declined due to its size. In 1975 an inspection, recording the picture as badly torn and fragmented, recommended it should be divided in two. Reluctant to do this, the Corporation again sought to give it away, to no avail. In 1983, the Area Museums Service for South Eastern England (AMSSEE) carried out emergency repairs to the painting. Their conservator, Rica Jones, reported: 'This picture will present extraordinary conservation problems purely because of its size ... It is possible for one person to restore a full-length portrait on his or her own from start to finish, whereas it is clear that some considerable manpower would be needed to lift this picture – and a good deal of technology to enable it to remain upright.'[5] AMSSEE faced the painting and reinforced the tears. It was then put on a new roller of 2.7m diameter, which allowed it to be rolled end to end without overlapping.

The picture was subsequently treated at English Heritage's Conservation Studio from 1985 to 1992, where cleaning and structural conservation was carried out.[6] Once treated, the picture was put into rented storage until the new Gallery was ready. It was transported on a smaller roller of less than 1000mm diameter, then stored on the larger roller (Figs 5 and 6).

The frame had suffered greatly and arrived back at Guildhall in 1993. After nearly 60 years of storage it was filthy, with numerous losses to the carved ornament and with large areas of delamination and loss to the whitening layers.

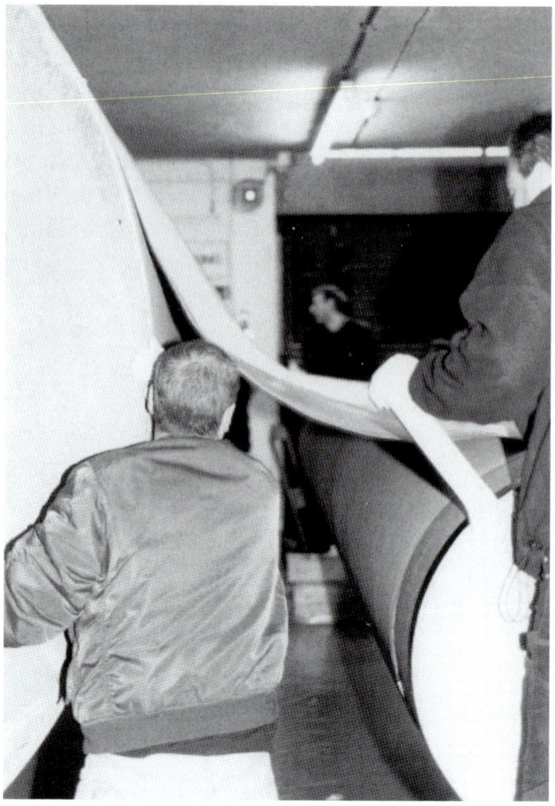

Figure 5 The canvas being transferred from its storage roller to the smaller roller for transport to the new Guildhall Art Gallery, 1999. (Guildhall Art Gallery, Corporation of London.)

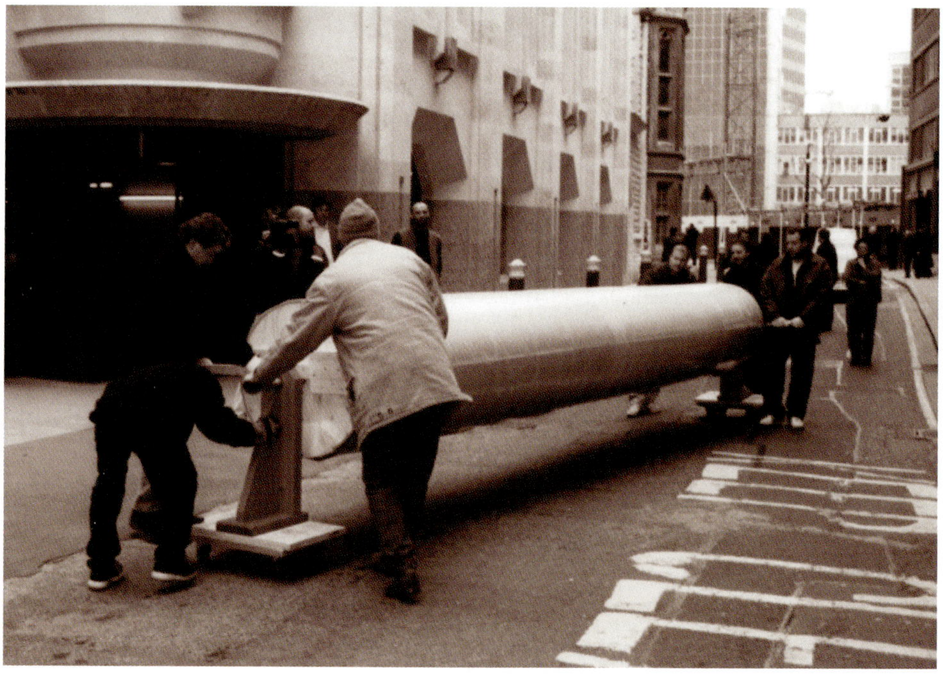

Figure 6 The canvas being moved into the new Guildhall Art Gallery on its transport roller, 1999. (Guildhall Art Gallery, Corporation of London.)

Analysis of cross-sections from the frame's surface decoration, prior to treatment, by Dr Nicholas Eastaugh detected six or seven separate gilding schemes. It was decided to remove all non-original material from the surface decoration, consisting of dirt and gilding layers which clogged the surface detail, to reveal the original burnished water gilding underneath. A corridor in the Guildhall studios had to be converted into a workspace to accommodate the great length of the frame members. The original whitening layer was consolidated with rabbit skin glue and various structural repairs were carried out on the carcass of the frame. All old carved and gilded restorations to the decoration were retained. The frame was then cleaned with Nitromors (dichloromethane) and all the major losses to the decoration were filled, water-gilded and burnished. When the rebate, which had been previously misaligned, was correctly positioned it demonstrated the frame's former height and how much was missing. To restore the old proportions, two new extensions were carved, gilded and toned to match the existing original. These were housed on the loose-tongue tenons of the reduced side members and allowed the whole of the canvas to be shown. With the frame's rebate remaining fundamentally weak and the new stretcher for the canvas now being larger than the original, the rebate still could not be used and the black batten step from the frame's sight edge to the painting remains. All the new gold was toned to match the rather patchy surface of the cleaned original gilding.

The new Copley Room within the Guildhall Art Gallery has been built to accommodate the picture and has a viewing balcony at mezzanine level, as the picture's size resulted in it spanning two floors of the new building. Size also dictated that the canvas was stretched and the frame assembled in the Copley Room. Final restoration of the painting took place with it hung *in situ* prior to the frame being positioned in front.

Before the project commenced there was a great deal of discussion as to the best system for display. When previously hung there is nothing to suggest that the painting was other than fitted to the frame, as one object, in an essentially conventional manner. There are numerous old screw holes in the back of the frame and original stretcher to suggest that they were fitted together by metal plates. Indeed, a portion of one such fitting survives on the old stretcher. The splitting of canvas, stretcher and ends of the frame members may have resulted from this system being employed for such a large work, with the associated handling difficulties. The old stretcher, like the frame, had been reduced and was warped and split. It was decided that the previous method of fitting and hanging would not be reinstated. However, after much deliberation, the fabrication of a new traditional wooden stretcher was favoured over modern metal options. Wood was chosen for its relatively good rigidity for comparative weight with aluminium. The original stretcher was used as a model for the new one made by International Fine Art Conservation Services (IFACS), from single lengths of Douglas fir, chosen as a good quality straight timber available in long lengths therefore requiring no joins (Fig. 7).

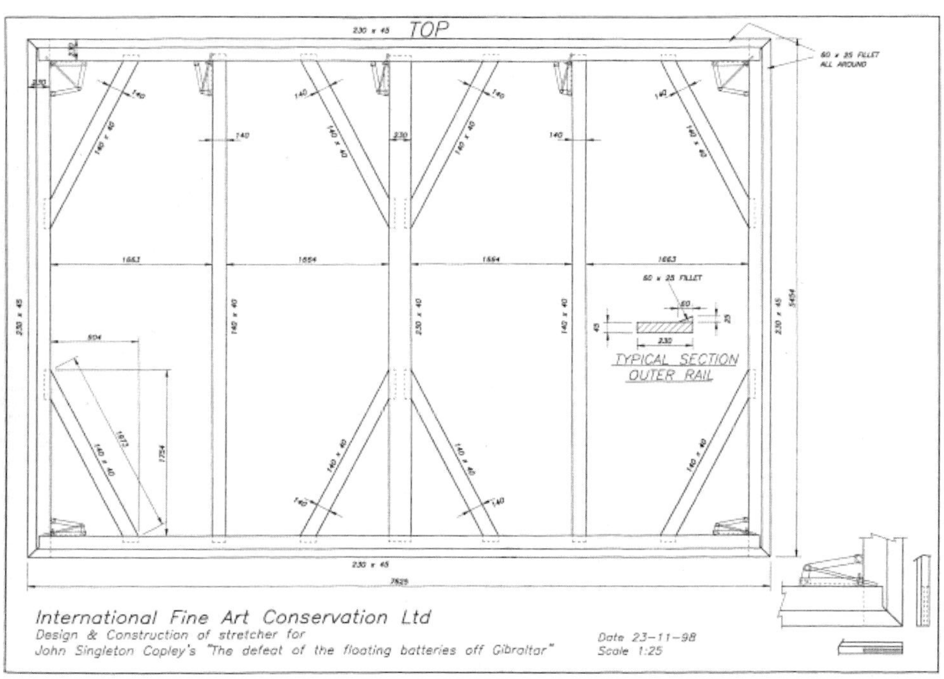

Figure 7 Front elevation diagram of the new stretcher, 1998. (Reproduced with the permission of International Fine Art Conservation Services.)

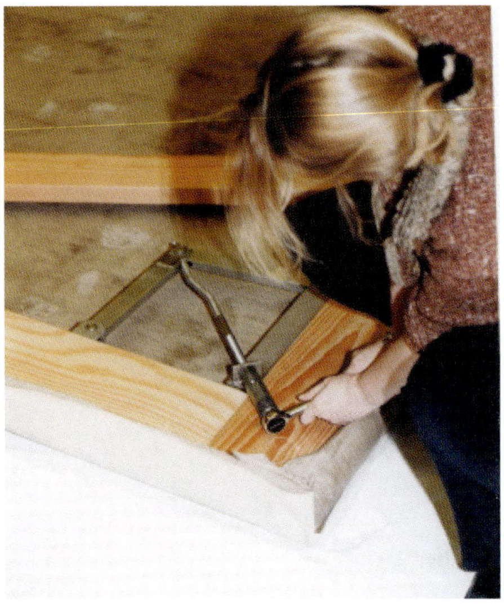

Figure 8 The canvas being stretched using the corner expansion mechanism, 1999. (Guildhall Art Gallery, Corporation of London.)

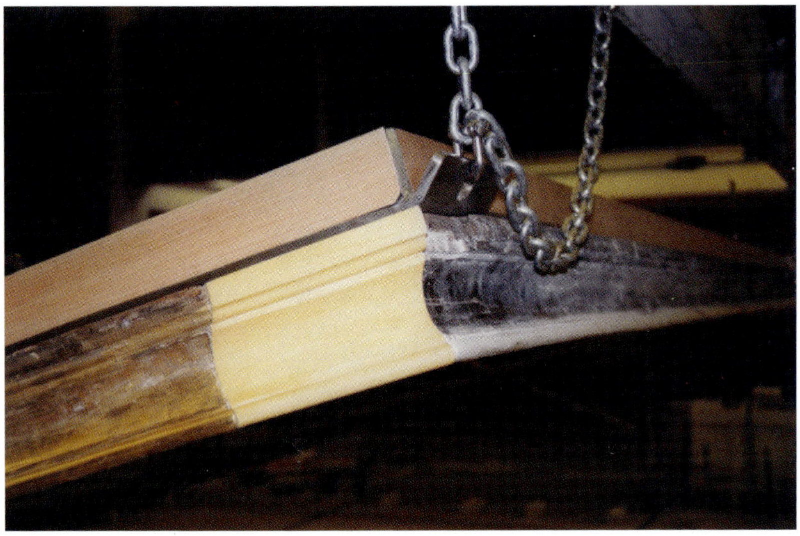

Figure 9 The partly restored frame showing its new build-up and one of the corner plates with its integral lifting eyes, 1999. (Guildhall Art Gallery, Corporation of London.)

The solution to attaining the correct tension for the stretched canvas was reached in consultation with IFACS, who designed and fabricated the expansion mechanisms. These are systems of stainless steel levers, each adjusted by a nut, bolted to each corner and at three other points along the top member (Fig. 8).

The decision was made to display the picture with a slight cant, rather than fixing it flat to the wall with the frame attached to the wall around it. This was primarily for aesthetic reasons but also affords a generous air space behind the canvas and a low amount of restraint. A backcloth of cotton was fitted with metal eyelets onto turn-buttons on the back of the stretcher. This material was chosen as being lighter and more manageable than rigid alternatives. Openings secured with Velcro allow for access to the expansion mechanisms without necessitating the painting's removal from the wall.

As the frame's mitres and old steel L-plates were not considered strong enough to support the frame's weight, a build-up of Douglas fir (section 80 × 100mm) was screwed onto the back of the members. This also provided a rebate for the new stretcher. The mitres were reinforced with new L-section corner plates designed with the consulting engineers[7] fabricated from 10mm thick stainless steel. These were sandwiched between the original frame and the new build-up (Fig. 9).

With these additions the frame could support itself on display; it was decided that this would not provide safe support for the canvas if painting and frame were fitted together in the conventional way. Also, the combined weight of around 800kg would have been more difficult to manoeuvre and hazardous to the still-fragile whitening layer of the frame's top edge. With all this in mind it was decided to support the canvas and frame independently of one another on five 2-tiered brackets at the bottom and suspend their tops from two hanging rails. In the new display, both stretcher and frame are attached from the tops of their side members to their respective rails by stainless steel hanging fittings. These fittings comprise of marine D-shackles, closed-link chain and adjustable 'bottle-screws' with the threads locked into the bodies. These enable the painting and frame to be moved into contact with each other but to be structurally independent. The upper hanging rail, used by the frame, provides support at two additional points along the long span of the top member, which would otherwise be unsupported along its length. The stretcher is also supported at its top-centre from the lower hanging rail. The brackets and hanging rails were also designed in conjunction with the consulting engineers. The wall on which the painting hangs is formed of suspended stone

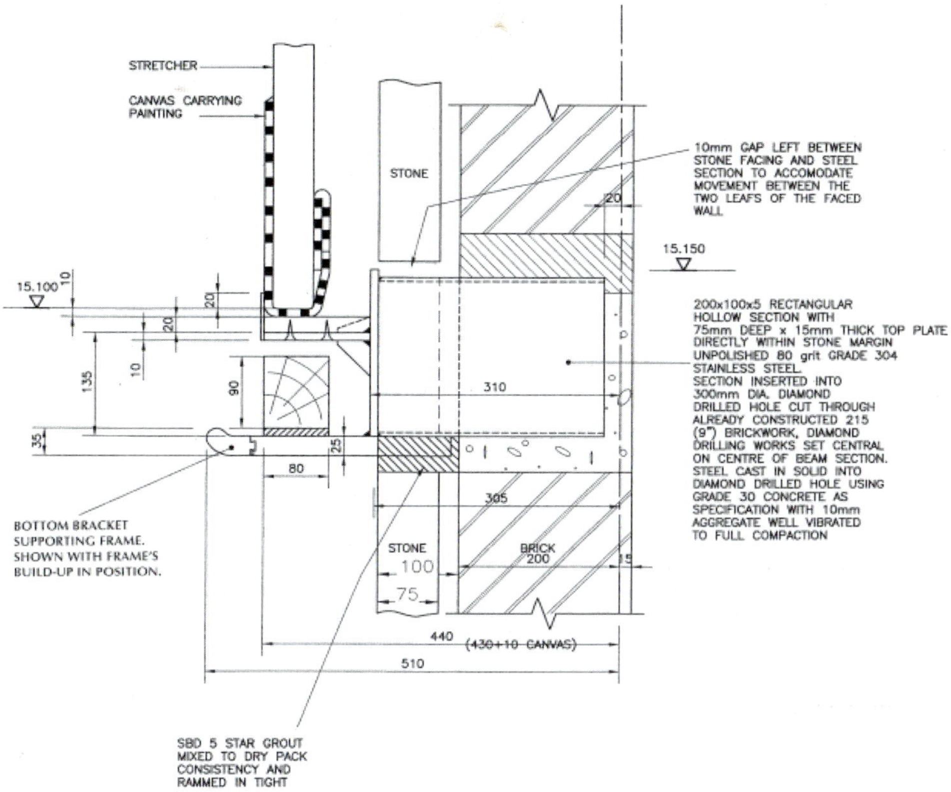

Figure 10 A sectional diagram of the supporting brackets for canvas and frame in the current display. (Detail reproduced from a drawing by Oscar Faber Consulting Engineers, 1997.)

and is not load bearing. All the hanging rails and supporting brackets therefore had to be designed to be built into the Gallery's underlying superstructure before the stone was installed. All brackets, rails and hanging fittings were load-tested or rated to a safe working load of at least 1 tonne (Figs 10 and 11).

Health and safety was a major consideration while dealing with such a heavy work, often at heights. Thorough planning and training were essential. It was unrealistic to reduce all the processes to below the assessment category of 'substantial

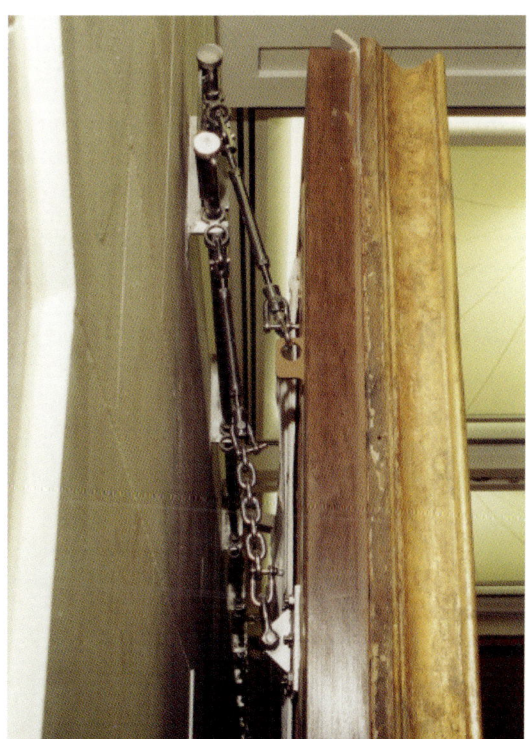

Figure 11 The top of the picture in the current display showing the two hanging rails and adjustable hanging fittings, 2000. (Guildhall Art Gallery, Corporation of London.)

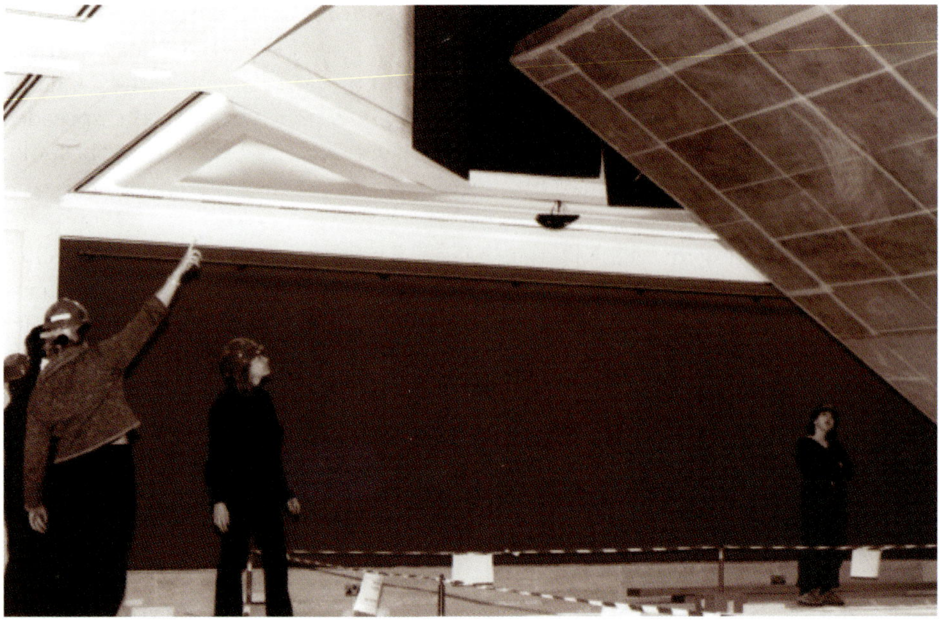

Figure 12 The stretched and faced picture being hoisted in the Copley Room, 1999. (Guildhall Art Gallery, Corporation of London.)

risk', but all risks were minimised as far as possible. Final restoration of the painting took place with it vertical *in situ*, with the frame being treated simultaneously, laid horizontally on benches (Fig. 12).

The entire picture surface was made accessible from three levels of scaffolding to allow the team of seven conservators access to fill, texture, retouch and varnish the painting. Only brush varnishing was possible over the large surface for health and safety reasons. On-site solvent extraction and filtration had to be provided necessitating the provision of five separate extractor tubes capable of reaching 7m to the top working positions.

The Gallery floor is of sprung wooden sections within a marble grid. The Gallery staff was informed that lifting machinery could not be used on this surface, even if the load were to be spread. It proved impossible to overrule this decision so the consulting engineers devised a system of runway beams temporarily fitted into the ceiling. From these, two pairs of especially low-speed electric hoists (maximum speed 1m/min) controlled two spreader beams able to lift and travel with the painting or frame from points along their top and bottom simultaneously (Fig. 13).

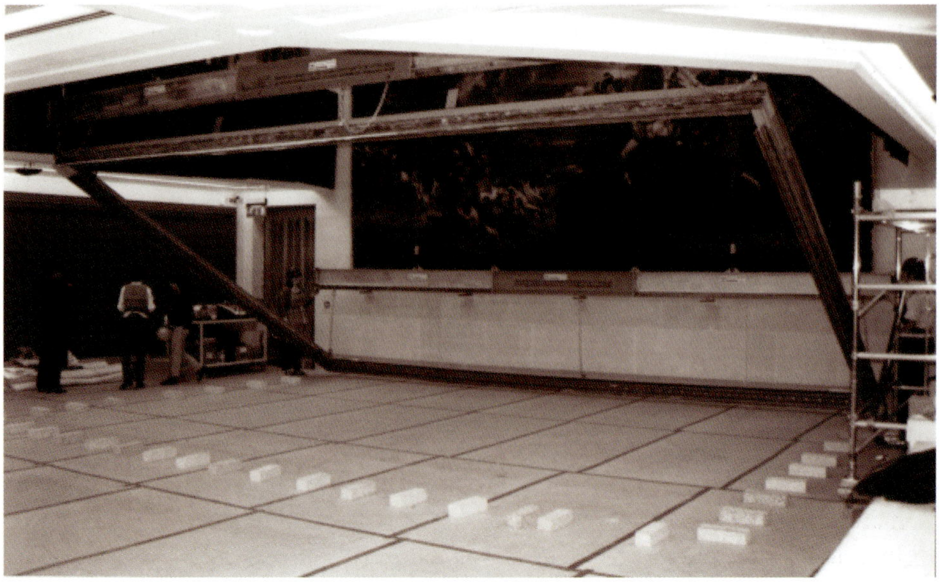

Figure 13 The frame being hoisted with the painting *in situ* in the Copley Room, 1999. (Guildhall Art Gallery, Corporation of London.)

The hoists and spreader beams were all load-tested to 1 tonne – this proved essential as during testing the hoists did not travel properly under load and the runway beams quickly had to be fitted with additional components. Chains connected the integral lifting eyes in the frame's corner plates to the spreader beams during hoisting. The stretcher was attached to the beams from six bespoke stainless steel eye-brackets bolted through the stretcher's side members, near each corner and the centres at top and bottom.

With the painting and frame hung independently of one another, the stretcher had to be rigid. The choice of timber resulted in as robust a structure as could have been achieved using other materials with a comparable section and weight. Its bowing when first being lifted from horizontal was overcome with two additional fixing points being added at the top and bottom centres. When stretching the huge canvas, the hoists enabled an unusual, and useful, modification to usual practice. The stretcher was suspended from the hoists in contact with, but not resting on, the canvas. This allowed good tension to be achieved as the canvas was not trapped beneath the weight of the 'hovering' stretcher. In theory, final tensioning of the canvas could be completed while the painting is hanging, but the expansion mechanisms along the bottom of the stretcher do not function when the picture is vertical due to the weight of the canvas and stretcher upon them. This problem was not overcome but the canvas retained good tension.

After the amendment to the runway beams, the hoists proved a very controllable and versatile means of manoeuvring the picture's components. Records were kept of processes leading up to display, including a video, but the problem remains that the complex hoist system will be a daunting prospect for subsequent members of staff to master when those originally involved in the project move on. This system was only adopted due to architectural decisions, which were taken without Gallery consultation. If money had not been available for this system then perhaps a simpler solution would have been sought, with a more pragmatic approach to the building's utility. Storage of the hoists, runway and spreader beams is difficult. The hoists may prove to be problematic to recommission after indeterminate years of being mothballed. Thus, in the future, the painting risks falling into the category of big pictures that are neglected due to the difficulty of removing them from display for treatment, etc.

The protection of the painting while hanging is a matter of ongoing discussion. The Gallery has lighting that can only be reached by scaffolding for servicing, perhaps involving the removal of metal ceiling panels. This, together with other potential housekeeping tasks, presents dangers to the picture. Unfortunately, many aspects of the building were established before conservators could influence decisions. Presently there is no provision for any protection of the picture during Gallery maintenance and a system will need to be formulated in advance of any works. No specific disaster plan dealing with the picture has been devised and currently it will be exposed to emergencies with only on-the-spot initiatives to afford it protection. Disaster planning should start from a position of attainable reality. Currently the picture could not be removed from the Gallery in much less than a week. Can the largest paintings stand much of a chance in a worst-case scenario? What can be done to improve matters? More research needs to be undertaken to establish what protection can be given to this large work against the various dangers to which pictures of all sizes are subject.

The conservation project was completed by September 1999. Since late 2000 the painting has begun to betray a memory of Copley's initial composition incorporating spandrels (Fig. 1). It is not entirely clear what has caused this alteration; however, it appears that the varnish has sunk to a greater extent in the spandrels and they now show up as matt areas. This effect was not noticed during conservation and has never been recorded in the notes of any past observers.

In conclusion, perhaps it is unreasonable to expect a picture of this size to be

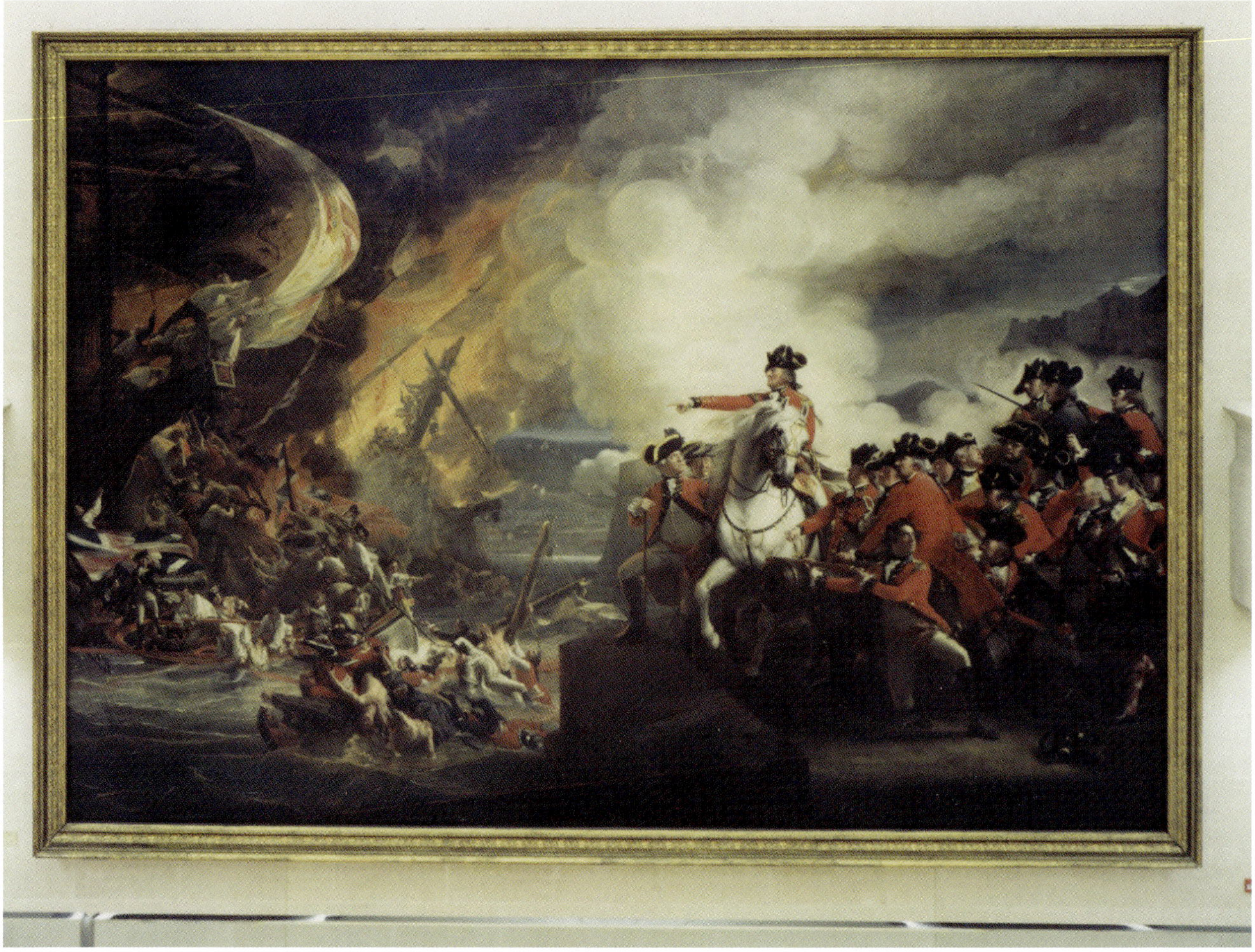

Figure 14 The picture as it is presently displayed in the new Guildhall Art Gallery, 2000. (Guildhall Art Gallery, Corporation of London.)

afforded support by a traditional frame. Often such large works are fixed rigidly into their frames by metal plates screwed into the frame and stretcher. This creates a situation in which both can adversely affect each other, but not actually provide significantly more mutual support when being moved or on display. Pictures fixed flat to a wall can have their frames applied independently to the wall around them, but thought must be given to possible restraint to movement of the object while on display and restriction of air circulation behind. The Copley's current form of display has continued to be stable to date, with the frame and painting structurally independent from one another while presenting a canted, cohesive aspect. Despite 200 years of mixed fortunes, the picture survives as the centrepiece of the new Guildhall Art Gallery (Fig. 14).

Notes

1. C. Dibdin (1786) 'Reminiscences,' *Cuttings on Art*, II, p. 151, Victoria and Albert Museum.
2. Jules David Prown (1966), *John Singleton Copley: In England 1774–1815*. Washington, DC: National Gallery of Art, p. 331.
3. *General Purposes Committee Journal*, Vol. 2, Feb. 1792–1795, Corporation of London Records Office. Also a report submitted to this Committee 30 April 1794, Corporation of London Records Office.
4. Jacob Simon (1996), *The Art of the Picture Frame*. London: National Portrait Gallery, p. 146.
5. Letter from Rica Jones, AMSSEE, to J. Hoole, Barbican Art Gallery, 27 February 1983.
6. For details of both the AMSSEE and English Heritage treatment of the painting, see the paper by Woodcock (in this volume, pp. 144–52).
7. Oscar Faber Consulting Engineers.

Bibliography

Journal of Court of Common Council, Vol. 74, 1793–1794, Corporation of London Records Office, CFI/995.
Knight, V. (1999) *The History of Guildhall Art Gallery*. London: Guildhall Art Gallery.
Neff, E.B. (1996) *John Singleton Copley in England*. London: Merrell Holberton.

The authors

Gerry Alabone, formerly of the Guildhall Art Gallery, London, is Head of Frames Conservation, Tate, London. Louise Dandy, formerly of the Guildhall Art Gallery, London, is an independent frames conservator based in Kent.

The Defeat of the Floating Batteries off Gibraltar by John Singleton Copley: A Painting Waiting for a Wall

SALLY WOODCOCK

Introduction

The post-war conservation history of John Singleton Copley's largest work is a good illustration of the mixed fortunes of large-scale paintings once they are removed from their stretchers, a process often undertaken purely to allow them to be moved from one location to another. The fact that it has survived when so many large works of art have been destroyed or allowed to deteriorate beyond repair is a result of luck, ample resources and good timing as well as a team of curators and conservators determined to reinstate one of the Corporation of London's early commissions in the Guildhall Art Gallery.[1]

Narrow escapes and near misses

After its safe evacuation a month before one of the most violent bombing raids on the City of London almost totally destroyed the Guildhall Art Gallery in 1941, by 1947 *The Defeat of the Floating Batteries off Gibraltar* is recorded as being stored in the barn of R. Free & Sons in Newbury, rented by the Corporation as a picture store. In order to move the painting it had been removed from its stretcher and attached to a narrow cardboard roller, which forced the painting to overlap itself. Although the store was inspected on an annual basis, it seems unlikely that the painting was unrolled on each visit and it is not until 4 July 1953 that it is certain that the painting, as well as the premises, was inspected in detail. On that occasion, Mr J.L. Howego, the Guildhall's Print Room and Art Gallery Assistant, noted that although the thick coat of varnish had protected the paint surface, rats had been nibbling at the edges of the canvas, although had not encroached on the painting itself, and damp had caused the brown paper to adhere to the paint surface in places. The numerous cuts and slits in the canvas were reported as dating from before World War II, although photographs of the painting hanging in the Gallery in 1935 do not support this. It is more likely that the soft board roller, affected by the damp, had collapsed, causing or exacerbating the damage; the fact that the painting overlapped itself on the roller over 2½ times must also have contributed to the deterioration.

In 1953 it was offered on loan to the National Maritime Museum but it was declined on the grounds of inadequate available wall space. At one point it was suggested that the Governor of Gibraltar might be able to accommodate it on the island and the Permanent Secretary to the War Office also tried to find room for it in the Royal Artillery Mess at Woolwich, but all these attempts to house it were unsuccessful. The Royal Exchange, the Mansion House, Gresham College, a livery company's hall and Lloyds were all considered as potential locations, but the large size of the painting meant that none of these suggestions came to fruition. By 1 October 1960 it is recorded as being stored in the warehouse of Pitt and Scott, fine art handlers, in Holloway.

By 1969, the Corporation's attitude to finding a new location for the painting appears to have changed in light of the prospect of the Guildhall Art Gallery being rebuilt. In that year the National Portrait Gallery, apparently unaware of both its size and condition, approached the Guildhall Art Gallery asking to borrow the painting, but this request was declined by J.L. Howego on the grounds that 'Our new gallery is still a few years off, but it would hardly be worth the trouble and expense of getting it out of store, restoring and framing it and sending it out on loan, only to claw it back shortly afterwards.' In 1983, when the new Guildhall Art Gallery once again seemed a more distant prospect, the position was reversed. The Director of Libraries and Art Galleries asked the Director of the National Portrait Gallery whether it would be possible to hang the painting post-conservation but received the reply that 'there is just not any room here for a picture of that immense size'. It is therefore likely that the 1969 loan proposal would have come to nothing, even if the Corporation had been willing to lend the painting.

On 4 June 1975 a representative from Brangwyn Studio, a commercial framing and restoration workshop in Farnham, inspected the painting and recorded it as being stored 'in a packing case, rolled, paint surface outwards on a drum cylinder'.[2] The painting was described as badly torn and fragmented, a state ascribed in part to the storage method and in part to the age of the canvas. The paint layer was described as 'reasonably sound', although the varnish was recorded as being yellowed with surface grime and it was noted that strips of linen canvas would have to be removed from the edges. The Studio's solution to the difficulties of handling so large a painting was drastic: 'it is recommended that the painting be divided into 2 parts measuring approx. 18 ft × 12 ft 6" and hand relined to new canvas, two strong stretcher-frames with expandable cross-bars and wedges to be provided to support the paintings'. Fortunately this recommendation was ignored, although it was passed on to the relevant Corporation committee.

In the early 1980s the Metropolitan Museum of Art in New York expressed interest in exhibiting the painting on long-term loan, post-conservation. On 17 February 1983, John Brearley, the Museum's conservator, visited Pitt and Scott's warehouse to inspect the painting. A subsequent letter in the Guildhall Art Gallery's records describes his report as quite positive: 'It has obviously suffered some mechanical damage by being rolled for so long a time, but he feels that Mr. Berger will be able to deal effectively with those problems in his lining of the painting.' 'Mr Berger' was Gustav Berger, a New York conservator with extensive experience in conserving large-scale paintings, including a number of panoramas. Unfortunately, John Brearley's report is not preserved in the records, although it appears to recommend that the painting be protected by facing the painted surface. In March 1983 the Metropolitan Museum suggested that Dianne Dwyer, another of their conservators, come to London to carry out a cleaning test as the Museum was concerned about how the painting would react. The Corporation responded by pointing out that no loan arrangements had been finalised and that in the interim alternative sites were still being sought as it would prefer the painting to remain in the UK. Accepting this aspiration, the Metropolitan Museum cancelled the proposed visit.

In the same year, approaches were made to the National Trust to determine whether the painting could be hung in any of its houses, but again, no wall was found large enough to accommodate it. The same response was received from Sir Oliver Millar, Surveyor of the Queen's Pictures, when enquiries were made to see if any of the royal palaces open to the public could take it.

Resuscitation: Area Museums Service for South East England

In February 1983 Rica Jones, the Conservation Officer at the Area Museums Service for South Eastern England (AMSSEE) was also approached to provide an estimate for the conservation of the painting.[3] She too recommended that the painting be faced, regardless of whether or not treatment followed. She was unable to examine the reverse of the painting and therefore could not comment on the presence of seams, but noted that their apparent absence was surprising in a painting of this size. The report described the twill weave of the canvas running from top right to bottom left and noted that the painting had been strip-lined onto a plain-weave linen canvas with strips approximately 300mm deep being adhered with animal glue. The date of this intervention is unrecorded. Pronounced buckling in the support, particularly around the edges, was observed where the glue of the strip lining had stiffened and shrunk, and the central area had many tears.

Areas of paint loss around the tears as well as areas of abraded paint were noted, mainly as a result of unrolling and rolling, mostly in the left third of the picture, where the buckling was particularly severe. The varnish was recorded as being thick and very discoloured, and the report notes that 'large areas of the dark background paint are suffering from medium-shrinkage, which might indicate a soft paint film'.

As there was still no possibility of displaying the painting after treatment, it was decided to face it for protection as an interim measure. Warehouse space had to be hired from Pitt and Scott in order to carry out this operation and a new roller and case was constructed. AMSSEE conservators, although unable to carry out the major conservation treatment the painting required, were available to apply the protective facing. Their report also noted the need for a new wooden storage roller, to avoid the painting overlapping itself, requiring a diameter of approximately 2.7m. The large roller was suggested by Rica Jones in order to stabilise the painting as it was unclear how long the painting would have to remain in storage before full restoration treatment. The splits in the canvas had been caused by compression of the threads (the previous roller had sagged for many years under the weight of the painting) and therefore it was important to provide a roller that supported it with as little stress as possible.

The painting was faced with Japanese mulberry tissue (Usumino H1005J from Falkiners Fine Papers, London) and a facing adhesive made of unbleached beeswax, dammar resin and white spirit (25:50:75) was brushed on cold and allowed to dry naturally. Margins of 40mm were left either side of the tears to prevent the wax from penetrating the canvas and reducing the efficiency of any future lining adhesives. The tears were reinforced by strips of heavier grade Usumino, adhered with the same adhesive and left to dry. Strips of nylon gossamer fabric, impregnated with BEVA 371, were placed loosely across the tears and ironed down on either side, again leaving an untreated 'bridge' over the tears. The AMSSEE conservators' report noted that the painting would require much relaxation and preliminary treatment before lining could take place, and this was borne out by the experience of the English Heritage (EH) conservators, described below.

Broken canvas on the lower edge was realigned and held in place with the wax-resin adhesive and eltoline tissue before being faced as described above. Strips of eltoline tissue (50mm deep) impregnated with wax-resin adhesive were ironed onto the picture edges for further protection. The former strip lining was removed from the upper and lower edges to allow the distortion it had caused in the original canvas to relax; however, on the shorter edges it was retained in order to be able to attach the picture to the roller. It was extended with canvas strips (Ulster Weaving Co. no. 3151) attached with two lines of canvas thread in herringbone stitch. The AMSSEE report noted that the strip-lining glue originally used, tentatively identified as compo (usually a composition of whiting, glue, resin and linseed oil), retained much of its shear strength, but had lost almost all of its peel strength. Wooden batons (50 × 50mm), each slightly wider than the picture, were stapled and nailed to the strip lining. Twelve people were required for safe handling of the painting as the canvas had to be held under tension while rolling. Once it could be handled, the painting was turned over using the roller so that the reverse could be examined. At some point in the past, 50mm-wide masking tape had been applied along the tears on the reverse; this was removed and the tears were temporarily supported with strips of linen canvas (no. 3151), previously impregnated with BEVA 371. Areas where the reverse of the canvas had been scored were reinforced with nylon gossamer, heat-sealed with BEVA 371.

Before the painting was rolled up, cleaning tests were carried out close to the left edge. It was found that both propan-2-ol and acetone removed the varnish safely (propan-2-ol slower and acetone more quickly). Once the treatment was complete, the painting was rolled and held under tension by nailing through the wooden batons into the drum. Webbing was wound around the rolled painting for extra support and the whole was wrapped with polythene for protection before being cased.

Remedy: English Heritage

In September 1985 the Historic Buildings and Monuments Commission (HBMC), now English Heritage, offered to complete the structural conservation of the painting and accommodate it on the floor of the Commission's studio in Regents Park. The painting was therefore transferred to a transport roller for delivery on 3 September. The frame, which appears to have been taken to HBMC but not worked on by the conservators there, was taken to the Guildhall Art Gallery conservation studios for treatment in 1993.

The conservators at EH allowed the canvas to relax for two months before treatment and removed the facing to facilitate this (Fig. 1). Once the facing was removed, major tears with frayed edges were revealed, overlapping each other in some cases and misaligned in others. A platform of plywood, cushioned with polystyrene lining paper, was constructed to support the painting and in order to maintain humidity levels in the canvas, sheets of Melinex were spread over the surface and taped down to create a microclimate. After two months, although the canvas had relaxed in many areas, there were still areas of distortion.

The thick varnish layer was removed to allow further relaxation, the conservators reaching the centre of the canvas by means of padded bridging boards or cushions to spread their weight (Fig. 2). Once clean, the surface was protected with a layer of facing paper. The painting was again sealed in a microclimate, resulting in considerable further relaxation, and then turned over to allow the reverse to be cleaned by brushing and scraping away the accumulated dirt. Areas of distorted canvas were treated by spraying them lightly with deionised water and then ironing the reverse of the canvas, the heat and moisture allowing the canvas to be manipulated back into position. Starting at the centre of the painting and working out to the edges, the entire reverse of the painting was ironed in this manner.

The tears in the canvas were realigned and repaired using epoxy adhesive. Where canvas was missing, inserts were applied. Once complete, the front surface was again checked to ensure correct alignment of the tears. It was decided to attach a double lining to the reverse because of the size and weakness of the original canvas. Rica Jones' initial impression had been correct: the original canvas is a single piece. As suitable linen canvas was not available in this size, a lightweight

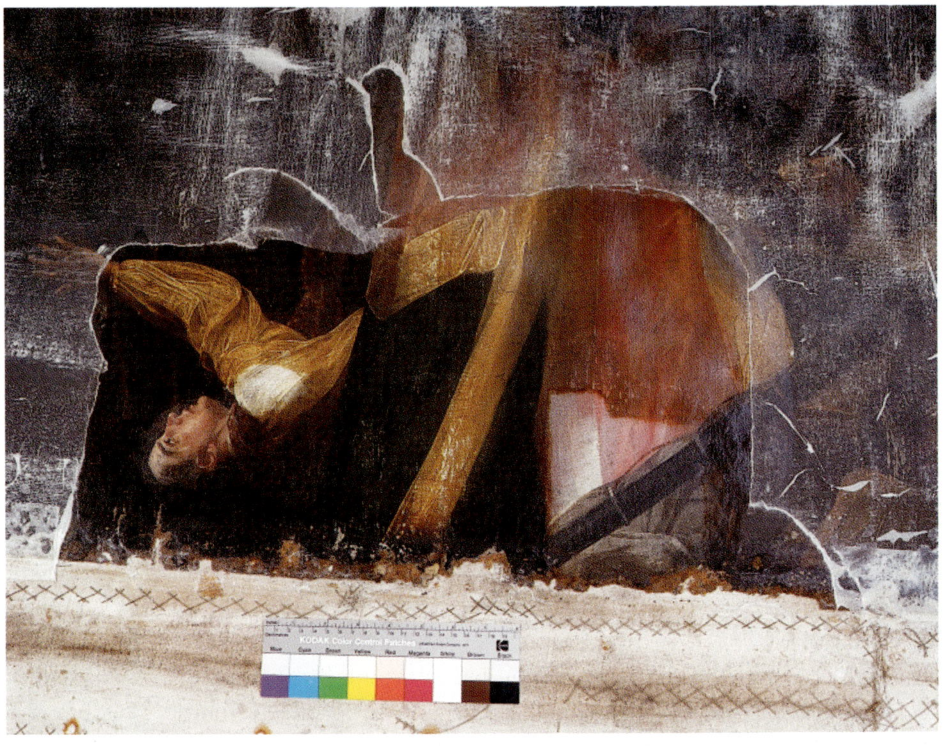

Figure 1 Detail of painting at English Heritage's studios during removal of facing with varnish removal tests in lower part; note the canvas edge added by AMSSEE (© English Heritage).

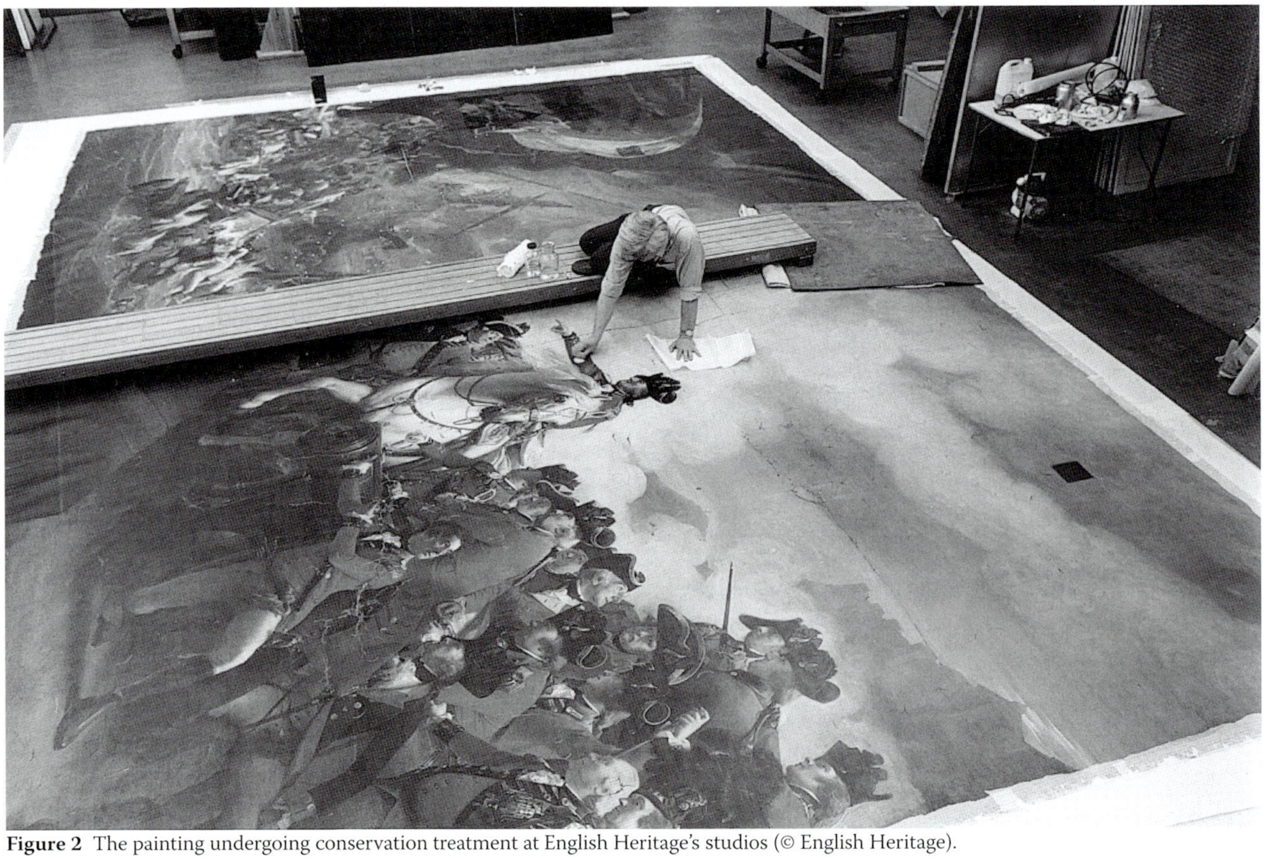

Figure 2 The painting undergoing conservation treatment at English Heritage's studios (© English Heritage).

Belgian cotton was chosen as an interleaf fabric – it was available in the required dimensions and is strong with an even weave. This was sandwiched between the original canvas and the lining canvas, a heavier weight linen. As the maximum width of the lining canvas was 2.75m, three sections had to be used, butt-joined together. The painting was lined with BEVA 371, hand-ironed from the reverse. The joins in the lining canvas were reinforced with additional strips of canvas. Once the treatment was complete, the painting was transferred to the warehouse of the art handlers Momart, in December 1992, and was stored there until the rebuilding of the Guildhall Art Gallery was completed.

Revival: Guildhall Art Gallery

Although there had been some discussion in 1984/5 concerning the possibility that the EH studio would undertake the cosmetic conservation of the painting once the structural work had been carried out, eventually it was decided that the final phase of the treatment would be carried out *in situ* by the Gallery's own conservators once the new Guildhall Art Gallery was at a sufficiently advanced stage to accommodate it. In the event, this was not possible until 1999.

The painting was brought into the Gallery on a transport roller and unrolled onto a floor protected with plywood and cushioned with felt followed by a layer of Tyvek (DuPont) to allow it to be moved with little resistance (Fig. 3). The use of a hoisting system suspended from the ceiling gave the conservators a level of dexterity and precision in moving both the stretcher and the stretched painting that could not have been achieved using a traditional block and tackle system or lifting platforms.[4] This proved especially useful when stretching the canvas as the stretcher could be lowered and suspended horizontally above the canvas, in contact with, but not putting any weight on the canvas during stretching. This allowed good tension to be realised. Contrary to expectations, the initial stretching achieving surprisingly good tension and the process only had to be carried out once.

Once stretched the painting could be hoisted to a vertical position, with the frame simultaneously being treated horizontally in the room behind. When vertical and resting on foam blocks on the floor while still attached to the hoists, a

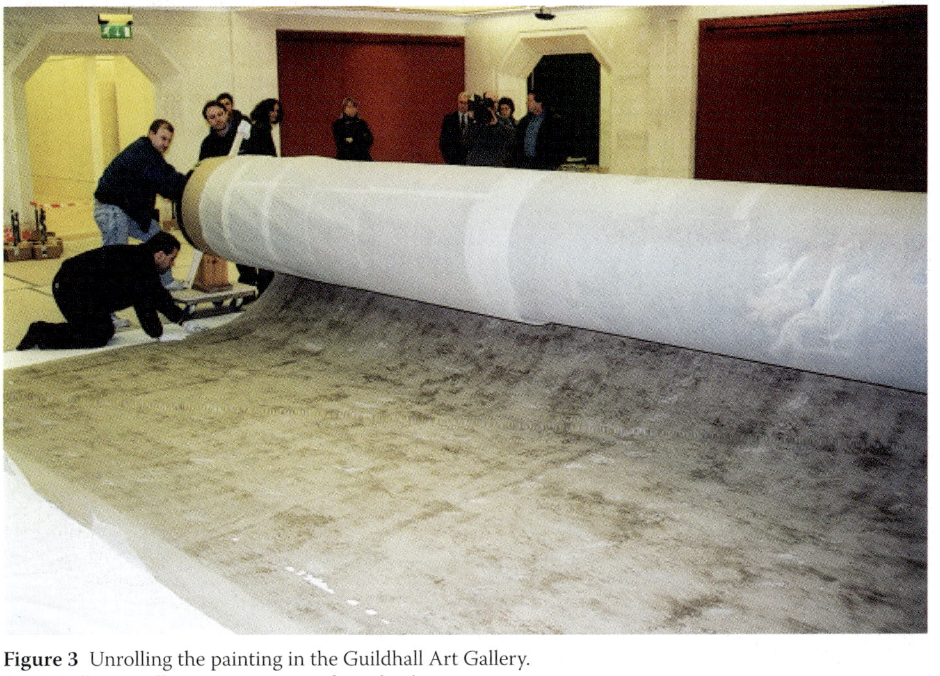

Figure 3 Unrolling the painting in the Guildhall Art Gallery. (Guildhall Art Gallery, Corporation of London.)

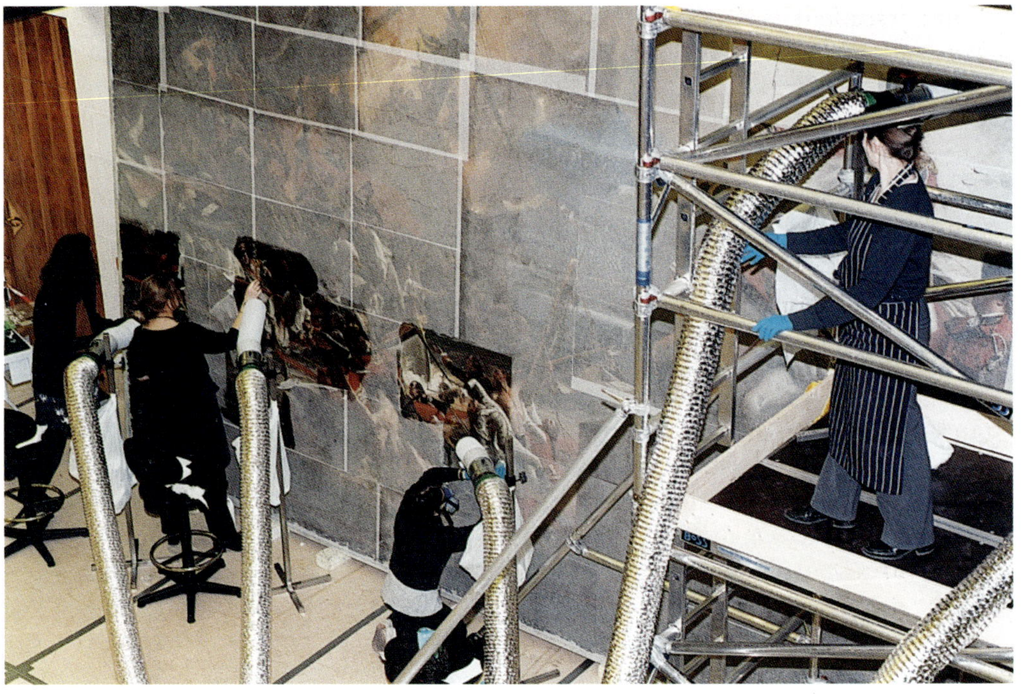

Figure 4 Removing the facing applied by English Heritage. (Guildhall Art Gallery, Corporation of London.)

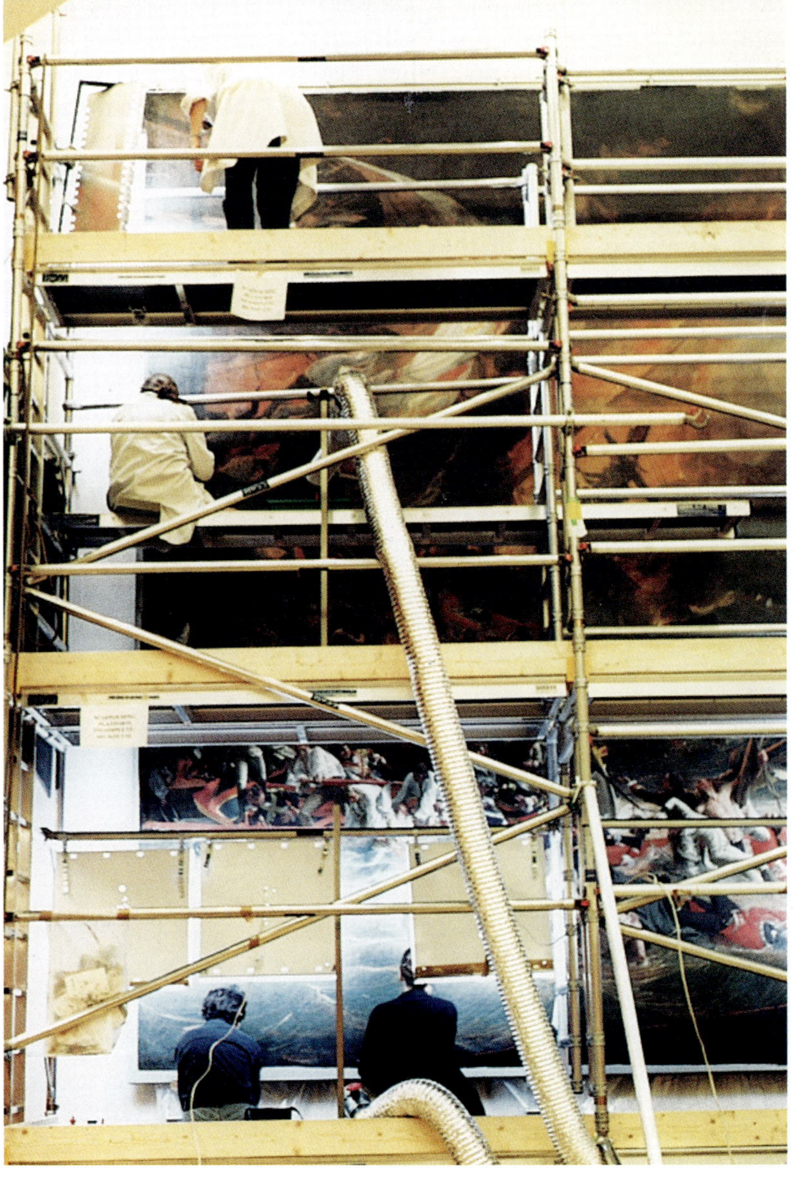

Figure 5 Detail of three-tier scaffolding, lights and local exhaust ventilation. (Guildhall Art Gallery, Corporation of London.)

temporary scaffolding tower was erected to enable removal of the facing from the upper sections of the painting (Fig. 4). Once hoisted to its permanent hanging position, a three-level scaffolding (S.G.B. Youngman) was erected in front of the painting to allow access to the entire surface. The scaffolding was provided with lights, fitted with Phillips TLD 95 fluorescent bulbs (240V fitted with circuit breakers) to provide good colour rendering. In addition, solvent extraction and filtration was provided (Rentavent Ltd) with five separate flexible extractor tubes attached to carbon filter boxes and fans in acoustic boxes to reduce the noise, located at the base of the scaffolding (Fig. 5). The tubes were capable of reaching 7m to the top of the scaffolding and were extremely effective in ensuring that health and safety requirements were met. A team of seven conservators, including two members of the Gallery conservation staff, was employed to treat the painting from March to July 1999, filling, retouching and varnishing.

The only part of this treatment affected by the size of the painting was the varnishing. Both the isolating varnish of Paraloid B72 (Rohm and Haas) in Shellsol A and the final varnish of MS2A (Linden Nazareth) in Stoddard solvent had to be applied by brush as spraying was not possible within the confines of the Gallery. Varnish trials were carried out using 10%, 15% and 20% solutions of B72 covered with a coat of MS2A to simulate the final effect. The 20% solution of B72 gave the most satisfactory saturation and although it was rather thick and therefore fairly difficult to brush out, it had the advantage of not dripping. Simultaneously, on each level of the three-tier scaffolding, teams of two conservators brush-varnished from left to right to a pre-orchestrated plan, 'leap-frogging' each other to maintain complete and even coverage.

Conclusion

The *Defeat of the Floating Batteries off Gibraltar* endured the threats of war, dismemberment and export in the twentieth century, its large size proving a liability in both contributing to its physical deterioration and making it a difficult work of art to accommodate. Where an anonymous work of lesser artistic merit may have been discarded, Copley's fame and the quality of his work, once indecipherable beneath the darkened varnish, almost certainly contributed to his painting's survival. Its continued existence has been secured by systematic, incremental conservation treatment in three studios over almost two decades, championed by the curator of the Guildhall Art Gallery who was determined to resurrect a picture that had spent over half a century waiting for its wall.

Acknowledgements

The conservation treatment was carried out at the Area Museum Service for South Eastern England by Rica Jones, Deirdre Mulley and Krystyna Kelly; English Heritage by Jan Keevil and Ray Hemmett; at the Guildhall Art Gallery it was undertaken by Cressida Harwood, Sally Woodcock, Alexandra Walker, Daniella Spenippo, Liz Reissner, Andre Nottage and Julia Nagle. The author acknowledges the contribution of all those who have played a part in the treatment of this painting since 1983, in particular the staff of the Guildhall Art Gallery and Cressida Harwood, its former paintings conservator.

Notes

1. For a detailed discussion of the early history of the painting, see the paper by Alabone and Dandy (in this volume, pp 131–43).

2. Letter from Brangwyn Studio to the Director of Corporation of London Art Gallery, 25 June 1975.
3. Treatment was carried out by Rica Jones, Deirdre Mulley and Krystyna Kelly, among others.
4. See Alabone and Dandy (in this volume, pp. 138–9) for details of the hoisting mechanism.

The author

Sally Woodcock, formerly of the Guildhall Art Gallery, London, is a lecturer at University College London and an independent paintings conservator based in Cambridge.